TESTS, MEASUREMENT, AND EVALUATION

TESTS, MEASUREMENT, AND EVALUATION

A DEVELOPMENTAL APPROACH

ARTHUR BERTRAND and JOSEPH P. CEBULA

American International College

ADDISON-WESLEY PUBLISHING COMPANY

Reading, Massachusetts • Menlo Park, California
London • Amsterdam • Don Mills, Ontario • Sydney

Library of Congress Cataloging in Publication Data

Bertrand, Arthur, 1926-
    Tests, measurement & evaluation.

    Includes index.
    1. Educational tests and measurements.
2. Developmental psychology. I. Cebula, Joseph P.,
joint author. II. Title.
LB3051.B424   371.2'6   79-21032
ISBN 0-201-00778-9

ISBN 0-201-00778-9
ABCDEFGHIJ-MA-89876543210

PREFACE

The testing movement in America has come under severe criticism in recent years by those who claim that schools place too much emphasis on "standardized" instruments to measure intelligence and achievement. The most vocal critics, in fact, have called for a halt to standardized testing because they believe such tests are "dehumanizing" and do not provide an accurate assessment of individual differences. The resultant move away from standardized or "norm-referenced" tests and toward "criterion-referenced" tests has been dramatic.

This book takes the view that tests, in and of themselves, are not dangerous. However, the improper use of tests sometimes makes them seem dangerous. Both norm-referenced and criterion-referenced tests are valuable tools in testing, measuring, and evaluating. Along with systematic observation and teacher-made tests, they provide the classroom teacher with a helpful set of assessment tools.

The emphsis throughout this book is on teachers, whose front-line activities in the day-to-day challenge of the classroom make them a powerful force in the development of their students. And since teachers must interpret test scores directly to parents, they must know how tests are constructed, administered, and interpreted and they must understand as much as possible about the human characteristics they are attempting to measure.

With this in mind, the book takes a developmental approach to growth and learning. It emphasizes the need for teachers to understand each developmental stage of physical, cognitive, and personal growth and how each stage dramatically affects the others throughout a child's life.

Evaluation, in short, is a dynamic process to be carried on constantly as teachers go about the daily job of assessing the needs of their students. Systematic observation, teacher-made tests, and standardized tests are described in detail as effective ways to help teachers in their assessments and as valuable tools for determining teaching strategies.

The assessment of personal or affective, behavior, is especially emphasized. This aspect of evaluation has often been neglected, perhaps because of the difficulty in assigning quantitative values to "feelings," "attitudes," and "appreciations." Yet these are vitally important facets of growth and development. Good attitudes and feelings about self and life are *taught* and *learned* just as surely as arithmetic. In fact, they play a major role in enhancing or inhibiting the child's success in arithmetic and other "cognitive" subjects.

This book is written for future teachers and teachers already in the field. It supplies a background in testing, test construction, statistics, systematic observation, the writing of objectives, and future trends in developmental psychology. We believe that teachers who understand the nature of the child will be more successful evaluators of the child's physical, cognitive, and personal needs.

We are grateful for the encouragement and help we received in preparing this book. We wish to express special thanks to Dr. Richard Sprinthall for his willingness to read and criticize much of the text and to Dr. Brian Cleary, who contributed his broad knowledge of special education by writing Chapter 11, Assessing Children in Our Classroom Who Have Special Needs. We acknowledge our reviewers for the hard but professional look they gave the text and for their helpful suggestions for strengthening our presentation. We acknowledge, with gratitude, the patience, cheerfulness, and expertise of our typists, Brenda Chouinard and Diane Pelletier, and our secretary, Wilhelmina Perkins.

Springfield, Massachusetts   A. B.
December 1979   J. C.

CONTENTS

CHAPTER ONE

WHY TEST CHILDREN?

IMPORTANT POINTS TO WATCH FOR

Tests are tools used to measure and evaluate the growth and development of children.

Tests, in and of themselves, cannot hurt children; professionals who use tests inappropriately can.

The origins of testing and the systematic study of human behavior are very recent. There is much to be learned about both.

Our less than perfect understanding of human behavior and of ways to test it have led to some inappropriate testing practices.

Critics of the testing movement say that tests are dehumanizing, destructive of the ego, and unfair to certain cultural and racial groups. They also claim that there has been too much emphasis placed on the measurement of ability and not enough on the assessment of personal growth.

In the hands of good teachers, tests become valuable tools for the diagnosis of individual strengths and weaknesses.

In the hands of knowledgeable teachers, the *good* things about testing far outweigh the *bad*.

Alice was a fragile and lovely child, painfully shy, almost to the point of withdrawal. Her gentleness was both disturbing and attractive to other children. They were disturbed because she seemed remote from them and from the carefree activities typical of second graders. She seemed older, somehow more mature than they, almost as though she wanted to play but had grown beyond their childlike antics.

They felt attracted to her for almost the same reasons. Her gentle nature seemed to say to them, "I understand how you feel," especially when they were sad or when they had gotten hurt. Without saying a word, she told them by her way of watching that she enjoyed them and liked them. They showed her their art work and their faltering attempts at writing, and she smiled and seemed to say, "That's nice, thank you for showing me." Many of them, with the purity of children, seemed to understand her and make her a part of them.

Alice's teacher understood her, too. At least she thought she did. She saw Alice as a child different from the others, unable to keep up with usual second grade work and unwilling to participate. In her desire to help Alice, she sought to discover whether her shyness and silence were symptoms of some deeper problem. She asked that Alice be tested, and after some months, the school authorities finally gave her an intelligence test. Her I.Q. was found to be 77, a few points below the mandatory cutoff score which, by state law, separated the retarded from the normal. It was recommended that she be placed in a "special class," the designation for classrooms set aside for retarded children.

Alice'a teacher, stunned, wondered how this sensitive girl could be retarded, and how a single test could be allowed to uproot her from an atmosphere of relative security and thrust her into a roomful of strangers, many seriously troubled and unable to relate to her with warmth and affection.

Fortunately, her teacher was sensitive enough to children and knowledgeable enough about tests to insist upon additional diagnosis, hypothesizing that, even if the child had problems, retardation wasn't one of them. The results convinced her superiors that emotional distress, and not retardation, caused Alice's poor performance on the I.Q. test. A plan to deal with the reasons for this emotional distress was designed and implemented.

Alice's case is not unusual; its fortunate outcome is. Although she attended school in a northeastern state considered to be a pioneer in education, it was not unusual even in recent years to find children with emotional or behavioral problems labeled "retarded" and removed from the regular classroom. Sometimes it happened because teachers and principals simply could not handle the children in regular classes and sometimes the children were truly retarded. Always there were test scores involved: "Jimmy's I.Q. is only 79; how can he function with 'normal' children?" "Billy has an I.Q. of 80; no wonder he's a discipline problem." These were common statements.

GOOD TESTS AND BAD

Does it seem incredible that in our enlightened society we could make such tragic decisions? Are testing programs bad[1] and should all testing be abolished as some critics advocate? We believe not, for in spite of the unfortunate decisions that have been made because of tests, the over-whelming effect of testing has been beneficial. By coming to understand both the positive and negative aspects of testing, you will gain the sensitivity, knowledge, and competency to avoid the potential harm that could occur to students by misuse of tests, and at the same time realize the benefits of the competent use of these tools.

A TEST IS A TOOL

A few important statements need to be made about testing, and you should keep these thoughts in mind as you read this book.

Tests, like thermometers, in and of themselves are not bad. They become bad only in the hands of those who administer and interpret them poorly.

Tests do not hurt children. However, people who use tests can badly hurt children, as you will see in examples throughout this book.

A test is merely a tool, and like any tool, it must be used appropriately to be helpful. A carpenter who uses a chain saw and an axe to build fine cabinets will sell very few cabinets. Similarly a teacher who tests a first grader's arithmetic ability with a calculus exam is not likely to get very promising results.

Measurement, the work for which these tools are designed, is simply one of many ways to evaluate children. In later sections, we will detail the methods used in evaluating children. For now, let's consider a single example.

Alice was evaluated in second grade. The I.Q. test she took yielded a quantitative measurement of her intelligence, 77. Even if the test was an appropriate tool for Alice and the measurement an accurate expression of her ability to solve intellectual problems, it could not provide complete evaluation. Alice's teacher used other tools as well, including careful observation of the child's behavior, especially her ability to share and to engage in activities that require both physical coordination and social skill. She also used tests she made up herself; tools by which she measured Alice's ability to write, read, and speak. A test is only a tool, and it will do its intended job only if the tester knows what it is for and how it is properly used. The measurement that tests provide is only one aspect of the evaluation process.

Testing, measuring, evaluating—these are processes as old as re-corded history and among the most criticized and least understood of all teaching tasks. Yet, in spite of the criticisms, can you imagine teaching children multiplication without evaluating their background in arithmetic? Can they count? Can they add and subtract? They must be tested and their arithmetic ability measured before they can learn multiplication. This is the way each new learning experience must begin. Before teachers go to a new concept or a new skill, they must know whether children have the concepts and skills to build upon. Sometimes the task of measurement is simple, requiring the simple reminder that Timothy is very good at addition and subtraction, while Suzy is less confident and must be asked to do some specific things. By testing her on addition and subtraction, the teacher measures the degree to which she understands these concepts. The evaluation of her work helps her teacher determine whether she is ready for multiplication.

The criticisms leveled against testing are justified to some degree. Educators have been too quick to introduce faulty testing programs into their school systems and too slow to get them out. Test results too often have been used to place children in rigid categories: slow, average, fast, for instance, or retarded, normal, bright. Children have often had great difficulty escaping such categories, not because they couldn't but because those who interpret tests wouldn't allow it. Moreover, the anxiety many children feel when they take a test too often influences the test results. The effects of emotion on testing—fear, apprehension, excitement—have been ignored, and children have been severely penalized for allowing normal feelings to interfere with their ability to answer the questions.

What is it about testing, measuring, and evaluating that has caused such misunderstanding and such criticism? As educators, we need to understand much better than those who have gone before us the limitations of this aspect of teaching. One way is to know the origins of the testing movement and to understand what the first test makers had in mind.

THE ORIGINS OF TESTING

The testing movement as we know it is *less than 100 years old*, a small amount of time in which to build an exact science. The need for testing grew directly out of modern psychology, the study of human behavior which itself originated *less than 100 years ago*. When we consider the centuries over which man has built his theories of astronomy, physics, and mathematics, sciences that continue to change and evolve even today, how can we be so presumptuous as to expect near perfection of testing tools after a mere seventy or eighty years?

In that brief period, an enormous amount of activity ensued as researchers attempted to apply testing procedures to newfound theories of human development. In many instances, the individuals who contributed their efforts to the study of human behavior were the ones who developed methods by which to measure and describe the behavior.

One of the first and most famous of the early pioneers in the testing movement was an English scientist, Sir Francis Galton. At the turn of the nineteenth century, Galton had studied human behavior enough to recognize that individuals differ, not only in physical characteristics, but also in the ways they solve intellectual problems and in their emotional responses to life. The significance of this kind of pronouncement becomes clear when we realize how much the concept of "individual differences" permeates the literature of psychology and education today. He invented tests that clearly demonstrated individual differences and then developed the statistical procedures to describe them. In a very real sense, Galton was a pioneer both in the study of human development and in the methods by which people are tested, measured, and evaluated.

Like Galton, James McKeen Cattell, another turn-of-the-century pioneer, also concerned himself with individual differences and experimented with ways to measure individual responses to stimuli. During these early years, scientists were preoccupied with the ways in which people responded, and "reaction time" became a popular way to estimate intelligence. Cattell theorized that those whose sensory responses were faster and sharper were probably demonstrating a higher degree of intelligence. His tests measuring sensory motor abilities and his belief that he was testing intelligence led him to invent the term "mental test." Yet in many pioneering ventures, Cattell's ideas proved disappointing since no significant relationship emerged between the reaction time of students and the way they performed in school.

Perhaps the most important of testing pioneers was Edward Lee Thorndike, whose research in the learning process led to significant theories of how people learn and to the development of many tests. His contributions in both areas are considered enormously important since many of the developments in human psychology and testing arose from his work. Thorndike believed, as did Galton and Cattell, that understanding individual differences was the key to accurate statements about intelligence. The many tests he devised became important models for those researchers who followed him. Although many tests were modified and some were discarded, Thorndike's influence still appears on tests that are widely used and respected.

No discussion of the testing movement would be complete without mention of Alfred Binet. It was Binet who, with his assistant Theodore Simons, developed the first truly successful method for testing, measuring, and evaluating the intelligence of children. His was an individual test of intelligence rather than a group test, describing individual differences in quantitative terms. Revised versions of the Binet-Simons Intelligence Test are still widely used today.[2]

During the years when these investigators developed their theories and measuring devices, great attention was being given to the study of human behavior. Along with their colleagues they can truly be considered the founders of both the psychological and the evaluation movement as we know it today. It is important for those of us who will teach to know and appreciate their contributions, for many of our classroom teachings and testing activities are rooted in their pioneering work.

Historical Pictures Service, Inc., Chicago

SIR FRANCIS GALTON

Francis Galton was born near Birmingham, England, in 1822. His family was wealthy and highly educated. Among his relatives were many of England's most-accomplished and gifted citizens, including Charles Darwin, who introduced the modern theory of evolution, and Arthur Hallam, the subject of Tennyson's "In Memoriam." Galton even published a list of his wife's "connections," indicating that her father had been headmaster of Harrow.

In 1838 Galton took up the study of medicine at Birmingham General Hospital and later at King's College in London. In 1840 he shifted his career plans and transferred to Trinity College, where he majored in mathematics.

Following college, Galton went on several trips to Africa, exploring some areas of that continent for the first time. For his African explorations, Galton received the Royal Geographical Society's gold medal in 1854. After his marriage in 1853, Galton turned to writing. His first book, *The Art of Travel*, was a practical guide for the explorer, and his second book, on meteorology, was one of the first attempts to set forth precise techniques for predicting the weather.

During the 1860s Galton became impressed with his cousin Charles Darwin's book on evolution, *On the Origin of Species*. He was fascinated with Darwin's notion of the survival of the fittest, and he attempted to apply this concept to human beings, thus founding the field of *eugenics*, or the study of how the principles of heredity could be used to improve the human race.

In 1869 Galton published his first major work, *Hereditary Genius*, in which he postulated the enormous importance of heredity in determining intellectual eminence. He felt that "genius" ran in families, and he was able to point to his own family as "exhibit A." He also became impressed with the wide range of individual differences which he found for virtually all human traits, physical as well as psychological. Assuming that intelligence was a function of man's sensory apparatus, he devised series of tests of reaction time and tests of sensory acuity to measure intellectual ability. He is considered, therefore, to be the father of intelligence testing. Although Galton's tests seem naive by modern standards, his emphasis on the relationship between sensory ability and intellect foreshadow much of today's research on the importance of sensory stimulation in determining cognitive growth. Galton also invented what he termed the "index of

Adapted and used with permission of Norman and Richard Sprinthall, authors of *Educational Psychology—A Developmental Approach*, 2nd ed. (Reading, MA: Addison-Wesley, 1977).

co-relation" in order to analyze the test data that he was collecting. It was left to one of his students, Karl Pearson, however, to work out the mathematical equation for this index, which is now called the Pearson r, or product-moment correlation.

Following the publication of *Hereditary Genius*, Galton wrote other major works, including *English Men of Science, Natural Inheritance,* and *Inquiries into Human Faculty*. His range of interests in psychology was extremely wide, delving into such topics as imagery, free and controlled associations, personality testing, and, of course, the assessment of intellect.

Certainly Galton takes his place in history as being a hereditarian. He did not overlook environment completely, however. To gain understanding of the possible differential effects of heredity and environment, Galton performed psychology's first research studies on twins.

In 1909, just two years before his death, Galton was knighted. Galton's place in the history of psychology is ensured. More than any other person, he set psychology on the road to quantifying its data, and, of course, the whole testing movement in educational psychology owes a major debt to Galton's early work.

The work of these investigators made such an impact that a literal explosion of test development ensued. From approximately 1915 to 1930, numbers of testing instruments were devised to test everything from basic skills to subject matter knowledge and intelligence. Millions of tests were administered to children. Most were group tests, since school systems could not economically or practically administer individual tests. As in most "bandwagon" approaches, the enthusiasm and sometimes outright disregard for thoughtful and ethical procedures led to abuses. Controversies among researchers concerning the nature of learning and of human behavior and intelligence were thunderous at times, and stubborn individuals refused to modify their entrenched theories. Schools were flooded with both good and bad measuring instruments from inside and outside psychology and education, leading to a period of harsh criticism from those who saw this unchecked testing movement as dangerous to the welfare of the children. Fortunately, there were enough committed researchers to bring reason to the scene, and after 1930 these individuals led a serious campaign to examine and challenge the premises upon which many tests were constructed.

From 1930 to 1945, the new wave of self-evaluation and self-criticism produced significant changes in the ways in which human development and measurement were considered. Carefully standardized tests were developed from sound psychological principles. Those whose commitment to a better understanding of human behavior has made it possible for us to more adequately meet the needs of our youngsters.

CURRENT CRITICISMS OF TESTING

The abuses and often careless procedures that occurred in the earlier years of the testing movement have not, however, been completely forgotten nor

Wide World Photos

E. L. THORNDIKE

Born in 1874 as the son of a Protestant minister and brought up in the mill towns of Massachusetts, E. L. Thorndike completed his undergraduate studies in classics at Wesleyan University. A somewhat singular and solitary person, he demonstrated early in his life a capacity for hard work, long hours, and precision. Almost a classic example of the protestant work ethic, Thorndike simply abhorred making even the slightest error and consequently was always striving for perfection in his work. He had enormous amounts of mental energy and virtually threw himself into the task of defining a scientific base for psychology.

At Columbia's Teachers College, he completed his doctorate in the department of philosophy, psychology, anthropology, and education in the late 1890s. At that time, departmental specialization was not yet established. The field of educational psychology was amorphous and resisted a generic definition. Academic psychology and the so-called brass-instrument laboratories and physical measurements represented one stance. At the other end William James at Harvard was lecturing on the art of teaching, separate from the science of psychology. In between there was a range of philosophers, educators, and psychologists all attempting to give definition and coherence to the field. This was educational psychology's moment of a "cultural revolution." A hundred flowers were blooming when the youthful but dedicated E. L. Thorndike appeared on the scene. Apparently he was not at all intimidated by the first-generation psychologists and educators. As a brand new assistant professor at Teachers College in 1898, he took pleasure in attacking his elders. He referred to this period as his early assertive years. "It is fun to write all the stuff up and smite all the hoary scientists hip and thigh. . . . My thesis is a beauty. . . . I've got some theories which knock the old authorities into a grease spot." For such a fledgling, still in his twenties, to have the inner strength to attack the heroes of the day both in print and in association meetings was most unusual. Possibly within himself Thorndike transformed the protestant ethic into a messianic vision not of religion but of scientific logical positivism. In other words, the dedication that a person might feel toward a religious mission was apparently shifted so that science became his religion.

For the entire 41 years of his professional life, Thorndike remained at

Adapted and used with permission of Norman and Richard Sprinthall, authors of *Educational Psychology —A Developmental Approach*, 2nd ed. (Reading, MA: Addison-Wesley, 1977).

Columbia Teachers College. He defined educational psychology as essentially the psychology of laboratory experimentation. His life work was to create a base of scientific knowledge through careful experiments, changing one variable at a time and using precise measures. He insisted that the operational definition was the only definition for science. If you couldn't see, measure, and directly record the phenomenon under investigation, then it was not scientific or even worthwhile. Look, see, and collect data were his bywords for investigators. In fact, he really viewed himself more as an investigator than a scholar. He once noted that he had probably spent over 10,000 hours in reading and studying scientific books and journals, but he devoted more time to his own experiments and writing. His bibliography runs to a prodigious 500 items. Science, he would say was to be built by research, not proclamation.

Thorndike's insistence on the operational definition as the only acceptable way to describe and define behavior directly influenced the construction of many early intelligence tests. Even now, most intelligence tests stress observation of behavior as the way to assess cognitive ability.

---

forgiven. There are still those, inside and outside the teaching scene, who harshly criticize the things educators do in the name of evaluation. Such criticism demands an open-minded, professional attitude in order to assess the evaluation process. Knowing about some of the specific criticisms and gaining some understanding of why they exist is perhaps the best way to maintain this attitude.[3]

Tests Are Dehumanizing

Critics assert that tests tend to reduce children to something less than full human status, that by assigning numbers and quantities to human attributes, teachers diminish children in their own eyes and in the eyes of society. When Galton developed his statistical procedures for interpreting test results, he was attempting to simplify and objectify the measurement of individuals' behavior by assigning numbers to their actions. While he probably could not foresee the lengths to which his followers would go in describing human behavior in quantitative and mathematical terms, he did, in fact, open a sort of Pandora's Box. However, psychologists' intense and continuing efforts to describe behavior in statistical and quantitative terms are not motivated by insidious reasons, but instead by the need to find ways of quantifying data for research and analysis. Unfortunately, when a mother hears that her child has an I.Q. of 98, she may well throw her hands up in despair at the news that her son is below average in intelligence. If no one explains to her the wide range of I.Q. scores within the "normal" category, she probably will suffer great anxiety. Clearly, parents and others become threatened by test results if they do not fully understand the meaning of the numbers. If educators do not do the job of interpreting such test data, they deserve the criticism. For too long, educators and psychologists deliberately withheld such information as-suming that it would be misinterpreted and could cause more harm than good.

Fortunately, good teachers and others who test children are sensitive to parents' needs to know as much as possible about their children. Further, the government has stepped into the picture, partly as a result of the criticism of testing, and has brought the force of law to bear. Children and their parents not only have a need to know, they have a right to know, and teachers are now required to provide full information. While it seems unfortunate that laws must be passed to ensure fair treatment of those whom teachers serve, accountability for explaining the numbers assigned to children when they are tested, measured, and evaluated demands that teachers do a more responsible job and helps reduce the criticism that testing dehumanizes the individual.

Tests Are Destructive of the Ego

Critics also assert that test results diminish the child's will to learn. This criticism is due largely to the use of test results in placing children in ability groups such as reading or in academic tracking in junior and senior high schools. Critics say that whenever youngsters compare themselves with others in a "faster" or "brighter" group, motivation suffers and the children tend to give up. Certainly this criticism is justified if a given test result locks a child in the "C" group or in reading level three or in a category called "underachievers" or "mentally retarded." The tendency to do this is far less common than it was a decade ago, since teachers are becoming much more knowledgeable about human development, particu-larly the fact that there is no such thing as a permanent condition of intelligence. Any evaluation of intellectual ability must be made with the knowledge that innate intelligence, together with the child's experiences, combine to bring about a given I.Q. score. Psychologists generally agree that any significant change in the environment may well produce a different score. Once again, the ways in which teachers interpret and use test results make all the difference. By clearly understanding the purposes for which a given test is designed, teachers are less likely to condemn children to feelings of inadequacy. Alice's case provides a good example of the thoughtless use of test results. Fortunately, it also reveals an en-lightened and sensitive teacher who recognized the limitations of a single evaluation and did something about it.

Tests Are Unfair to Some Children

Another criticism is that many children cannot perform adequately on tests because the tests do not reflect their life-styles or their cultural environ-ments. This long-standing criticism has prompted much revision so that tests reflect the language and cultural uniqueness of given groups. Some of the most widely used intelligence and achievement tests have been revised in this way, but the criticism is still valid in many instances. Perhaps one of the most dramatic examples of this shortcoming can be seen in the case of the Puerto Rican child who speaks little English but who must take an achievement test given in English. With the increasing ethnic populations of our urban schools, this problem has become serious. Translations of major tests into Spanish, French, or Portuguese are time-consuming. Moreover, since each language varies in subtle ways, the translated tests must also be carefully standardized through extensive use with large groups of the population in question.

The problem also exists with English speaking groups whose cultural backgrounds include unique expressions and perceptions. When a word on an intelligence test carries a different connotation for these children than for the population at large, their answers are often wrong because their expressions are simply different from those of children in the larger population. There have been unfortunate cases in which the low test scores of such children have been interpreted to mean they are less intelligent or less capable than others who better understood the language of the test.

Enlightened teachers are aware of cultural and language differences, and they interpret test results with these differences in mind. Whenever possible, they avoid giving tests to children who may misunderstand or misinterpret the language. Only by working diligently toward culturally unbiased evaluation can teachers diminish both the incidents of unfair testing and the criticisms.

There Is Too Much Emphasis on Ability Testing

Lastly, critics assert that most testing is done to determine how much subject matter children have learned and how many skills they have acquired. School systems, they say, are caught up in the belief that all children should be prepared for college and that tests should reflect this emphasis. Academic excellence is stressed, and tests of intelligence, achievement, and basic skills predominate. Thus, the extensive use of such tests places little or no value on other human attributes such as creativity, vocational ability, or personality. The testing program tends to determine the curricula, particularly of secondary schools, short changing many youngsters with abundant talent and excellent personal qualities.

Despite some school systems that emphasize college preparation, this criticism is becoming less and less justified. School authorities, teachers, and parents are recognizing the wealth of human qualities and talents that exist in any group of youngsters, and important changes are taking place, particularly in the availability of alternative routes to success, such as vocational training.

As our understanding of human behavior and how to evaluate it grows, teachers will come to know that a child is a creature of many characteristics. All of these must be attended to in order to help children develop and offer to life their best and most productive assets. Teachers cannot determine the characteristics they want children to display. If evaluation techniques are sensitive to this concept, all children will have a better opportunity to succeed, and the criticism that teachers are too narrow or limited in the tests they use will fade.

These are only a few criticisms of the testing movement in America; others and new ones will appear as long as teachers test, measure, and evaluate. In the face of such criticism teachers can neither assume, as educators sometimes do, a defensive posture that denies that such abuses exist nor follow the strident demands of the most vocal critics and do away with all testing.

It is true that some school administrators place far too much stress on academic achievement in order to please parents. Some secondary schools deliberately prepare youngsters to do well on college entrance examinations. Some teachers and psychologists regard the I.Q. score as a final and permanent assessment of individual potential. Yet it is equally true that most psychologists and educators test, measure, and evaluate children with an understanding of the complex nature of human development. They consider every factor that might cause them to inadvertently misinterpret or misrepresent a test result. They consider the child's environment and the effects it may have had on the child's performance. They also consider the child's intellectual performance, physical characteristics, and emotional makeup. When they administer a test and report the results they do so with all of these factors in mind. This kind of professional attention will finally make the testing movement comprehensible and acceptable. Since the greatest percentage of testing is done in classrooms, teachers have the major responsibility for presenting children, parents, and the public at large with an improved image of testing, one that honestly keeps both the weaknesses and strengths in perspective and that ensures that tests are used to improve children's educational experiences.

TEACHERS TEST TO MEET THE NEEDS OF CHILDREN

Understanding that testing, measuring, and evaluating are in their relative infancy as methods of assessing human behavior, will lead to their improved professional use. Everyone who works with learners in any capacity must approach the task of evaluation with caution and humility and with the learners' needs uppermost in mind. This is particularly true for classroom teachers, whose front-line contact with children is totally concerned with meeting their needs.

How can tests help meet children's needs? By themselves, they cannot, since tests are merely tools. But used appropriately and skillfully, they provide important information not only about what children know or don't know but also about how they learn. Some examples will demonstrate how good teachers use tests as diagnostic devices to help them determine a child's needs.

Ms. Adams plans to begin teaching decimals to her sixth grade class. She knows that success with decimals requires a great deal of knowledge of mathematics, such as understanding fractions and how to add, subtract, multiply, and divide them; and knowing the basic operations performed with numbers, including counting, addition, subtraction, multiplication, and long division. Recognizing that mathematics is a developmental subject in which new concepts build upon previous ones, Ms. Adams tests her class on their background in mathematics. She has two objectives in mind. First, she wants to know how many children are familiar with the mathematics necessary for success with decimals. Second, she needs to know exactly where each child stands along the continuum of developmental mathematics. She discovers that seven youngsters are ready to begin discussion of the nature and meaning of decimals, but eleven others are still shaky on multiplication and division of fractions, and a third group is still struggling with long division.

Ms. Adams has used a test as a tool to measure the mathematical ability of her class. The results tell her that she will have several groups working at different developmental levels. More specifically, the test diagnoses the strengths and weaknesses of each child. Mary does well until she reaches division of fractions, where she doesn't seem to grasp the concept of inversion. Here she will need special attention and practice. Jimmy doesn't understand that one fraction multiplied by another gives an answer that is smaller than either ($1/2 \times 1/2 = 1/4$). Sam seems to understand the nature and meaning of fractions but has trouble working the examples.

Children have special needs. They handle the test differently and have their own developmental levels. Ms. Adams understands this at least partly because of the test she gave, which has helped her diagnose the arithmetic abilities of each of her children. She now is ready to teach to those abilities based upon her assessment and evaluation of the individual needs of her children.

Children's needs are not always so easy to diagnose. Mathematics is a precise subject with clear-cut blocks of material to be learned, each with its exact steps and procedures. And it is relatively easy to construct fairly good tests of arithmetic ability. This is not the case in those subjects that call for judgmental answers or opinions or that require children to make interpretations and inferences. Not only is it much more difficult for children to learn and think in this way, it is also far more difficult to test, measure, and evaluate such abilities. If Ms. Adams were teaching a social studies unit on the United Nations, for example, she would need to evaluate her children's readiness to learn about that organization in somewhat different ways.

Studying the United Nations helps youngsters understand the necessity for cooperative interaction among all peoples. Ms. Adams knows that her children began to study human relationships in kindergarten and first grade when their teachers helped them understand the structure of the family and the neighborhood. Moving through the grades, they expanded their understanding to include the community, the city, and the state, each with its set of rules, laws, and customs. Just before the sixth grade, they learned how people struggled to open the West and how they cooperated to build a great nation with its unique government.

It would be easy for Ms. Adams to construct a test of the factual material the children had learned. What were the thirteen original colonies? When was the Battle of Gettysburg fought? Who was the twelfth president of the United States? Name three explorers who helped begin the Westward Movement. But would these questions tell her how much they really understand about the need for cooperation among people? Would they give her any clues to the children's attitudes and feelings about other races and nationalities and religions?

She knows that learning about the United Nations should help her children understand the desirability for people to work together for the common good. One of her most important objectives in teaching social studies is to have her class think deeply about such things, and she must find ways to judge whether this is happening. Factual questions alone will not help her. She must examine the children's affective behavior—behavior associated with feelings, emotions, and attitudes.[4] Such behavior is very difficult to test, measure, and evaluate. She probably will begin by making her own assessment of their ability to plan and work cooperatively as a class, noting individual behavior as the group begins its work on the United Nations.

Mary, for instance, seems to be very outgoing and quite able to relate well to most of the other children. John has difficulty sharing with others and prefers to work alone. Mike is very egocentric and thinks in terms of what is important to him. The children can be placed along a behavioral continuum, from egocentric, even selfish behavior to complete ability to share and cooperate.

As Ms. Adams and her class learn the history and structure of the United Nations and discuss its goals, she relates the behavior of nations to the behavior of people. As the children study the United Nations' past ordeals, including its modest successes and frequent failures, they may project their own personalities into the study and gain insight into their behavior towards others. Ms. Adams will observe whether John becomes more able to share or whether Mike becomes more willing to reach out to others. Observations such as these are the most widely used form of testing, measuring, and evaluating, and they will help her decide whether the children have increased their ability to relate to others. Although her written tests will include factual questions, they also will ask the children to tell how they feel about relationships among nations, why some nations have difficulty working together for peace and why they sometimes go to war, and how many countries find ways to live in mutual trust.

Having carefully examined their answers and closely observed their classroom behavior, Ms. Adams will try to evaluate the affective growth of her children. Such assessments are more difficult to make and the results are not nearly as clear as those in mathematics, yet her job demands that she continually assess her children's development in all areas. As difficult as it is to accomplish, evaluation of affective behavior is just as necessary and just as important in mathematics as in any other subject. The difficulty does not relieve her of her responsibility, not only to help her children develop more mature human relationships, but to measure and evaluate that behavior as well.

So whether we are evaluating growth in arithmetic, in social skills, or in any other aspect of learning, the process is the same; only the techniques differ, with different testing instruments and procedures used to measure different kinds of growth and behavior. To meet these varied testing needs, a bewildering array of tests have been published for every conceivable area of growth and development. There are many tests of intelligence; for instance, some are designed to test groups of children while others are designed to test children individually. There are specific aptitude tests, tests of basic skills, and tests of achievement. There are personality tests, tests of vocational preference, and tests of physical fitness.

The list seems almost endless, yet new teachers need to know how to choose the testing tools that will be most appropriate to a particular task. Some questions to consider are whether a given test lives up to the claims of its publisher; what its strengths and limitations are; and most important, whether the testing, measuring, and evaluating techniques chosen are based on sound psychological principles and, when used with sound professional judgment, will help meet children's needs.

The benefits of testing by far outweigh the disadvantages. Moreover, teachers' intelligence and professional judgment will continue to assure the appropriate use of testing, measuring, and evaluating procedures. Evaluation, however, presents an awesome responsibility. Teachers are learning increasingly more about human behavior and how to change it. The process of deliberately changing children's behavior reveals that each child's behavior varies from that of every other. No two children read with exactly the same ability. No two children respond in exactly the same way to a question about atomic structure. And no two children "feel" exactly the same about democracy or loyalty or the need for cooperation. All are highly individual in their needs and in their responses. Their responses, or behavior, indicate what they know and what they need to know. Observing and recording their behavior is the foremost source of vital information to help a teacher meet their individual needs.

The purpose of this book is to help you understand how to test, measure, and evaluate children's behavior, not just to gain mechanical proficiency in administering and grading examinations, but also to become familiar with the many facets of educational evaluation for which you will be responsible. The following chapters will help you keep the individual needs of children uppermost in mind. Whatever we discuss—the nature of intelligence, item analysis, the coefficient of correlation, musical aptitude—we will keep each topic in the context of children and their needs. In this way, perhaps the typically formidable aspects of testing such as statistics and the analysis of test data will become more meaningful and understandable.

Before we continue our discussion, we ask that you keep several important points about testing in mind.

1. Tests are merely tools with which to discover what children know or need to know.

2. Tests help us measure children's behavior.

3. The measurement of behavior provides one of many possible inputs by which to evaluate children.

4. Evaluation of children provides the information we need to meet individual needs.

We ask you to remember also that, in spite of the criticisms of testing, tests do not hurt children; only those who use tests poorly hurt children. We hope the material in this book will help you use testing, measuring, and evaluating procedures with caution, good judgment, and humility.

IMPORTANT POINTS TO THINK ABOUT

1. Review the beginnings of the testing movement and note the relative "newness" of testing as a science. Can you identify the major contributions of such early pioneers as Galton, Cattell, Thorndike, and Binet?

2. As you think about the current criticisms of testing described in this chapter, can you think about ways in which a good teacher might reduce their severity?

3. The history of the testing movement can be divided roughly into four periods of approximately fifteen years each, starting around 1900 and continuing through 1960. Can you describe briefly the characteristics of each period?

4. How would you describe the testing movement from 1960 to the present?

5. We contend that tests in and of themselves do not hurt anyone. The misuse and abuse of tests has done and can do a great deal of harm. Can you discuss ways in which tests are misused and abused?

6. Tests are merely tools by which we measure and evaluate the behavior of children. Can you describe how these tools might contribute to helping students succeed in school?

NOTES

1. Paul L. Houts, ed., *The Myth of Measurability* (New York: Hart, 1977); Leon J. Kamin, *The Science and Politics of I.Q.* (New York: Wiley, 1974).
2. A. Binet and H. Simon, "Application des methodes nouvelles au diagnostic du niveau intellectual chez des enfants normaux et anarmaux d'hospice et d'ecole primaire," *L'Annee Psychologique* 11.(1905).
3. George Weker, *Uses and Abuses of Standardized Testing in the Schools* (Washington Council for Basic Education, 1974).
4. David R. Krathwohl, Benjamin S. Bloom, and Bertram B. Masia, *Taxonomy of Educational Objectives*, Handbook II, Affective Domain (New York: McKay, 1956).

ADDITIONAL READINGS

L. J. Cronbach, "Five decades of public controversy over mental testing," *American Psychologist* (1975).

H. J. Eysenck, *The I.Q. Argument* (New York: The Library Press, 1977).

B. Hoffmann, *The Tyranny of Testing* (New York: Crowell-Collier, 1972).

Richard and Norman Sprinthall, *Educational Psychology, A Developmental Approach*, 2nd ed. (Reading, MA: Addison-Wesley, 1977).

CHAPTER TWO

WHAT DO TEACHERS NEED TO KNOW BEFORE THEY TEST?

IMPORTANT POINTS TO WATCH FOR

Understanding the developmental nature of physical, personal, and cognitive growth is essential to effective testing, measuring, and evaluating.

Physical growth can dramatically affect personal and cognitive development.

Good personal, or affective, growth is essential to ego strength and self-confidence and can play an important role in good cognitive development.

Adolescence is a particularly trying time for youngsters who need to enter adulthood with a feeling of security and independence.

Evaluation of personal, or affective, growth is difficult but essential to a thorough understanding of children.

Cognitive growth is the ability to receive stimuli and process them into meaningful intellectual structures by which individuals are able to solve more and more complex problems as growth proceeds.

Cognitive, or intellectual growth, is the result of the continued interaction of inherited ability with the environment.

Jean Piaget sees cognitive growth as proceeding through four well-defined developmental stages—sensori-motor, pre-operational, concrete-operational, and formal operational—each marked by a *qualitatively* more mature intellectual ability.

Physical, personal, and cognitive growth are all dramatically entwined, and each must always be considered because it might affect the other two.

18

Most growth and development, particularly the personal and cognitive, cannot be assessed directly but must be evaluated indirectly by observing behavior. *Behavior* is what we test and measure in order to understand and evaluate the child within.

In the previous chapter we stated that each generation of teachers knows a great deal more about human behavior than preceding generations. Since there is more to know, a vital part of professional training involves keeping abreast of the ongoing research in growth and development. Psychologists' expanding knowledge of behavior enhances the teacher's ability to evaluate children's needs and to develop effective teaching strategies to meet them.

TEACHERS NEED TO KNOW ABOUT INDIVIDUAL DIFFERENCES

Even the most elementary education and psychology courses stress the term "individual differences." Although the term may have become a cliché, the concept has made a strong impact on the teaching and learning environment. It is certainly one of the most significant of psychology's contributions, one which provides us with the tools for meeting "individual needs."

Differences among individuals are due partly to inherited qualities and partly to environmental conditions. Although the degree to which one or the other factor dominates in shaping differences is still a controversial subject, it is clear that children arrive in the world different from one another in many ways. Some differences, easily recognized, are physical—size, for instance, or hair color. Others are less obvious but easily determined—reaction time, for instance, and sensitivity to light and sound. Others, even less obvious, are largely inferred; perhaps the most important of these is what we call intelligence.

A CHILD'S BEHAVIOR IS SHAPED BY INHERITANCE AND ENVIRONMENT

Newborn infants are bombarded by thousands of sensory stimuli, which immediately begin to shape their inherited traits. The process continues throughout a life time, as the combination of inheritance and environment modifies and conditions behavior. When children reach school, they have unique personalities that resist a teacher's efforts to group them with others or force them to learn in a uniform way. A child's intelligence, physical appearance, personality, and language ability have combined to produce a unique individual, very much like everyone else in some ways but very different in many others. Teachers are responsible for recognizing the differences among children and developing learning experiences appropriate to each. Only when they acquire the skills by which to evaluate each child's differences can this be achieved.

THE CHALLENGE OF EVALUATING INDIVIDUAL NEEDS

Developing learning experiences to meet individual needs is challenging. As mentioned previously, before beginning to teach decimals, a teacher must know whether the children know fractions. There is no way to know this without some kind of testing to assess the arithmetic ability of all of the children in a class. Otherwise, teaching decimals will not be merely challenging, it will be downright frustrating to teacher and pupils alike. What must teachers know, then, to identify individual strengths and weaknesses effectively in order to fully individualize instruction? Is evaluation simply a mechanical process by which teachers give a test or ask some questions to find out what children know or don't know? Or should teachers think more deeply about the children and the long developmental process by which they arrived at this point in their lives?

THE DEVELOPMENTAL NATURE OF GROWTH

Effective evaluation and teaching are possible only when teachers have adequate understanding of the developmental nature of growth. Growth, whether physical, cognitive, or personal, consists of a series of fairly well-defined stages and plateaus. To know that children are not physically mature enough to reach the ceiling on a climbing rope, or that their coordination is not yet developed enough for them to perform on the parallel bars, is to have some understanding of the developmental nature of physical growth. At this point the children's teacher will provide physical tasks at a lower order and will patiently wait and watch for rope climbing and parallel-bar strength and coordination to develop further along the developmental continuum. Testing will play a major part in the teacher's decision to wait or to proceed, but testing without understanding the continuum may lead the teacher to make judgments that are inaccurate or unfair. "Tommy will *never* be able to climb that rope," or "Sally is so uncoordinated, she'll never be graceful like the others."

The same principle applies to cognitive growth. Teachers must understand how intellect develops, and when testing, they must be able to recognize that a response is wrong not necessarily because the child is unintelligent but perhaps because not enough experience has been gained to permit the correct answer.

Similarly, with personal, or affective, growth labeling a child as "selfish" or "insensitive" is permissible as long as a teacher recognizes that these traits are common to all children at certain points along the personal growth continuum. Assessments of "selfish" or "insensitive" behavior should be the result of careful testing of personal behavior, either through systematic observation or with carefully constructed measurement instruments. Knowing that these traits are common at a particular age gives teachers the patience and understanding necessary to guide a child toward more "giving" behavior later on.

The following overview of physical development is general and cites a number of authors from among many who have contributed to our knowledge in this area. However, the discussion of personal and cognitive development identifies a specific writer for each area, not to exclude the work of others but to simplify the discussion of developmental growth and to stress the importance of understanding cognitive and personal development for effective testing, measuring, and evaluating.

TEACHERS NEED TO UNDERSTAND PHYSICAL GROWTH

What has good physical health to do with learning? The learning process demands tremendous amounts of physical energy, not available in inexhaustible supplies. Thus good physical health is essential for its production in adequate amounts. The child in poor physical condition, who falls asleep in class or who seems listless and devoid of ambition tires more quickly than one in better shape. The unthinking teacher may call such children lazy, trying to force them to do more work but this may fail and perhaps so will the children.

The teacher who is aware of physical differences among children and who understands the developmental nature of physical growth will recognize the limitations of children whose poor health denies them the energy that other children seem to have in abundance. For example, the teacher may evaluate Jimmy's physical appearance and activities simply through observation or through sophisticated medical tests. Either form of evaluation, or both, will improve the child's chances for success. Knowing that Jimmy's lack of energy will limit him to shorter work sessions and frequent rest periods, the teacher can plan lessons to help Jimmy meet his physical as well as his learning needs—perhaps by seeing that he has a good lunch and nourishing snacks each day, or by working with the nurse and the physical education teacher to see that he receives adequate physical care and exercise. The teacher's careful testing, measuring, and evaluating of his physical growth will greatly improve Jimmy's chances for better health and therefore will provide more energy for the learning process.

Good teachers know that all aspects of growth are developmental, and they better understand the needs of their children because of this knowledge. They know, for instance, that physical growth is not merely the sum of the current height, weight, and other physical measurements of the child. The child has inherited a particular set of genes that determine many of the obvious physical characteristics such as hair and eye color and general body configuration. The genes also determine a child's general ability to move the various parts of the body and to receive and respond to stimuli. Heredity also determines the ability to see, hear, taste, smell, and touch, but it remains for the environment to produce the stimuli to which the responses will be made. The interaction of inherited physical traits with environmental stimuli produces a child's behavior. Inheriting a well-formed and healthy body with a well-developed central nervous system gives the child excellent chances for good physical development. If, however, the environment denies the opportunities for nourishment and exercise of inherited attributes, the child may become unattractive and poorly coordinated, physically weak and underdeveloped from lack of proper food and healthful activity.

PHYSICAL APPEARANCE CAN AFFECT EMOTIONAL GROWTH

As children move on to their later childhood years, they may differ greatly in physical development, and this can cause special learning problems. Teachers who work with children in the upper elementary and junior high grades must be particularly aware of such differences. They know that physical development around the time of adolescence not only includes wide variations in growth, but also that adolescence arrives at different times for different children. Sally, a fifth grader, towers over other children, boys and girls alike. Although she is in excellent health, she is painfully aware that she is different from everyone else, especially since she has begun to take on some of the characteristics of adulthood: her breasts are developing and she has had her first period. On the other hand, Tommy is in the eighth grade, but the other kids, having begun adolescence, tower over him. Even though he is in excellent health, he is physically more like a fifth grader and wishes, sometimes, that he were back there.

Youngsters like Sally and Tommy have special problems. One feels like a misfit because she has matured early and the other because he hasn't matured on time. Awareness of these as well as less dramatic physical differences among children is part of the evaluation process that good teachers carry on every day. By understanding the typical growth patterns for youngsters at different ages, they come to recognize those which differ significantly enough to cause problems. They know that Sally will be extremely self-conscious of her size. She will be preoccupied and anxiety-ridden about her appearance. The feelings she has about herself may be heightened by insensitive classmates who poke fun at her or perhaps exclude her from their activities. The sensitive teacher knows that Sally's anxiety about her appearance will affect her ability to learn, and that ways must be found to develop her patience and understanding while her classmates catch up with her.

Sally's teacher, and Tommy's, will use sound evaluation techniques based upon their understanding of the developmental nature of physical growth. These may include physical fitness tests that they administer themselves or schedule through the physical education department. Many tests of coordination, strength, and stamina are available and are widely used. The teachers will also ask for health reports from the school nurse and, when appropriate, will seek more specific assistance from a doctor to determine the presence of such conditions as chronic malnutrition or anemia. These and other physical conditions can play a major role in robbing children of energy to learn and grow adequately. However, careful and systematic observation are the teachers' major source of information, giving them important clues about the physical health of their children—clues that may enable them to improve opportunities for physical growth in the classroom or that will signal the need for the expertise of the nurse or family doctor.

Finally, their evaluation will help them meet the personal needs of each child as they find ways teach the children to understand and accept these temporary differences. Thus, sound evaluation techniques derive from sound knowledge of physical growth patterns and how these patterns affect learning.

TEACHERS NEED TO UNDERSTAND PERSONAL GROWTH

Physical growth is relatively easy to observe and evaluate. Other aspects of development, such as development of the personality, are not so apparent, yet they are perhaps more important than physical growth. Personality development plays a significant role in the child's ability to succeed, since it is the product of all other aspects of growth. Marked differences in physical characteristics, for example, can cause anxiety and emotional stress. How children view themselves and how they think others view them are often tied closely to appearance.

Knowing that children need to feel good about themselves in order to be comfortable and successful in school, teachers are constantly alert to the children's affective behavior. They realize that the behavior they see at a given moment results from a complex developmental process that began at birth and that continues long after the child leaves school. As professionals, they have come to understand this process, and their understanding helps them to evaluate effectively.

In a later chapter, we will show how teachers carry on the actual process of assessing the personal growth of their children. The next section will present a brief overview of Erik Erikson's personal development theory. As the various developmental stages are described, try to visualize children in a classroom engaging in the behavior typical of each stage. Consider how a teacher might help each achieve good personal growth.

ERIK ERIKSON'S THEORIES OF PERSONAL GROWTH

Psychology has contributed a great deal to our understanding of personality development and to productive ways of evaluating affective growth. One of the most significant contributors has been Erik Erikson,[1] whose research shows a well-defined set of developmental stages. Unlike Freud, who believed that the child's basic personality structures were complete by about age 6, Erikson theorized that personality development continues throughout life. He agreed with Freud, however, on the great importance of the early years to later emotional and personal success. A child, for instance, who experiences a warm and loving environment during the first 18 months, will tend to develop a more positive and trusting outlook than one who is neglected. The latter may become distrustful and negative, traits which will be carried into the classroom and which may inhibit learning.

Early Childhood

The first stage or period in Erikson's theory is one of *trust and mistrust*, when the child is totally dependent upon the mother's care. This 18-month interval is followed by a period known as *autonomy and shame*. Lasting approximately from ages 1 1/2 to 3, this period is marked by constant activity and exploration as the child begins to assert a degree of autonomy from the mother. The degree to which children are allowed to explore and investigate will help determine whether they become secure and self-assured about themselves and the world, or filled with shame about their exploratory behavior. Since these characteristics are present later in the classroom, strongly affecting the child's ability to learn, a teacher's awareness of these characteristics helps in understanding the reasons for such behavior.

Once children have negotiated the period of autonomy and shame and have developed some degree of self-direction, the third childhood period, that of *initiative and guilt* begins. Between 3 to 6 years of age, they become intensely aware of their roles as male or female, and they try to identify with adult models. The degree to which they are allowed to express themselves and act out their perceived roles without censorship or ridicule will help determine their ability to take initiative later without fearing reprisal or humiliation. If they are secure in their roles, their feelings and self-concepts will be well established, and they will come to school more able to tackle "grown up" learning tasks.

Kindergarten and first grade teachers must be particularly understanding of the childhood stages of personal development, for during the first six years or so of life children come face to face with many of the challenges of independent behavior. Teachers must be ready to recognize the highly dependent child who was never allowed self-directed exploration. They must be sensitive to the developmental deficiencies of such children and ready to provide experiences that will gradually bring the child to a greater feeling of self-worth and independence. They need to find ways to encourage the child's initiative without fear of shame or guilt and the awareness that at least part of the world is safe and comfortable. Even more important, the teachers in these earliest grades must recognize that their efforts to develop children's self-assurance will influence youngsters' subsequent and more challenging learning experiences, experiences that will require increased personal strengths and independence.

Teachers who understand early and preschool development can evaluate more effectively the personal strengths and weaknesses of their kindergarten and primary grade youngsters. Knowing what behaviors to expect, they will quickly recognize those that signal inadequate personal growth. Effective evaluation is essential if they are to help children achieve good affective growth and successfully overcome personality deficiencies acquired in early childhood.

Personal Growth in the Elementary Grades

Erikson calls the second major stage the *juvenile period*, which lasts roughly from 6 to 12 years of age. Teachers are most familiar with this stage, for they watch it develop daily. Not only do they watch it, they play a major role in the development of personality during these years. Called the period of *mastery and inferiority*, this stage describes how children begin to turn from previously egocentric and childlike behavior toward important associations with others. The classroom, the neighborhood, and the juvenile group provide opportunities for socialization, especially for learning to give and share with others rather than simply taking. The new environment is one to be mastered and, during these years, children have many opportunities for developing mastery, in school subjects, in athletic skills, in the entire world of growing and living things. Effective teachers in the elementary grades are sensitive to the need for mastery, and they provide the materials and opportunities for children to indulge their emerging curiosity and feelings of independence, particularly through their increasing proficiency at reading and other learning skills. If the children are relatively self-assured, they will approach the job of learning with enthusiasm, and their successes with learning in turn will increase

Harvard University News Office

ERIK ERIKSON

Born at the turn of the century, Erik Erikson spent his early years in Europe. As a son of well-to-do parents, his education was both formal and informal. Like other upper-class children, when he finished his regular school work, he traveled the continent. He described this period as his own "moratorium." Later in his professional career he developed a theory of human development in stages across the entire span of the life cycle. For adolescents and young adults he noted the importance of a moratorium, a temporary life space, between the completion of general academic education and the choice of a life career. He noted at the time of his own young adulthood it was fashionable to travel through Europe, gaining a perspective

on civilization and one's own possible place in it. He chose the avocation of portrait painting as an activity during this time. It permitted maximum flexibility for travel and yielded some productive output as well. Obviously talented, he soon gained a reputation as a promising young artist, especially for his portraits of young children.

The turning point in his life came when he was invited to a villa in Austria to do a child's portrait. He entered the villa and was introduced to the child's father, Sigmund Freud. There began a series of informal discussions as he completed his work. A few weeks later, he received a written invitation from Freud to join the psychoanalytic institute of Vienna and study for child analysis. Erikson has commented that at this point he confronted a momentous decision, the choice between a continued moratorium, with more traveling and painting, and a commitment to a life career pattern. Fortunately for psychology and particularly for our eventual understanding of children and adolescents, Erikson ended the moratorium.

After completing his training, he migrated to this country and served from 1936 to 1939 as a research associate in psychiatry in Yale. From 1939 to 1951 he served as professor at the University of California and then moved to the Austen Riggs Clinic in Pittsburgh. With each move, his reputation grew in significance. His theoretical framework was adopted in toto by the White House Conference on Children in 1950. The conference report, a national charter for child and adolescent development in this country, was almost a literal repetition of

Adapted and used with permission of Norman and Richard Sprinthall, authors of *Educational Psychology: A Developmental Approach*, 2nd ed. (Reading, MA: Addison-Wesley, 1977).

his thoughts. In 1960 he was offered a university professorship at Harvard in recognition of his national and international stature in the field of human development. The career that started so informally that day at Freud's villa culminated with almost unprecedented eminence as a professor in the country's oldest and most prestigious institution of higher education—all without the benefit of a single earned academic degree. Ironically, he was offered only associate status in the American Psychological Association as late as 1950. This oversight was partially removed in 1955 when he was elected as a Fellow of the Division of Developmental Psychology, without ever having been a member.

His work has been a major contribution to our understanding of healthy psychological growth during all aspects of the life cycle. In addition to the high quality of his insight, Erikson possessed a genuine flair in linguistic expression both spoken and written. In fact, one could almost compare his command of the English language with the benchmark established in this century by Winston Churchill. In many ways Erikson's scope was as broad and comprehensive as that of Churchill. Erikson's genius has been his ability to see the threefold relationship among the person, the immediate environment, and historical forces. Thus each human is partially shaped by environmental and historical events, but each human in turn shapes the environment and can change the course of history.

Erikson's long and distinguished career is an outstanding example of his own theory of development. He has achieved a sense of personal mastery and professional integrity with "an acceptance of his own responsibility for what his life is and was and of its place in the flow of history."*

Certainly his contributions to our understanding of the personal growth of children add immeasurably to our ability to assess the personal and emotional strengths and weaknesses of our youngters.

---

self-confidence. On the other hand, if the school environment is threatening or too difficult, mastery will be impossible and feelings of inferiority will result. As teachers observe their children, they constantly evaluate these aspects of affective behavior. Their understanding of the need to gain mastery of the environment will help them promote good personal growth in their children during the first five or six grades.

Adolescence—Personal Growth in the Upper Elementary and Secondary Grades

Teachers in the upper elementary and secondary grades see youngsters move into and through the third of Erikson's stages, *adolescence*. While the juvenile stage requires mastery of many kinds of activities, the adolescent stage requires increased opportunities for independence and responsibility as teenagers struggle for a sense of identity. Even those who have come gracefully and successfully through the childhood and juvenile periods with relative self-assurance often struggle with the transition events of adolescence. They must confront and survive both the world within them and the world without. The physiological changes that mark entrance to adulthood generate confusion in many adolescents. More often than not, their questions about their dynamically changing physiology are not answered fully, if at all. At the same time, the world outside makes increasing demands upon them to be responsible and grown up, often without allowing them adequate opportunities to test their ability to do so.

Teachers who work with adolescents must know about the psychology of this often traumatic period of personal development. Their observations and evaluations will give them clues to the ways in which individual adolescents handle the difficulties of adolescence. Even the most stable of them must come to grips with the contradiction of adult demands for responsibility without having achieved the status of real adulthood. Childhood rules and regulations tend to persist and adolescents resent the inconsistency of those adults who preach honesty and morality but who may drink to excess, lie on their tax returns, and get their traffic violations fixed.

With some understanding of adolescent psychology, teachers of young adults will be sensitive to their need to assume adult roles. Straightforward classroom discussions about the confusion and inconsistencies of adolescence will show them that others are also struggling to understand themselves and that they can begin to assume a greater degree of freedom to learn independently. Watching carefully the ways in which individuals learn responsibility is an important part of the evaluation process. It is the principal means by which teachers help each young adult develop a sense of identity and independence without losing sight of essential relationships and moral values.

EVALUATION OF PERSONAL GROWTH IS DIFFICULT BUT ESSENTIAL

Helping children at all levels come to know and accept themselves is incredibly challenging. Teachers find it difficult to evaluate affective growth, and yet they have no choice but to do so, for personal development is learned as surely as geography or spelling. Teachers' responsibility for evaluating personal growth is not lessened by the difficulty in understanding it. By understanding personality development, teachers can better identify each child's place along the continuum of personal growth. Has Bill achieved mastery over the important elements of his life? His school work? His relationships with his classmates? Or does he have feelings of inferiority because some things in life have mastered him instead? Are the demands of junior high too much for Tommy, who must behave in more adult ways but who is still physically and emotionally a fifth grader? By understanding his desperate need for identity, perhaps his teacher can lessen the demands upon him until he is a little better able to be independent and responsible.

In following chapters, we will explain in detail how affective learning is evaluated, instructional objectives stated, and teaching strategies planned for the optimal development of affective learning.

TEACHERS NEED TO UNDERSTAND INTELLECTUAL GROWTH

A third area of human behavior, and the one of most direct concern, is *cognitive growth*. Cognitive growth means the way in which children learn, more specifically, the ways in which children use intelligence to internalize their experiences. Until quite recently, psychology considered intelligence to be quantitative in nature and inherited at birth. Thus, since a person's cognitive ability was thought to be predetermined, a child had fixed intelligence and could learn just so much. Retarded children, for instance, were treated as slow learners because of their limited quantity of intelligence, and curricula were established to accommodate their slowness. Accordingly, Alice, who was discussed in the first chapter, could not be expected to perform intellectual tasks equal to those of more intelligent children because her quantity of intelligence was some twenty points less than that of normal children. Had her teacher been unaware of recent changes in cognitive theory, Alice might well have been placed in a special class, one which might never have provided the stimulation for her to show her true ability.

The study of intelligence, that quality or ability that allows us to remember, to think, and to solve intellectual problems has had a controversial history, and some dispute still lingers.

Is Intelligence Inherited?

Around the turn of the century, when the testing movement was in its infancy, serious differences of opinion among those who pioneered in the study and testing of human behavior created great animosity among the new experts![2] There were those such as Sir Francis Galton, who believed that intelligence was a completely inherited trait and a function of an individual's sensory equipment.[3] Galton, a cousin of Charles Darwin, was the first to devise a test of intellectual potential based upon his belief that since people varied in their sensory ability to discriminate among stimuli, such "individual differences" were inherited and could be measured. A child who could discriminate more accurately than another the subtle differences in musical pitch and tonal quality, for instance, would be thought to have inherited more aptitude for music.

Other researchers brought Galton's hereditarian views to America. One was James McKeen Cattell,[4] who studied with Galton and who devised a sensory motor test and coined the term "mental test." G. Stanley

Hall,[5] a prominent psychologist and President of Clark University, was perhaps America's most influential advocate of the inheritance theory. By 1916, L. M. Terman,[6] one of Hall's students, had created a total revision of the famous Binet intelligence test, and his studies of gifted children gave strong impetus to the hereditarian point of view.

Is Intelligence a Product of Environment?

However, there were those who felt just as strongly that intelligence was not inherited but rather was the result of environmental influence. For them, behavior was the clue to mental ability and all behavior occurred in response to the environment. The early behaviorists believed, furthermore, that the responses could be measured and cognitive ability evaluated.

John B. Watson[7] was one of the earliest and most influential of the behaviorists; it was he who declared, "Give me the baby and I'll make it climb and use its hands in construction of buildings of stone or wood. . . . I'll make it a thief, a gunman or a dope fiend . . . . Make him a deaf mute, and I will build you a Helen Keller. Men are built, not born." This astounding theory of learning, in which man was thought to be nothing more than a complex machine to be manipulated, had powerful followers. Edward L. Thorndike[8] compiled a set of "learning laws" by which man acquired knowledge and new behavior. His theories were refined by B. F. Skinner[9] the most influential behavioristic psychologist, whose "operant learning" theory currently dominates many curricula.

Although most hereditarians and environmentalists have since come to agree that learning ability is a product of both inheritance and environment, they did so only recently. In fact, the degree to which each influences behavior is still the subject of long debates and learned papers.

With the controversial state of these psychological theories, it is easy to understand why testing, measuring, and evaluating procedures are sometimes suspect. If psychologists cannot agree on the origin of mental ability, how can they devise a test to measure it?

Is Intelligence a Quantity or a Quality?

More recently, particularly through the work of Jean Piaget,[10] psychologists have made a dramatic reassessment of the nature of intelligence, providing teachers with an exceedingly different theory of intelligence that views the child as inheriting a basic learning ability that is nurtured dramatically by the environment. In this view, the child's intellect is described as developmental and composed of clearly-defined stages, each being qualitatively rather than quantitatively different from the last. Each depends for full development on successful development of the preceding stage.

In recent years, then, teachers have come to understand cognitive growth as the ability to receive and process stimuli into meaningful intellectual structures by which individuals are able to solve increasingly complex problems as growth proceeds. By describing intellectual structures in *qualitative* terms, they are able to understand that a full developmental nurturing of the intellect will require a curriculum that is flexible and responsive to the qualitative nature of the mind.

Flexibility of curriculum also means flexibility of evaluation. If each child is qualitatively different from all others, each must be tested, measured, and evaluated without rigid preconceptions of how much the child should know at a specific time.

JEAN PIAGET'S THEORY OF COGNITIVE GROWTH

A brief discussion of Piaget's developmental theory illustrates some of the latest thinking about cognitive growth. Such thinking makes the task of nurturing and evaluating children's cognitive ability look more promising.

Piaget described intellectual development much as Erikson described personal growth—as composed of successive stages. He believed that there is a close relationship between biological and intellectual growth. As he watched young children mature in their ability to adapt physically to their environment and, over a long series of developmental stages, to control it, he recognized that the intellect was undergoing the same kind of development. Although adapting at first, the intellect gradually gained experience through interaction with the environment and eventually acquired increased control over an environment that had originally dominated the individual. Teachers who understand intellectual development in this way know that children at various ages reveal varying degrees of mastery over the environment in the way they solve problems. By watching and describing the way children handle problems, teachers are evaluating cognitive growth. The evaluation might result from daily observation of the children at work and play or from their performance on a formal intelligence test. Either way, they are describing the *behavior* of children, behavior which provides clues to the quality of their intellectual ability.

Cognitive Development in Early Childhood

To know what kind of cognitive behavior to watch for and to evaluate, teachers need to know how and when each level or stage of cognitive growth develops. For instance, very young children react largely sensorially and physically to the immediate environment, which provides most of the stimuli during this *sensori-motor* period, lasting from birth to approximately age 2. Piaget has found that during the first few months, responses are immediately and grossly muscular. More controlled responding follows as children mature physically and acquire greater ability

Jean-Pierre Landenberg

JEAN PIAGET

Jean Piaget was born in Neuchatel, Switzerland, in 1896. Piaget was a curious, alert, studious, and extremely bright child. By age ten he had published his first scientific paper, a description of an albino sparrow he had observed in a local park. Between ages eleven and fifteen Piaget worked after school as a laboratory assistant to the director of a natural history museum and in the process became an expert on mollusks and other zoological topics. When he was fifteen, he was offered the job of curator of the mollusk section at a Geneva museum. He received his degree from the University of Neuchatel at age eighteen, and his Ph.D. in natural sciences three years later. Piaget had published more than twenty papers in the field of zoology before reaching his twenty-first birthday. In short, Piaget demonstrated a rare intellectual precocity during his childhood and adolescent years.

Despite his early interest in natural science, the yound Piaget read widely in sociology, religion, and philosophy. While studying philosophy he became especially interested in epistemology, the study of how knowledge is obtained. With his background in zoology, Piaget became convinced that biological principles could be utilized in understanding epistemological problems. His search for a bridge between biology and epistemology brought him finally into the world of psychology.

After receiving his doctorate, Piaget sought training in psychology and so left Switzerland to study and gain experience at a number of European laboratories, clinics, and universities. During this time he worked for awhile at Binet's laboratory school in Paris, where he did intelligence testing on French school children. He became fascinated, not by a child's correct answer to a test item, but by a child's incorrect responses. He doggedly pursued the incorrect answers in the hope of learning more about the depth and extent of children's ideas and mental processes. His goal was to understand how children of various ages came upon their knowledge of the world around them. This became Piaget's lifework, to find out how children go about the business of obtaining knowledge.

Later Piaget took detailed, minute-by-minute notes of the mental growth of his own three children, Jacqueline, Lucienne, and Laurent.

In 1929, Piaget went to the University of Geneva, where he became the assistant director of the J. J. Rousseau Institute, and in 1940 he assumed the duties of director at Geneva's Psychology Laboratory.

Piaget has written a tremendous

Adapted and used with permission of Norman and Richard Sprinthall, authors of *Educational Psychology: A Developmental Approach*, 2nd ed. (Reading, MA: Addison-Wesley, 1977).

number of books and articles on cognitive growth in children. He believes that intellecual growth is a direct continuation of inborn biological growth. The child is born biologically equipped to make a variety of motor responses, which then provide the framework for the thought processes that follow. The biological givens impose on the developing child an invariant direction to the development of cognitive processes. The ability to think springs from the physiological base. Clearly, Piaget has kept his early training in natural science clearly in mind as he has gone on to develop his system of cognitive growth.

Now in his twilight years, Piaget still is actively seeking asnwers to some of psychology's most fundamental questions. According to his biographer, friend, and former student, David Elkind, Piaget still rises early, about 4 a.m., and writes at least four publishable pages before teaching his morning classes. His afternoons are devoted to taking long walks and thinking about his current studies and research, and his evenings are spent reading. As soon as his classes are over for the summer, Piaget goes to his mountain retreat in the Alps. As fall approaches, the mountain air turns crisp, the leaves begin to change color, and Piaget comes down the mountain, laden with new material for several articles and books. Piaget has been coming down that mountain for over fifty autumns, and the volume of his writing has been enormous. Just as Freud's name has become synonymous with the study of emotional growth, Piaget is psychology's foremost expert on cognitive growth. He has provided teachers with a clearly defined theory of cognitive development; one which permits an excellent framework by which we can better observe and evaluate the intellectual potential and progress of our children.

---

to respond in more refined ways. Increased physical ability allows more motion, and as the infant begins to move away from the captive environment of crib and playpen, the world expands enormously and with it the number of stimuli to which the infant can respond. This rapid expansion of available stimuli is one of the most important aspects of the sensori-motor stage. With so many more opportunities to respond and react to the environment, children must learn the vital ability to make choices. Since they cannot respond to all stimuli, they must decide which are most desirable. In addition to selecting from among thousands of stimuli, children also learn that many different responses are possible. The child learns to *discriminate*, choosing not only the appropriate stimulus but also the correct response. The tremendous importance of discrimination becomes very clear a little later on in life when the formal learning process begins.

Teachers quickly identify those youngsters who have had poor early childhood experiences during the sensori-motor stage of cognitive development. These children often have problems with discrimination, particularly in reading, and remedial work becomes necessary.

The sensori-motor stage, then, provides the child with fundamental responding mechanisms which are absolutely necessary for successful growth. At about age 2 if all has gone well, the child will be ready to move from the sensori-motor stage, with its relatively primitive quality of cognitive growth, to the *pre-operational stage*. The quality of thinking moves to a higher plateau during this stage, which lasts for approximately five years. Children become very mobile during these years and are no longer bound by their immediate sensory environment. Their travels around the house, into the neighborhood, and beyond enable them to begin to store internal images and to develop rapidly expanding vocabularies. Their ability to use more and more words helps in the development of the intuitive process, a process so necessary to problem solving later on. As a result of increasing language ability and thousands of new experiences, they engage in a great deal of fantasy, which helps in building a rich imagination and in storing memories. Most behavior during this period is haphazard, without much thought of the consequences. However, kindergarten and first grade teachers must realize that imagination and memory are extremely important to learning during the child's school years and that the pre-operational stage marks the period during which the child gathers the experiences necessary to successful entrance into the third, or *concrete-operational stage*.

Cognitive Development in the Elementary Grades

Children at age 6 or 7 qualify, so to speak, for entrance to Piaget's concrete-operational stage when they begin to systematically recall some of their experiences and are able to verbalize them accurately and to selectively explore and test them. This ability is essential to successful learning. Without accurate recall and good language ability with which to describe memories, children are hard pressed to use their experiences to solve new problems.

It is no coincidence that children begin the challenge of formal schooling at about the time these cognitive abilities begin to emerge. Even though kindergarten and first grade youngsters continue to exhibit vivid imaginations, the discipline of school demands that they begin to relate to the environment in a more structured and logical manner. During the four or five years of the concrete-operational stage, cognitive quality changes dramatically as children learn to perform specific and "concrete" operations on memories they bring to school and on the experiences they encounter there. Their conclusions, in turn, become more and more logical with practice. Performing concrete operations in a logical and structured way makes it possible for them to learn the fundamental skills necessary to read, write, and compute accurately and to reach into their storehouse of cognitive memory for clues to testing and solving new problems.

The concrete-operational stage is well known to elementary grade teachers, who need to assess the quality of each child's cognitive ability. If children entering kindergarten have already gained a wealth of experiences through traveling to many places with their families and through exposure to many books at home, their language ability will probably be superior to that of many other children. Such children will be confident about moving immediately into structured and disciplined learning situations because they have developed the cognitive abilities to do so. However, children who have had few of these kinds of experiences will be unable to succeed in disciplined and structured learning situations. They do not have the large number of memories and the language development necessary for these activities. In other words, their cognitive growth is still pre-operational, and the teacher will have to spend considerable time helping them make up for lost time and experience.

Cognitive Development in the Upper Elementary and Secondary Grades

Toward the end of the concrete-operational period, most children have gained a great deal of language ability, and this increased skill in verbalizing experiences allows them to form increasingly complex mental associations. The quality of cognitive growth changes once again as they begin to solve problems without the need for such concrete tools as pencil and paper and spoken language. Their increased mental ability carries them into the highest level of intellectual functioning, described by Piaget as the *formal-operational* stage. The quality of cognitive growth becomes so refined during this period that children are able to transcend the overt activity of the first three stages, performing all the operations necessary to solve problems by purely intellectual means.

Piaget has provided teachers with a logical way of understanding how children proceed through the stages of cognitive growth. Knowing Piaget's developmental theory they can ascertain the cognitive level of each, by carefully testing, measuring, and evaluating each child's problem-solving behavior. If Mike is studying the United Nations in grade seven but still thinks at the concrete-operational stage, a teacher could not expect him to make sound judgments about world peace. His study of the United Nations should include its mechanics and organization, aspects he can understand by examining charts, graphs, and other concrete materials. Mary, on the other hand, quickly grasps the global concept and is able to discuss international relations with good verbal skill and an obvious grasp of more intellectual matters. Her cognitive power and Mike's are at different levels, and their teacher must understand this if each is to learn optimally. While helping Mike work from the concrete-operational level toward the formal-operational, the teacher will encourage and challenge Mary to continue developing her cognitive power at the formal-operational level. To do this successfully with Mike and Mary and all the other youngsters in the class, the teacher must understand the developmental nature of cognitive ability in order to evaluate the cognitive power of each child.

ALL GROWTH IS DEVELOPMENTAL

We have only scratched the surface in this brief discussion of developmental nature of growth. In addition to physical, personal, and cognitive growth, which we consider most important, psychology has begun to provide important new information about other kinds of growth patterns. One area, moral development, has to do with the ways and reasons why children make moral choices at different ages. Lawrence Kohlberg[11] has done significant work in the study of moral development and his theories will be important. Another area has to do with language acquisition, that most vital of learning activities. Eric Lenneberg,[12] B. F. Skinner,[13] and Noam Chomsky[14] are three major contributors to the growing understanding of how children acquire language.

Psychological research has also yielded significant findings about the importance of early childhood experiences to later success in learning because of its importance to understanding subsequent physical, personal, and cognitive growth. Information now available about human behavior is far more abundant than even a few years ago, and it is based more on solid research than ever before.* This information is vital if teachers are to provide meaningful learning experiences for each of their children.

We would like to make an important point about the continuum of cognitive growth. At any time in the lives of children, each will occupy a specific position along a personal continuum of growth and development. While we can make some general statements about the place each 6 year old should be occupying, the differences among children will not allow the assumption that all 6 year olds are about to enter the concrete-operational stage or that all of them have arrived at Erikson's stage of mastery and inferiority. To think this way would be the same as believing that intelligence is fixed at birth. Such thinking would force each child into the behavior considered appropriate at a given age. Instead, a teacher must recognize that Tommy has had many more enriching experiences than Jane and is much farther along the cognitive continuum. In fact, he has begun first grade already able to perform many concrete operations, such as reading his name and even writing it, recognizing many other words, sounding them out, and identifying specific letters. He knows how to

---

*For an excellent and very readable discussion of current psychological theories of human growth and development, we strongly recommend that you read Sprinthall and Sprinthall's *Educational Psychology: A Developmental Approach*, 2nd ed. (Reading, MA: Addison-Wesley, 1977).

count and write numbers up to ten and can use a pencil and paper to add and subtract.

If a teacher failed to recognize Tommy's stage of development and forced him to work at a lower level, he would become bored and begin agitating for more challenging activity. And yet, quite recently, this happened in many classrooms, with all children doing the same things in the same ways because the teacher's manual and curriculum guide specified the behavior expected of all children at that age. Because teachers did not have the benefit of the important findings about human behavior that have become available in recent years, children did not learn as effectively as they could have.

Suppose Jane, whose first five years were devoid of the enrichment of books in the home or of travel to the many places Tommy had been, is forced to begin full-fledged concrete operations on words and numbers when she enters first grade? Without the experiences and memories so necessary to success at the concrete-operational stage, she will become frustrated, and the pain of failure will be her most lasting memory of first grade.

PHYSICAL, PERSONAL, AND COGNITIVE GROWTH ARE CLOSELY ENTWINED

Even knowing exactly the cognitive position Tommy and Jane held when they entered first grade, a teacher would have to understand something else equally as important—the extent to which each child's physical and personal development was compatible with the cognitive, and how all three were interacting to produce the complex behavior of each. Behavior results from each child's cumulative experiences. Physical growth, personal development, and cognitive power are not independent of each other; one can never really be considered in isolation from the other two.

Thus, in spite of Tommy's superior cognitive power he may be a physically awkward boy, unable to engage successfully in the activities that require coordination. Perhaps he has been sheltered by parents who were overly fearful of his getting hurt or of tearing his clothes. His superior intellectual ability will be small comfort to him when he fails to master the physical dimensions of development, and his personal development will be inhibited by such failure. Instead of mastering the personal dimension of his environment, he acquires painful inferiority feelings abou himself. His ego and self-image diminished, he fails not only physically but personally as well. These combined and interacting failures will eventually affect his cognitive behavior. While we could never predict with certainty the precise effect, certainly Tommy's total personality, with its dynamically interacting dimensions of physical, personal, and cognitive growth, will be something less than satisfactory to him.

Knowing the total personality and ability of any child is not a matter of guesswork or of preconceived notions of what children should be doing at some point in their lives. It is a matter of a truly professional understanding of physical, personal, and cognitive growth. Just as important, it is a matter of understanding how all three constantly interact to produce the individual child. It is a matter not only of knowing how the child got this way but also of how to recognize the specific roles each of these dimensions has played. This can be done effectively only through a constant program of observation. Testing, measuring, and evaluating children's behavior in whatever ways are appropriate to discover why they behave as they do will provide the necessary insight to help bring about optimum development of all facets of personality.

BEHAVIOR IS WHAT TEACHERS TEST, MEASURE, AND EVALUATE

As we move on to more specific materials and information concerning the evaluation process, keep in mind that while we are able to measure some physical aspects of growth directly, such as height, weight or strength, most are not so easily identified. Muscle coordination, for instance, must be evaluated in terms of skill at certain activities such as games, athletic contests, or gymnastics. In other words, evaluation is the result of observation of *behavior*, behavior which gives us clues to the child's physical ability.

There is no direct way to measure personality development; we can merely make inferences about the personality of each child from observable actions. In fifth grade, does Sally accept assignments with confidence and independence? Or does she ask dozens of questions about the assignment? Does she relate openly and confidently to other children? Or does she withdraw when others are around? Her behavior and not the inner feelings themselves is observable, providing clues to what is going on inside.

Cognitive growth must also be evaluated by observing behavior. A child's brain cannot be hooked up to a complicated electronic device to measure cognitive quality. Teachers simply have to observe how each child handles each learning task. In doing so, teachers are not seeing cognitive power itself, but cognitive power as it has evolved in a particular child at a specific point. And when a poorly developed personality inhibits success in cognitive growth or, conversely, when cognitive failure causes destruction of ego strength, teachers do not see the actual interaction of these facets of development but the results. The results are visible only through behavior.

What teachers test, measure, and evaluate, then, is *behavior*, behavior which provides indirect insights into the various facets of growth and development for which teachers are responsible. Such behavior must be meaningful not simply as a trigger to preconceived notions of what the child *is* or *should be*, nor as a trigger to responses that are inappropriate or destructive of good development. If teachers understand as fully as possible the developmental nature of physical, personal, and cognitive growth, they can come to know how to identify behavior that signals where the child is at some point along the developmental continuum. If teachers can then infer, from the behavior of children, how each facet of growth is affecting the others and how all three dynamically interact, they are then using the skills of testing, measuring, and evaluating in a truly professional manner—to structure the learning environment in ways most likely to meet the individual needs of each child.

IMPORTANT POINTS TO THINK ABOUT

1. Think about how individual differences develop in each child and how inheritance and environment influence these differences. Can you imagine yourself in a classroom with a group of children all very much alike but very different as well? What are some differences you might observe in their physical growth? personal growth? cognitive growth?

2. Physical, personal, and cognitive development interact dynamically to produce the individual children. Can you describe how one growth factor might affect the others?

3. Piaget's developmental theory of cognitive growth describes intelligence as qualitative rather than quantitative. Can you visualize examples of cognitive behavior at each of Piaget's qualitative levels—sensori-motor? pre-operational? concrete-operational? formal/operational?

4. Erikson's theory of personality growth is also developmental. Can you visualize examples of personal growth at the juvenile period? How will you recognize the child who is successfully acquiring feelings of mastery? How do children manifest feelings of inferiority?

5. Think about the special problems of adolescents. Can you describe some of the traumatic, often destructive experiences related to adolescence? How would you evaluate them in order to develop a more constructive environment for adolescents?

6. Physical, personal, and cognitive growth are thought by some leading psychologists to occur along a well-defined continuum. Can you describe a well-developed child in grade one? grade five? grade eight? grade twelve?

7. Most growth is assessed indirectly, rather than directly, by observing behavior. Can you imagine the behavior of a child who is physically unattractive but very bright? How might an unattractive appearance affect cognitive and personal development?

NOTES

1. Erik Erikson, "Identity and the Life Cycle," *Psychological Issues*, Vol. I (New York International Universities Press, 1959).
2. J. D. Matarazzo, *Wechsler's Measurement and Appraisal of Adult Intelligence*, Ch. 3 (Baltimore: Williams and Wilkins, 1972).
3. *Ibid*.
4. *Ibid*.
5. *Ibid*.
6. *Ibid*.
7. *Ibid*.
8. *Ibid*.
9. *Ibid*.
10. J. Piaget, *Science of Education and the Psychology of the Child* (New York: Viking, 1970).
11. L. Kohlberg, "State and Sequence: The Cognitive-Developmental Approach to Socialization," in D. Goslin, ed., *Handbook of Socialization Theory and Research* (Chicago: Rand McNally, 1969).
12. E. Lenneberg, *Biological Foundations of Language* (New York: Wiley, 1967).
13. B. F. Skinner, *The Behavior of Organisms: An Experimental Analysis* (New York: Appleton-Century-Crofts, 1938).
14. N. Chomsky, *Reflections on Language* (New York: Pantheon Books, 1975).

CHAPTER THREE

THE IMPORTANCE OF OBJECTIVES IN EVALUATING CHILDREN

IMPORTANT POINTS TO WATCH FOR

Good instructional objectives are vital in helping us plan for children's individual needs.

Effective planning, through the use of objectives, in turn, is important to effective testing, measuring, and evaluating of learning.

Long-range objectives over the course of a year or longer establish the broad framework for learning activities. These objectives are usually called *educational goals*.

Objectives for shorter periods such as units are called *terminal instructional objectives*; those for very short periods such as single lessons are known as *instructional objectives*.

The three major characteristics of useful objectives are *performance*, *conditions*, and *criterion*.

Instructional objectives are important in planning and evaluating both *cognitive* and *affective* learning.

Cognitive and affective learning are closely related, and instructional objectives should be written to include both whenever appropriate.

Teachers who understand the developmental nature of learning and who are sensitive to children's individual needs are well on the way to becoming effective evaluators. They know that, in spite of the ready availability of commercially prepared tests, the most important testing, measuring, and evaluating activities will be those they carry on daily. Teachers are the day-to-day participants in the dynamic interactions of

41

physical, personal, and cognitive elements of growth discussed in Chapter 2. They are responsible for monitoring and nurturing this growth and for describing it as it occurs. When they describe it, they do so in terms of behavior, behavior which gives them clues to how much and how well the children have learned.

THE ASSESSMENT OF LEARNING IS NOT A HAPHAZARD PROCESS

Day-to-day assessment of learning is not haphazard. Good teachers do not wait for behavior to happen; they influence its occurrence first by knowing their children's needs and then by developing curriculum activities to meet those needs, activities which will bring about new behavior to be described and evaluated in turn. From this new evaluation will come a revised assessment of needs and revised curriculum activities. Although the process sounds circular, it is the most effective way for teachers to accomplish their major objectives: to determine their children's needs and then find ways to meet them. Teachers determine needs by testing, measuring, and evaluating behavior and meet them by teaching new behavior. This objective will be realized most effectively by determining in advance what that new behavior should be. Alice, in Chapter 1, primarily needed emotional security since her lack of emotional strength made academic progress extremely difficult. Her behavior provided her teacher with important clues that helped the teacher not only to understand Alice's needs but also to structure subsequent learning activities with the child's need for security in mind. For example, her teacher planned a private arithmetic lesson in which she could give Alice close and supportive attention in order to guard against triggering an emotional withdrawal. By the end of a half hour, she would expect Alice to be able to add the primary facts $1 + 3$, $3 + 2$, $4 + 1$, $4 + 2$, and $4 + 3$ without help.

OBJECTIVES HELP MAKE BEHAVIOR HAPPEN

In setting her objective in advance, basing it strictly on her knowledge of Alice's needs, and using it to plan the lesson, Alice's teacher increased the likelihood that Alice would succeed. When Alice did recite the primary addition facts at the end of the half hour, her bahavior clearly indicated that learning had taken place. It also served to verify that the teacher could find ways to meet Alice's needs. Thus began a long and difficult but rewarding series of learning experiences for Alice, each carefully constructed from the clues her behavior provided.

Although teachers have traditionally recognized the need for instructional objectives, much more attention has been given this activity in recent years. With more knowledge about human behavior and the developmental nature of growth and learning, teachers have found it necessary to become more thorough and precise in planning teaching strategies. This expanded knowledge about behavior makes teachers more responsible for seeking ways to develop appropriate and productive lessons, units, and other learning experiences for groups and individuals alike.

Our discussion about objectives should begin with a reminder of that responsibility. Anything that occurs in the classroom affects the learning process. If teachers are careless and haphazard, learning will be haphazard also. If they pay less attention than they should to planning lessons, children will learn less than they should. Although much incidental learning takes place in any classroom, most occurs because teachers make the effort to plan carefully. And good planning always begins with the question "What are my reasons for teaching this particular material?" In asking this question, teachers have begun to think about the most important instructional objectives—how children will be affected by teaching, in what ways and directions they will grow, and whether the choice of subject matter and teaching procedures helps them become more skillful, knowledgeable, understanding, sensitive to others, physically coordinated, self-reliant, and independent. These questions are based upon prior evaluations. Since teachers cannot lead children to new growth without knowing how they have grown so far, they must evaluate their children's developmental status before they begin planning.

THREE KINDS OF OBJECTIVES

Three kinds of objectives are vital in teaching strategies. The first, educational goals, concerns changes in children's behavior over a long period of time, several months to a year. The second, terminal instructional objectives, describes the behavior anticipated at the end of a shorter period of time, such as several days or weeks. The third, instructional objectives, describes the behavior expected at the end of a given lesson.

EDUCATIONAL GOALS—THE SEVEN CARDINAL PRINCIPLES

Anticipation about children's behavior at the end of a school term involves long-range educational objectives or *goals*, usually stated in broad, general terms. Although teachers expect growth in a single area such as increased reading skill, their responsibility during a school term is for growth of the total child. Increased reading skill or any other single objective must always be consistent with overall growth and development.

Long-range educational goals are defined in the curriculum guides of school systems and in professional materials such as college texts on teaching methods. Traditionally, teachers have been expected to know and to aim toward them as part of their professional responsibility. As long ago as 1918, the extremely influential Commission on the Reorganization of

Secondary Education[1] listed as the following aims of American education, the Seven Cardinal Principles:

Health
Command of the fundamental processes
Worthy home membership
Vocational efficiency
Good citizenship
Worthy use of leisure time
Ethical character

The Seven Cardinal Principles became the foundation for curricula throughout the nation, making an enormous and long-lasting impact on classroom teachers as well as teacher training institutions.

In 1938, another attempt at setting national educational aims and policies led to the establishment of the Educational Policies Commission. The commission's publication, "The Purposes of Education in American Democracy,"[2] restated the Seven Cardinal Principles as the following four aims:

Self-relationships
Human relationships
Economic efficiency
Civic responsibility

Most school districts borrow freely from such principles as they attempt to set forth the goals and objectives they want their teachers to aim toward. They often begin with such all-encompassing statements as: "Our major educational objective (goal) is to teach our children to understand, appreciate, and acquire the ideals inherent in the American way of life."

Usually such statements are followed by descriptive details of the American way of life: "respect for the rights and privileges of others," "the achievement of economic, emotional, and social competence," "acquisition of the skills necessary to productive labor," or "development of the attitudes and skills necessary for effective citizenship in America."

Such broadly stated goals offer an initial framework for planning in various subject areas. Social studies, for instance, afford teachers an opportunity to teach children the attitudes and skills necessary for effective citizenship. Through the social studies, the kindergarten teacher as well as the senior high school teacher assume responsibility for helping their children learn how to be good citizens. For instance, the kindergarten curriculum guide for a typical school system might well include the following long-range educational goals for teaching social studies at this level:

The children will acquire good citizenship habits by learning the importance of their role as a member of a group, by understanding how good citizens work together for mutual growth and happiness, and by coming to understand how others in the family and community work to make their lives more comfortable and secure.

The senior high school teacher in the same school system might work toward the same citizenship skills according to these long-range educational goals:

The children will acquire good citizenship habits by practicing the democratic process through class elections, by learning the structure and operation of city, state, and national government, by participation in the student government of the school, and through volunteer work in civic and social service projects in the community.

Notice that these social studies goals, although somewhat less broad than the Seven Cardinal Principles, are still very general. Good citizenship is a widely accepted and often-stated educational goal, but teachers need to know more specifically how to identify good citizenship, how to encourage it, and how to evaluate it. While teachers may agree that good citizenship attitudes and skills are important for children to acquire, they must also be able to describe the kindergartner or senior high student who is a good citizen. Even knowing that two skills of good citizenship are common courtesy and the willingness to share, teachers must be able to determine which children really understand the principles of good citizenship or which have acquired healthy attitudes towards good citizenship.

MAKING OBJECTIVES MORE SPECIFIC

Problems such as these indicate the need for a discussion about instructional objectives. For a long time, teachers and administrators alike have been confronted with broad, general statements of educational goals and objectives. Although good teachers have always worked hard to teach such objectives, they have found it extremely difficult to determine whether and to what degree understanding was acquired, attitudes changed, or good citizenship values learned. Even in the realm of observable behavior teachers have often been vague in describing the skills to be learned. Whenever educational objectives are not clearly stated, they are likely to be misunderstood or else understood to mean different things to different teachers. If they are too broadly stated, interpretation of such terms as values and attitudes might be different for different teachers. Vague and unclear objectives lead to inconsistent teaching strategies, making teachers hard pressed at the end of a unit to evaluate how much was learned. Thus, evaluation is a key ingredient of effective teaching. Learning to state educational or instructional objectives with clarity and precision will make teaching more effective and evaluation more precise.

The need for stating educational objectives in more specific terms was dramatically highlighted in the 1950s when the Russians were suddenly discovered to have surpassed America in scientific discovery. With their launching of Sputnik, they galvanized an array of critics who blamed the nation's schools for the lag in scientific progress. They demanded a return to the basics and to a toughening of public school curricula and teacher education programs. The attack on the schools forced educators to be more accountable for their teaching and less fuzzy in setting their goals and objectives. The ensuing attempts to build accountability into the educational process led directly to the long overdue examination of objectives. Long-range goals such as those stated for the social studies unit were considered acceptable as general aims, but more precise and clearly stated objectives were said to be needed both for effective learning and for accurate evaluation. One of the most influential contributors in the area of objectives has been Robert F. Mager, whose 1962 book, *Preparing Objectives for Programmed Instruction,*[3] instigated a revolution in the writing of educational objectives.

To begin a discussion of the second and third types of objectives, we need to establish the characteristics of good objectives, both terminal instructional objectives and instructional objectives.

1. Performance

An objective is useful to the extent it specifies clearly what children must be able to do when they demonstrate mastery of the objective.

Very simply, this means that the *behavior* expected of the children at the end of the teaching-learning experience should be stated in the objective. If the lesson is on geology, for instance, the objective must state that the youngsters will demonstrate in writing, orally, by demonstration, or by some graphic means such as charts and drawings, that they know the difference between sedimentary and igneous rock formations, or that the Colorado River took thousands of years to carve the Grand Canyon.

The characteristic of *performance*, then, means exactly that; both *terminal instructional objectives* for a fairly long-term study or unit, or *instructional objectives* for very short-term learning experiences such as single lessons, must specify the expected *performance* or *behavior* that will demonstrate that youngsters have learned what the teacher set out to teach them.

2. Conditions

An objective is useful to the extent it clearly states the conditions under which the learning must occur.

It should establish the ways in which the children will go about the learning process and any special conditions under which they will demonstrate their knowledge at the end of the learning experience. For instance, if children will be required to base their *performance* on firsthand study of the geological formations near their school, these conditions should appear in the objective. Evaluations will be based on their answers (performance) about their visits to local quarries or river beds.

The characteristic of *conditions,* then, means that objectives clearly identify how the children will acquire their knowledge and then report it.

3. Criterion

An objective is useful to the extent it specifies the quality or level of performance expected.

This means that teachers should determine and state how much and how well children will be expected to understand the subject matter. Since children cannot be expected at any level to learn all there is to know about geology, teachers must decide just how much geological information they are to learn. For instance, they may be expected to identify and describe *three* types of rock formations and *two* kinds of erosion or to draw a chart showing the various stages in the formation of a river valley.

In short, the characteristic of *criterion* keeps the youngsters working and learning within reasonable limits. It establishes the amount and kind of information they are to assimilate while specifying the quality of learning we will expect of them.

Both *terminal instructional objectives* and *instructional objectives* should include the three characteristics of *performance, conditions,* and *criterion.* Let's look more closely at these characteristics in some specific examples.

Terminal Objectives

Beginning a kindergarten social studies unit on good citizenship, a teacher will look ahead to the children's behavior at the end of six weeks. Terminal objectives should specify clearly what this *terminal behavior* is expected to be. One terminal objective might read:

> At the end of the two-week unit, the children will demonstrate their knowledge of good citizenship practice by cooperatively planning and presenting a skit on the importance of firefighters. The skit will include the six rules of fire safety learned in class and at least five ways in which we can cooperate to make the firefighter's job easier and safer.

The objective states the performance expected (planning and presenting the skit), and the conditions (the skit must be planned *cooperatively* by the entire class), as well as the criterion or level of performance expected (the skit will include six rules of fire safety and five ways to cooperate with firefighters).

For a senior high class a terminal instructional objective might be stated in this way:

At the end of two months, the four students in group B will demonstrate their knowledge of the democratic process by preparing a chart based on their interviews with state legislators showing clearly how the recent bill reducing the voting age to 18 became a law. The chart will include both the typical route a bill must take and the major hurdles this particular bill encountered along the way.

Once again, the three characteristics of a useful objective are present.

Performance: preparing the chart.

Conditions: the chart must be based on personal interviews with legislators.

Criterion: the chart must clearly show both the typical route of a bill and the major hurdles this one faced.

Instructional Objectives

The daily activities of the kindergarten unit require that instructional objectives be stated in much the same way. For instance, on Wednesday of the third week, the kindergarten class will visit the fire station and learn about the duties of firefighters. The instructional objectives might read something like this:

From their discussion with firefighters, the children will be able to:

Name four rules of fire safety.

Identify three fire hazards found in the home.

Explain how to call in a fire alarm accurately.

Describe the procedure to be followed during a fire.

These instructional objectives demonstrate the same three characteristics of useful objectives.

Performance: The children's terminal behavior will be to *name, identify, explain,* and *describe.*

Conditions: The children will perform the behaviors of *naming, identifying, explaining* and *describing* on the basis of their *discussion with firefighters.*

Criterion: The specific information, skills, or learning the children will *name, identify, explain,* and *describe* are: four rules of safety, three fire hazards, the procedure of calling in fire alarms, and things to do during a fire.

The instructional objectives for a single lesson at the high school level will be similar.

During the fifth week of the high school unit, one lesson will be devoted to a discussion about a community's responsibility for its poor. The instructional objectives might be:

> As a result of our discussion on poverty and welfare, the students will be able to describe three specific programs by which this city cares for its poor and at least two sources of state and federal funding for these programs.

Consider the three characteristics of good objectives in this example.

Performance: What will the behavior of the children be? To *describe* something they have learned during this lesson.

Conditions: On what learning condition will the children base their descriptions? On their *class discussion* of poverty and welfare.

Criterion: Exactly *what* and *how much* will the children describe? *Three specific programs for the poor and two funding sources for them.*

WRITING OBJECTIVES FOR COGNITIVE AND AFFECTIVE LEARNING

A review of the distinction between two types of learning, *cognitive* and *affective*, will clarify how to write objectives for each.

Cognitive behavior involves the development of intellectual skills and abilities. In Chapter 2, we explained that Piaget's stages of cognitive development are based on the theory that children's intellectual ability evolves in a relatively systematic way as they gain experience and learn how to use those experiences to solve new problems. In very young children, such activities may be observed as simple responses to stimuli such as an affirmative shake of the head when a ride in the car is offered. A little later, as more experience and increased language facility are acquired, the child may initiate the discussion, asking to go for a ride. The quality of cognitive ability, in other words, expands and changes with increased age and experience and includes such behavior as simple remembering of facts already learned as well as the more complex behavior of using remembered facts and information to solve intellectual problems.

While *cognitive development* has to do with the way people acquire information and use it to solve intellectual problems, *affective development* has to do with the way people feel about what they have learned and how their attitudes and values are shaped. Affective development is less tangible than cognitive and yet it, too, follows a rather systematic pattern of development. Children learn values and acquire attitudes just as surely as they learn multiplication facts and acquire the skill to solve complex math problems. They learn, as a result of the same kind of experiences that foster cognitive growth, to form beliefs and to develop appreciation for their world. Therefore, teachers cannot expect children to develop sensitivity toward others and to use their knowledge in the best interests of humanity unless they teach them to do so. Affective learning is as important as cognitive and teachers share responsibility for helping to bring about both.

However, good affective development does not follow naturally from good cognitive growth. Demanding that children demonstrate a thorough assimilation of the multiplication facts will not guarantee a healthy attitude toward mathematics. In fact, children who are turned off to math because of the incessant and often meaningless drill and repetition they must endure are all too familiar. Instead of gaining an understanding and appreciation for the theoretical meaning of mathematics, many learn only to manipulate numbers and to avoid math courses when possible.

OBJECTIVES FOR COGNITIVE BEHAVIOR

The objectives in the preceding pages called for the acquisition of cognitive behaviors such as information or skills rather than affective behaviors, such as understanding or appreciation of community resources. However, a poorly written objective is unlikely to bring about improvements in either cognitive or affective behavior. For example, a teacher might plan a lesson designed to result in increased cognitive knowledge about good citizenship, and state the objective as follows:

> Through a discussion of our community, the children will learn how people work together for mutual growth and happiness.

Perhaps and perhaps not. The objective is very vague and, though it does state the *condition* (discussion of our community) on which the children will base their answers about good citizenship, it does not state the specific behaviors, or *performance*, in which the children should engage, behaviors that will show whether and how much they have learned about good citizenship. The third characteristic of good objectives is missing also, the *criterion* or expected level of performance. As a result, measurement of what they have learned will be less than precise; the teacher will have difficulty describing what took place. Unable to describe accurately how much and how well the children learned, this teacher will find that efforts at planning the next lessons are haphazard at best. Without accurate evaluation, the teacher can neither determine what the children have learned nor proceed systematically with effective teaching strategies.

The same objective might be reconstructed to make it somewhat more likely to produce the desired cognitive behavior:

> The children will discuss the role of firefighters and will learn how these community helpers contribute to the well-being and safety of the community.

Though a little more specific in naming an important community helper, the objective still does not express precisely how and what the children will learn. Omitting *performance* and *criterion* leaves much to be desired.

Naming the specific behavior expected from children sets instructional objectives in behavioral or performance terms. Beginning them with a verb helps teachers determine in advance the action they wish the children to take in order to demonstrate that learning has taken place. The rewritten objective, then, is stated as it was earlier.

Following a visit to the fire station, the children will be able to:

> *Name* the four rules of fire safety.
>
> *Identify* three fire hazards found in the home.
>
> *Explain* how to call in a fire alarm accurately.
>
> *Describe* the exact procedure to be followed during a fire.

This time, all three characteristics of good objectives are clearly stated. Each performance indicates specific facts to be acquired and specific behaviors to measure. Each performance begins with an action verb, demanding *demonstrated, observable* behavior to assure the teacher that learning has occurred. In other words, we have to see it to believe it.

For a final example of an instructional objective for cognitive learning, we'll return to the high school social studies class and its unit on good citizenship. The overall goal is to help the youngsters acquire the knowledge and habits of good citizenship through discussion and investigation of community activities. Following several lessons about the responsibility of a community for its poor (one of which is identified in the objectives on page 49) the class needs to know more directly the work carried on in community social service agencies. The objective might be stated as follows:

> The children will describe the work done for the poor in the Community Center for Senior Citizens.

This objective does not merit high marks for precision, yet surprisingly, many teachers write their objectives in this way.

This objective does have the characteristic of *performance*, though weakly, since it uses the verb "describe" to indicate the performance or behavior to observe at the end of the lesson. However, it lacks the characteristic of *conditions* since it does not specify the learning activities on which the youngsters will base their *performance*. Are they to read about the center? Are they to visit it? Are they to invite workers at the center to visit their class? The objective also fails to include the characteristic of *criterion*, at least with any degree of precision. How much are they to describe? Are they to describe the specific jobs of the staff members? Are they to describe the activities of the senior citizens who use the center? The conditions for learning must be set with more precision on the basis of the exact cognitive information the class should acquire. The objective must specify clearly what that information will be, how the children will report it, and what learning activities they will engage in to acquire the information. With these things included, the objective looks like this:

> Following a visit to the Center for Senior Citizens during which the class will speak with both staff and senior citizens (conditions) the youngsters will describe in written reports (performance) the counseling, nutritional, and occupational therapy activities carried on at the center (criterion).

Certainly the children will observe other ways that the center carries on the community's responsibility to the poor in addition to the three they are asked to investigate. The objective does not preclude additional information but channels the children's learning activities in ways to ensure that the most important things are learned.

As the children name, describe, identify, or explain the things they have learned, their cognitive behavior clearly indicates how much and how well they have learned. When instructional objectives state the learning outcomes a lesson should achieve and specify the responses, or behavior, that will indicate that learning has occurred, the job of evaluation is simplified. Children show by their actions how much and how well they have learned, and teachers can proceed systematically to the next learning experiences.

While precision is important and carefully stated behavioral objectives aid tremendously both in teaching strategies and in evaluation, the specific behavior that results is not an end in itself. It is a means to a greater, more encompassing, end. Children can list, describe, count, name, and define endlessly, but if they do not change in deeper and more significant ways, all of their isolated behaviors will be of little consequence. Instead, teachers need to work toward the attainment of broader goals those which involve significant changes in children's *affective* behavior.

OBJECTIVES FOR AFFECTIVE BEHAVIOR

Affective behavior is difficult to evaluate because it involves an area of learning that is not as clearly observable as cognitive. It is relatively easy to assess whether children remember a set of facts or a mathematical formula. It is equally easy to assess how well they use these bits of information to solve more complex mathematical problems. Cognitive behavior is generally overt and can be observed quite readily, particularly if instructional objectives determine this behavior. Affective behavior, on the other hand, includes such nebulous characteristics as beliefs, values, attitudes, appreciations, and understandings, none of which are easy to describe accurately.

Although educational and psychological literature is filled with theories about emotional, attitudinal, and moral development, this development cannot be quantifiably evaluated as memory and arithmetic ability can. But just because affective behavior is difficult to test, measure, and evaluate doesn't mean that teachers can ignore it to concentrate exclusively on the cognitive.

Earlier we stated a long-range educational goal as: "To teach our children to understand, appreciate, and acquire the ideals inherent in the American way of life." If teachers believe that this is a worthwhile objective, they must make an effort not only to teach children to appreciate and value the American way of life but to evaluate the effectiveness of such teaching as well. Since they can't probe children's minds to see how their attitudes toward democracy are developing, teachers must look to the possible kinds of behavior that will provide clues that children's attitudes and feelings are changing.

Which learning activities about the American way of life might get children to express, through their behavior, that they believe or feel differently about the subject than they did before? For instance, learning about the rights and privileges of others should help children develop respect. Specifically experiencing courtesy and sharing might help children understand and appreciate how pleasant social interaction can be when people are respectful of each other's rights and freedoms. Accordingly instructional objectives such as the following might be prepared around the theme of respect.

> Throughout our unit on the American way of life, the children will discuss and practice courteous behavior toward one another. They will help establish their own rules and guidelines for behavior during class discussions, group research projects, and other activities relating to the unit. Attitudes toward courtesy and respect will be considered changed and improved when children consistently and willingly:
>
> - Use the expressions: please, thank you, excuse me, and so forth.
> - Demonstrate helpful behavior towards others in all activities.
> - Listen courteously and without interruption when others are speaking.
> - When asked, comment constructively and courteously on their classmates' work.
> - Demonstrate willingness to assume responsibility for assignments during group research projects.

The characteristic of *performance* is evident in the expectation that the children will establish their own rules and in the behaviors listed at the end of the objective. The characteristic of *condition* is evident in the learning activities of class discussions, group research projects, and other activities.

The characteristic of *criterion* is evident in the words *consistently* and *willingly*.

None of this terminal instructional objective mentions "cognitive" activity such as the study of democratic institutions, yet it suggests behavior that can be observed and evaluated. Suppose, for instance, that when Jimmy started the unit, his behavior could hardly be described as courteous or respectful. The rights and freedoms of others were of little or no importance to him, and his demanding, selfish behavior clearly indicated his self-centered attitudes toward his classmates. Such attitudes are to be expected, particularly among very young children, but as the unit progresses, Jimmy's behavior should improve. If he demonstrates that he is fulfilling the instructional objectives, his teacher can feel fairly comfortable in saying that his attitude seems to be changing, although less quantitative terms, such as "much improved" or "somewhat improved" will be needed. Jimmy's teacher can be even more certain of this evaluation when Jimmy's courteous and respectful behavior carries over to other subjects and activities through the day.

If affective behavior must be taught and evaluated, it must be translated from terminal instructional objectives into shorter-term instructional objectives. On any given day, for instance, a teacher can determine whether there is evidence of attitude change toward courtesy and respect. By considering what behaviors (performance) to call for in an objective, what activities to schedule on which to base an evaluation (conditions), and the degree or frequency (criterion) to expect the performance from which to infer attitude change, a teacher can assess changes in attitudes. Will the following instructional objective accomplish the task?

> The children will hold an election for class officers during which candidates will make short speeches and the class will question them. Throughout this lesson, as a result of previous lessons and discussions about democratic behavior, the children will listen courteously to the candidate, ask questions respectfully, and make critical comments in a way that will not hurt the candidate's feelings.

The objective includes the characteristic of *performance* by specifying the behaviors of individual children as they carry on their election. Does Jimmy raise his hand more often than he did in the past? Does Tommy make his comments with less sarcasm than previously? Does Kim listen more courteously and with fewer facial expressions of disdain than usual? With these specific, observable behaviors in mind a teacher can accurately determine whether attitudes toward courtesy and respect have changed.

The characteristic of *conditions* is evident in the words "throughout this lesson" and in the phrases that specify *how* the behaviors will be performed: listen *courteously*, ask questions *courteously*, and make critical comments *in a way that will not hurt the feelings of others*.

COGNITIVE AND AFFECTIVE OBJECTIVES ARE BOTH ESSENTIAL TO GOOD TEACHING AND EVALUATION

Objectives, then, must set forth either cognitive growth or *affective* development, and in some cases both. (Cognitive) growth can be measured directly by observing children's responses, and teachers can make quite certain of how much and how well children have learned by establishing, *in advance*, the behavior they expect. Testing them on their recall of the subject matter or asking them to describe or identify characters in literature means asking them to demonstrate their cognitive growth. Instructional objectives that establish specific behaviors for a lesson to bring about increases the chances that the lesson will be effective and will not need to be repeated.

Other objectives that have to do with the tenuous and elusive aspects of affective growth and development yield less immediate and easily measured growth. More often, they must be written in longer-range terms and in language that expresses expectations in terms of "improved attitudes," "increased sensitivity," "deeper awareness," or perhaps "fuller appreciation." While these are not expressions that lend themselves to the language of instructional objectives, they, too are expressions of behavior like those in the cognitive area. Since human growth and development cannot be fostered adequately by stressing cognitive objectives and ignoring affective goals, both must be deliberately and conscientiously planned for in any teaching strategy. Both must be thoroughly tested, measured, and evaluated; both must be described in terms of the changes that have taken place in the child's behavior. Changes in each domain can then be described in the language appropriate to it.

BLOOM'S TAXONOMY OF EDUCATIONAL OBJECTIVES

There are sources that classify objectives in both the cognitive and affective areas. Such classifications, or taxonomies, are useful to teachers because by matching their objectives with the taxonomy, they can avoid teaching merely facts in favor of teaching more sophisticated intellectual processes. One of these is the *Taxonomy of Educational Objectives, Handbook I: Cognitive Domain* (1956), edited by Benjamin S. Bloom.[4] Cognitive objectives are listed in six major categories:

1.00 Knowledge
2:00 Comprehension
3:00 Application
4:00 Analysis
5:00 Synthesis
6:00 Evaluation

These are broken into such subsections as:

1:00 Knowledge
  1:10 Knowledge of specifics
    1:11 Knowledge of terminology
    1:12 Knowledge of specific facts
  1:20 Knowledge of ways and means of dealing with specifics
  1:30 Knowledge of the universals and abstractions in a field

The Taxonomy of Educational Objectives, Handbook II: Affective Domain (1964), edited by David Krathwohl[5], categorizes objectives in the affective domain as follows:

1.0 Receiving. Sensitivity to the existence of certain stimuli.
2.0 Responding. Active attention to stimuli; for example, going along with rules and practices.
3.0 Valuing. Consistent belief and attitude of worth held about a phenomenon.
4.0 Organization. Organizing, interrelating, and analyzing different relevant values.
5.0 Characterization by a value or value concept. Behavior is guided by value.

Measuring the objectives for the kindergarten class in social studies against these taxonomies, we can see that the anticipated cognitive knowledge would be classified within the first three levels of Bloom's taxonomy.

1:00 Knowledge: the children will acquire knowledge of community helpers and of good group behavior.
2:00 Comprehension: the children will understand the need to work together.
3:00 Application: the children will learn to apply their knowledge and understanding of good group behavior in everyday classroom living and in such specific activities as carrying on elections.

In the affective area, the objectives can be classfied within the first two levels of Krathwohl's taxonomy.

1.0 Receiving: the children will exhibit sensitivity to the rights and needs of others.
2.0 Responding: the children will actively respond to information learned about good group practice by being more courteous and respectful.

The upper levels of both taxonomies call for behavior somewhat beyond the capabilities of kindergarten children. However, the high school social studies objectives reach these higher levels. The high school youngsters, as a result of their increased experience with school and their environment, have greater cognitive abilities. They should be able to begin analyzing the information they gather and synthesizing it into new constructs, activities that correspond to levels five and six of the cognitive taxonomy. A few of the children will have reached Piaget's formal operational level of cognitive thinking and will be able to evaluate knowledge in terms of its relevance to broader, more universal issues. Objectives at level six of the cognitive taxonomy recognize this ability.

In the affective area, the high school objectives include levels three and four of the affective taxonomy. The youngsters should have begun the process of *valuing* (level 3.0), should have demonstrated some consistency of attitude about responsibility, and should have begun to understand the *organization* (level 4.0) of value systems and their interrelatedness and relevance to life. Their volunteer work in social agencies and their involvement in civic projects should show evidence of *characterization* (level 5.0) in which at least a few will demonstrate that good group behavior is guided by the values they have acquired during their learning experiences.

Teachers can better assess the level of their objectives by becoming familiar with both taxonomies. In Chapter 4, we will reconsider them as we discuss the importance of objectives in the preparation of good tests.

COGNITIVE AND AFFECTIVE EVALUATION ARE INTERRELATED

Although writers have dealt with cognitive and affective evaluation by separating the two, this is at best an artificial device contrived to make the evaluator's work more precise. But since human development cannot in actuality be compartmentalized, affective and cognitive learning must be treated together, particularly by teachers in their day-to-day work in the classroom. Teaching entirely toward cognitive objectives may well cause neglect of values teachers are pledged to develop. Teaching values entirely may well lead to children who have great feelings for life but who don't know enough about it to get a job. It would be an exercise in futility to argue whether the development of good attitudes turns children on to learning or whether exciting subject matter creates good attitudes. A great deal of research must yet be done to answer such questions. However, most writers agree that affective and cognitive behavior are deeply entwined and dynamically affect each other. If so, then teachers must do all they can to foster *both* kinds of growth. They need to exercise great care in describing what they think has happened in both the affective and the cognitive domains, particularly when discussing affective growth since its characteristics are less clear than those of cognitive development.

COGNITIVE AND AFFECTIVE OBJECTIVES FOR A UNIT IN SCIENCE

We conclude this section by showing how cognitive and affective learning might be interrelated with a set of objectives to include both. We said earlier that long-range educational goals are usually stated in very general terms and include such affective words as "values" and "attitudes." Yet teachers ought to be able to demonstrate, through immediate objectives, how changes in values or attitudes might be measured and described.

Even such a cognitive subject as science can include objectives for growth in both the cognitive and the affective domains.

Educational Goals

Suppose our sixth grade science curriculum guide states that children should study the subject matter and methodology of science in order to

Understand and appreciate the importance of scientists and their discoveries.

Develop a strong personal interest in both the natural and physical sciences.

Acquire respect for the scientific method by learning how scientists experiment, discover, and invent.

Develop a system of values and attitudes toward science that will help them make intelligent and humane judgments about scientific applications.

These are statements of educational goals appropriate not only for a sixth grade class but for any grade. They include both cognitive and affective statements. References to subject matter, methodology, and the way in which scientists work are cognitive and require that children understand the intellectual processes of gathering data, acquiring scientific skills, and making intelligent decisions while investigating and discovering. References to appreciation, interest, respect, values, and attitudes are affective and require the emotional process of developing feelings about science. Eventually, they should become informed decision makers with sensitivity to both the benefits and hazards of science. Some may become constructive workers in the field of science and make important contributions to human welfare.

To achieve these objectives, teachers must consider the many subjects among the physical and natural sciences and choose one, perhaps a unit on electricity, a typical science subject for grade six. The general educational goal translated into language appropriate and specific to electricity might read as follows:

Through a study of electricity, the children will learn how this discovery affects our lives. By learning how electricity is generated, the children will come to appreciate the work of scientists and will become knowledgeable about how people learn to control their environment through science.

Terminal Objectives

The educational goals stated, the next step is to set the *terminal objectives*, what kinds of behavior expected by the end of the unit, to help the teacher evaluate the children's cognitive and affective growth. These objectives might be stated as follows:

As a result of lectures, field trips, discussions, and research about electricity, the children will be able to:

Describe static electricity.

Describe how an electromagnet works.

Construct an alternating current circuit.

Construct a direct current circuit.

Name the parts of an electric cell.

Name the parts of an electric generator,

List ten ways in which electricity is used in homes.

Describe the scientific method of discovery.

Describe five ways in which electricity makes life more meaningful and comfortable.

State five ways in which people have learned to control the environment through the use of electricity.

Describe the need to exercise good safety rules when working with electricity.

Express feelings of appreciation for the discoversies and benefits of science.

Although others could be added to these, or these might be stated somewhat differently, the objectives account for both cognitive functions and affective behavior, both of which are integral parts of the ongoing instructional plan.

Instructional Objectives

In addition to the terminal objectives, which are derived from long-term educational goals, the teacher will need to prepare short-term objectives for each lesson. These instructional objectives, derived from the terminal objectives, are written in the same manner but with more attention to specific learning experiences and behaviors.

Imagine that on Tuesday the teacher will present a lesson about the electrical properties of the atom. As a result of the discussion and demonstration, the children should be able to:

Describe positive and negative electrical charges.

Describe the presence of static electricity in three ways.

Show by diagram the electrical structure of an atom of hydrogen.

Describe how atoms become electrically unstable.

Discuss the desirability for safeguards and ethical constraints when developing atomic energy.

Express feelings of appreciation and respect for science and for the work of scientists.

Each objective is stated in precise detail:

Performance: describe, demonstrate, discuss, show by diagram, express.

Conditions: on the basis of the demonstration and class discussions of the atom, the children will do all of the above.

Criterion: the children will demonstrate this knowledge and affective growth.

OBJECTIVES ARE VITAL TO THE TEACHING-LEARNING PROCESS

Objectives, then, whether stated as long-range goals or as shorter-term instructional objectives, are vital components of the teaching-learning process for two reasons. First, they force teachers to plan more carefully the strategies they use to help children learn and grow. Thorough planning keeps them on the track and makes their teaching flow more smoothly; this, of course, helps assure optimum learning opportunities.

Second, carefully stated objectives stand as a benchmark against which teachers can determine how much and how well the children have learned. Without clear-cut objectives, instructional strategies will be haphazard at best; neither teachers nor children will see clearly the pathways to the growth that educators are pledged to foster. With objectives, teachers not only have a set of clearly marked directional signs, they also will have the means, at the end of each lesson, at the end of units, and at the end of the year, by which to test, measure, and evaluate children's cognitive and affective development.

IMPORTANT POINTS TO THINK ABOUT

1. Effective teaching and evaluation require good planning. Good planning, in turn, requires the setting of objectives. Can you visualize (or remember) a classroom in which the teacher seems to have no plan and in which the learning experiences simply move haphazardly from one thing to another?

2. Can you visualize (or remember) a classroom in which everyone knows the plan and in which the subject matter is presented and learned in clearly identifiable segments?

3. Think about teaching mathematics in grade three. Can you compose a long-range objective (educational goal) that would provide an appropriate framework for teaching mathematics?

4. During the year in that third grade, imagine that you must plan for a four-week unit in long division. Can you compose an appropriate terminal instructional objective for the unit?

5. In the third week of your unit, you find that you must plan a single lesson on estimating. Can you write a good instructional objective for this lesson?

6. Now imagine that you are a teacher of English in grade eleven. Can you prepare a good statement of educational goals for teaching English? A good terminal instructional objective for a six-week unit on the writings of John Steinbeck? An instructional objective for a single lesson on writing poetry?

7. For each of the terminal and instructional objectives above, can you clearly identify the three essential characteristics of *performance*, *conditions*, and *criterion*?

8. Think about the cognitive *and* affective growth you would like to see your sixth-grade class achieve through a five-week unit on health education. Can you prepare good terminal and instructional objectives that incorporate behaviors in the cognitive and affective areas?

NOTES

1. W. M. French, *America's Educational Tradition, An Interpretive History*, Ch. 9 Boston: D.C. Heath, 1967).
2. *Ibid.*
3. R. F. Mager, *Preparing Objectives for Programmed Instruction* (Belmont, CA: Fearon, 1962).
4. B. S. Bloom *et al.*, eds., *Taxonomy of Educational Objectives: Handbook I, Cognitive Domain* (New York: McKay, 1956).

5. D.R.Krathwohl, *et al.*, eds., *Taxonomy of Educational Objectives: Handbook II, Affective Domain* (New York: Mckay, 1964).

ADDITIONAL READINGS

N. E. Gronlund, *Stating Objectives for Classroom Instruction* (New York: Macmillan, 1978).

P. Hanna and J. Michaelis, *A Comprehensive Framework for Instructional Objectives* (Reading, MA: Addison-Wesley, 1977).

CHAPTER FOUR

TEACHER ASSESSMENT TOOLS FOR IMPROVING INSTRUCTION
OBSERVING CHILDREN IN THE CLASSROOM

IMPORTANT POINTS TO WATCH FOR

The most important and useful tool for the assessment of learning is classroom *observation*.

For classroom observation to be truly effective in evaluating children, it must be systematic, objective, selective, unobtrusive, and carefully recorded.

The checklist is a valuable device for the day-by-day recording of observed behavior.

The rating scale not only records daily behavior but helps teachers evaluate the degree to which children are meeting instructional objectives.

The anecdotal record is a more thorough recording device than the checklist and rating scale. It allows for more complete and detailed statements about behavior and the conditions surrounding it.

As the discussion of instructional objectives pointed out, planning teaching activities carefully requires close attention to children's needs. Knowing in advance the knowledge, skills, understanding, and affective behavior that children should acquire simplifies the job of writing good objectives. Just as important, good objectives simplify the job of evaluation by which children's needs are determined in the first place.

Based upon the importance of objectives to good classroom evaluation, this chapter will begin our discussion of how to carry on the day-to-day job of assessing children's needs. Although an array of published tests is available, we will leave these for separate chapters. For now, we will concentrate on the day-to-day assessment tools that teachers need to fulfill a vital part of their ongoing teaching responsibilities.

OBSERVATION OF CHILDREN

Perhaps the most common assessment tool teachers use and the one by which they gain the most information is systematic observation. The complex task of meeting children's needs combines close attention to the physical, emotional, and intellectual development of each child. This way teachers can determine how each growth component interacts with others to form the unique personalities of their students.

The story of Alice illustrates the need for constant attention to all the interacting developmental factors. With an understanding of the developmental nature of the physical, emotional, and intellectual components, Alice's teacher used sound observational techniques to recognize that Alice was not retarded. These observations led to the important decision to get more information before allowing the child to be placed in a "special" class.

Despite Alice's very real and very painful problems, she was only one among 23 other children. Although the other 22 were luckier than she in the ways in which their growth patterns interacted and developed, each was still unique and, in many ways, very different from all the others. Sound observational techniques help to preserve the uniqueness of each child in a class.

Observation Should Be Systematic

Just watching children each day will not provide all the information a teacher needs to make accurate decisions about how much or how well they have learned. A few children, because of their outgoing and, sometimes, aggressive behavior, often call attention to themselves. Teachers are more aware of these youngsters and more likely to remember their behavior. Eventually, a pattern may evolve that the teacher will note and use in evaluating them. Others who are not so noticeable tend to attract less attention, but quiet children need as much attention as the very active ones and, in some cases, even more.

Sam, for instance, is one of Alice's more active classmates. Constantly seeking attention, he is always on the move and rarely lights in one place for more than a few minutes. The teacher observes Sam's behavior more consistently than that of the others because she has no choice. If she did not watch him continually, the classroom would be a shambles by noon, not because Sam is bad but because his development combines excellent physical strength and coordination with a decided lag in intellectual achievement and emotional development. Thus he is frustrated because he does not read as well as the others, and his physical behavior helps him defend himself against those who tease him. Knowing that Sam's aggression is his way of achieving the attention he cannot get from academic success, the teacher is tolerant and tries to close the gap between his emotional level and his intellectual abilities. He is fortunate to have a teacher who does not simply punish him each time he acts out. With great patience, Sam's teacher carefully plans instructional objectives not only to help him achieve success in reading, but even more important at this time, to give him a feeling of personal success. For a while, in other words, Sam's *affective* growth needs much more attention than does his intellectual development.

Ned, on the other hand, is a very quiet child, physically well developed, but unlike Sam, emotionally well adjusted. He has many friends and his social interaction is very fulfilling. He has more than adequate intelligence but, for some reason, does not do very well in his school work. Because he is unobtrusive in the classroom, his behavior is less noticeable. While it is easy to pay less attention to a Ned than to a Sam, good teachers know that *all* of the children must be constantly and *systematically* observed and their behavior noted; not just mentally noted but recorded accurately.

Systematic observation requires careful attention to several factors if it is to be useful in gaining an accurate assessment of any child.

Observation Should Be Objective

It is not easy to be objective with a child like Sam. Behavior like his provokes powerful emotional responses, challenging teachers' ability to maintain their composure and to keep their subjective reactions from interfering. However, in attempting to keep an accurate record of Sam's activities for later evaluation, his teacher must refrain from including statements of her "dislike" that serve only to invalidate observations, and limit attempts to meet his needs. Remembering that there are reasons for such behavior helps teachers keep their observations as free as possible from bias. The more objective teachers can be, the more effectively they can plan for children's growth.

It is equally difficult to observe Ned's behavior without strong emotional responses. He is such a likeable youngster with such a happy outlook on life that his teacher tends to feel sympathy for his inability to read well, sympathy that may interfere with objective assessment.

Teachers perceive every child with some degree of emotion such as affection, sympathy, annoyance, or dislike—all of these must be recognized as detrimental to effective observation and evaluation. While it is probably impossible not to have such feelings, they create very real problems when they affect the objectivity of observations.

Observation Should Be Selective

If teachers had only a few children to teach and unlimited time to observe them, the issue of selectivity would be unimportant. But the fact is, teachers are hard-pressed to find enough time to systematically watch even important behavior. This is particularly true of the junior and senior high grades with teachers meeting as many as six groups every day.

Although teachers observe continually, they cannot see everything that each child does. Skillful teachers, recognizing this, identify critical behaviors in children that seem to disrupt their learning activities or the learning activities of others. Timothy, for instance, another of Alice's classmates, is always the center of laughter and horseplay. By focusing on the things he says or does to others, the teacher might well notice a definite pattern of witty asides or comical actions. With this pattern in mind, Timothy's teacher should be able to include the instructional objectives for Timothy, activities that will channel his humor into productive learning. Perhaps she can capitalize on his wit by getting him to write funny stories for the class. In this way, he can learn that his teacher approves of his sense of humor and that it can make his classmates happy without interfering with their learning activities.

Being selective means that teachers do not waste valuable time on insignificant observation. They watch for those actions that seem to make a significant difference in the child's ability to grow and learn. Once satisfied that the observed behaviors do, in fact, inhibit learning, the teacher has gathered the information necessary to make an intelligent evaluation and to find ways to help change the behaviors.

Observation Should Be Unobtrusive

Letting observation become apparent may well defeat its purpose. Nothing causes some children to avoid certain responses more than knowing someone is watching. Others, when they know they are being observed, over emphasize their actions in order to continue the attention. In either case, the teacher will not see the child's normal behavior, and the observations will not be as helpful as they should.

The school environment is an excellent place to observe without being observed. Both teacher and child belong there and accept each other's presence. Unobtrusive but systematic observation in this natural setting yields much information about children's personalities and learning styles.

Observation Should Be Carefully Recorded

It is not enough to watch casually the behavior of a youngster and then try to remember each event later on. Too much happens in every classroom to allow precision in memory. Inaccurate memories are not effective in the preparation of instructional objectives. Instead, an ongoing, written record helps teachers preserve important information.

Recording observations is not difficult, but it does require thought and planning. Although each teacher develops a unique system of record keeping, we would like to briefly discuss three rather common and effective methods: the checklist, the rating scale, and the anecdotal record.

The checklist The checklist is the easiest of the three and requires only that a teacher develop a simple chart with enough spaces in which to list performances or behaviors and to make the checkmarks. Such a chart helps assure that the teacher is selective in observing behaviors and has eliminated any subjective feelings from each recording. Figure 4.1 shows a typical checklist.

By analyzing the checklist at the end of a given period, Sam's teacher can quickly verify her observations. She won't have to trust her memory to verify that Sam's behavior is getting worse. The record will also assist her in planning a strategy to help him change his behavior.

Checklists can be developed for any behavior. Figure 4.1 obviously was designed to verify and record simple affective behavior. Another checklist might help determine the degree to which the basic cognitive skills of reading are being learned. Still another might be constructed to keep track of children's work habits. Observing and recording youngsters' specific acts is called *performance assessment*. Some writers feel it is useful to pay particular attention to children's performance because their observable acts provide clues to cognitive and affective changes.

Imagine, for instance, that Ned's work habits leave something to be desired. He tends to be sloppy in his penmanship, and his written papers are disorderly. The teacher might prepare a list of good writing performances and attach it to each of his papers for several days. In this way, both he and his teacher can see evidence of progress. The checklist might look like Fig. 4.2.

Sam		
Physically Hurts Other Children	Destructive of Property	Temper Tantrum
Mon. ✓✓✓✓	✓✓✓	✓✓✓
Tues. ✓✓✓✓	✓✓✓✓✓	✓✓✓
Weds. ✓✓✓✓✓✓	✓✓✓✓✓	✓✓✓✓
Thurs. ✓✓✓✓✓✓✓	✓✓✓✓✓✓	✓✓✓✓✓
Fri. ✓✓✓✓✓✓✓✓	✓✓✓✓✓✓	✓✓✓✓✓✓✓

Figure 4.1

```
┌─────────────────────────────────┐
│         Writing Habits          │
│ _____   Prints words neatly    │
│ _____   Prints on a straight line │
│ _____   Leaves even margins    │
│ _____   Spells accurately      │
└─────────────────────────────────┘
```
Figure 4.2

A similar checklist for reading skills might be constructed like Fig. 4.3

```
┌─────────────────────────────────┐
│         Reading Skills          │
│ _____   Recognizes silent E effect │
│ _____   Recognizes vowel digraphs │
│ _____   Recognizes initial consonants │
│ _____   Recognizes consonant blends │
│ _____   Sounds words phonetically │
└─────────────────────────────────┘
```
Figure 4.3

Checklists are often included in curriculum materials, such as Fig. 4.4, taken from an elementary grade science textbook.[1] The behaviors the authors have listed are keyed directly to the terminal instructional objectives of the unit.

The list also includes both cognitive behaviors and immediately observable performances. All learning, whether cognitive, affective, or physical, involves behavior. Some can readily be observed, such as penmanship performance, while others must be inferred, such as understanding algebra. In this discussion of checklists and in the section on rating scales, we have chosen to mix some of our cognitive objectives with some specific performances, as in Fig. 4.5 and Fig. 4.6. In Fig. 4.7, we have combined checklists for both cognitive and affective behavior. The point we would like to stress is that cognitive and affective behavior occur *together* and are closely related. When teachers observe and record specific *performances*, they are simply trying to verify that children can perform the acts that indicate whether they have assimilated and remembered some specific cognitive skills or whether they have grown in some specific affective way.*

---

*For a thorough discussion of performance assessment techniques, see Bruce Tuckman, *Measuring Educational Outcomes* (New York: Harcourt Brace Jovanovich, 1975).

UNIT 1   TINY WORLDS

Student's name

Checklist of Objectives

1. Points out parts of microscope.													
2. Focuses microscope so specimen is clearly seen.													
3. Adjusts microscope for high or low power.													
4. Explains that microscopes enlarge images of objects.													
5. Distinguishes between cotton and nylon by the way they are woven.													
6. Distinguishes between threads of cotton and nylon and describes them.													
7. Identifies gauze, cotton thread, and piece of cotton as the same material.													
8. Explains why microscope can be used to learn how things are put together.													
9. Defines a crystal.													
10. Recognizes and draws salt, sugar, and Epsom-salt crystals.													
11. Identifies each substance in mixtures of salt, sugar, and Epsom-salt.													
12. Uses term "dissolve" in meaningful way.													
13. Identifies salt crystal with microscope.													
14. Demonstrates that recrystallized salt resembles crystals before dissolving.													
15. Prepares slide that reveals cell structure.													
16. Locates cell coverings in onion skin.													
17. Identifies cell coverings, nuclei, and cytoplasm in stained onion skin.													
18. Differentiates between onion cells and salt crystals.													
19. Classifies organisms as plants, animals, or protists, and gives reasons for doing so.													
20. Makes simple drawing of organisms viewed in sample of water.													
21. Distinguishes at least four kinds of microscopic animals.													
22. Prepares acceptable slide of water organisms.													
23. Determines which microscopic animals have body parts.													
24. Identifies four microscopic animals by matching viewed animals with pictures.													
25. Finds cell covering, nucleus, and vacuole of viewed paramecium.													
26. Distinguishes three kinds of algae when viewed with microscope.													
27. Uses microscope to see intracellular structure of algae and draws picture showing cell coverings.													
28. Rationalizes that algae are alive.													
29. Uses microscope and sees bundles of chlorophyll in green algae.													

Figure 4.4   From *Elementary Science—Learning By Investigating* (Brewer, Garland, et al.), 1st edition, c. 1972, by Rand McNally & Co.: pp. 18, 19.

Writing Habits	Exc.	V. Good	Good	Fair	Poor
Prints words neatly					
Prints on a straight line					
Leaves even margins					
Spells accurately					

Figure 4.5

Check	Reading Skills	Always	Usually	Rarely	Never
_____	Recognizes silent E effect				
_____	Recognizes vowel digraphs				
_____	Recognizes initial consonants				
_____	Recognizes consonant blends				
_____	Sounds words phonetically				

Figure 4.6

The checklist has its obvious limitations. The checks indicate the number of times Sam acted up or that Ned demonstrated the reading skills, but they do not record the severity of Sam's behavior or the degree of Ned's skill in reading. One way of gathering this additional information is by using a rating scale.

The rating scale Rating scales indicate how Ned's reading skills compare with standards set for the class or how well he is meeting an instructional objective for neat papers. These scales may be used alone or combined with a checklist as in Fig. 4.5 and Fig. 4.6.

Checklists and rating scales can be helpful in keeping track of children's behaviors and in indicating how appropriate or how severe the behaviors are at any given time. When used consistently, they keep both the children and the teacher on the path toward improvement. They are effective in helping teachers observe and record virtually any kind of behavior, affective, physical, or cognitive. They are also relatively simple to construct, especially if the teacher keys observations to instructional objectives. Accordingly, the following checklist/rating scale could be developed for a tenth grade social studies unit.

If youngsters are to acquire good citizenship habits through their study of how a community cares for its poor, the instructional objectives for this type of unit would provide for growth in both the affective and cognitive areas. Through their cognitive study of community services, they should develop affective feelings about their responsibility towards others. The combination checklist/rating scale might look like Fig. 4.7.

The anecdotal record A more accurate method of recording behavior is the *anecdotal record,* a written observation of children's behaviors. Although somewhat more time consuming, this method notes not only the behavior but the conditions surrounding it. It is a more thorough way to record behavior and preserves more information.

Although they take more time than checklists and rating scales, anecdotal records are relatively easy to construct and maintain. Once again, while each teacher finds a unique way to keep them, some guidelines are helpful in making the anecdotal record effective.

SOCIAL STUDIES GROWTH COMMUNITY AWARENESS				
Name				
	Excellent	Good	Fair	Poor
Knows the city's organization for care of its poor.				
Knows the services available to welfare mothers.				
Knows the city's philosophy toward care of its aged poor.				
	Consistently	Usually	Occasionally	Rarely
Expresses concern for more humane treatment of the poor.				
Expresses a desire for active involvement in social services programs.				
Indicates realistic understanding of the city's expenditures and resources for the poor.				

Figure 4.7

1. Determine what to observe. As in the checklist, determine which behaviors to record. Thorndike and Hagen[2] suggest that it doesn't make sense to record behaviors that are more easily obtained by other methods. For instance, intellectual ability, academic achievement, and skills are best determined through standardized tests. However, behaviors that are more personal or affective lend themselves well to observation and anecdotal reporting. How is Timothy relating to his classmates as he engages in his special brand of humor? Is his behavior natural for him or does it seem to be a bluff to mask feelings of insecurity? By carefully determining the activities to be observed, teachers find it relatively easy to make a few concise remarks about what happened. Choosing behaviors that are significant such as a child's face-to-face encounters with certain other children, provides clues about meaningful aspects of a child's development.

2. Keep the anecdote in context. Recording a given behavior in isolation from the surrounding scene will not tell very much about the reasons for the child's behavior. In other words, teachers do not just observe the child, they observe the child interacting with the environment—what causes the behavior, which children trigger the behavior, how and why they are able to do so. In short, what is it about the situation that will clarify both the child's reactions to others and others' reactions to the child?

3. Keep the anecdote specific. The more precisely and simply a teacher reports behavior, the easier it will be to recall it clearly and precisely. General and long-winded comments about behavior cloud the real issue. For instance, recording that Timothy was in great humor today while working with Tomilee will not be very useful at the end of the week when the teacher begins to analyze the record. However, if the record says: "Timothy immediately broke into a joking routine as Tomilee came into the room. He seemed unsure and nervous while talking to her and could not seem to get serious about the assignment they were sharing," along with a series of similar statements, this will piece together an accurate picture of Timothy, a picture that will help his teacher evaluate his behavior effectively and plan ways to channel it into productive activity.

4. Keep the anecdote objective. Timothy's teacher will have to be careful to avoid expressing emotional responses in the record of Timothy's behavior. "Timothy kept me in stitches all day with humor" does not say much about Timothy, but it says a great deal about his teacher's reactions toward him. Timothy's affective development is important, not his teacher's. Objectivity forces teachers to concentrate on the child they wish to study and to avoid clouding the picture with irrelevant material.

If teachers wish to express their feelings about the incident or to make evaluative comments, these should be parenthetical in form and kept separate from the recording of the incident itself.

5. Keep the recording process simple. Keeping anecdotal records should not become a clerical nightmare that takes valuable time from the teaching process. They should be kept, in fact, only when there is something important to observe and record such as the behavior of a Timothy or an Alice or a Sam, children who need close watching in order to help them. Or teachers might record the children's responses to them in order to find better ways to plan their own behavior. At any rate, keep the record as brief as possible without losing the major thread.

To illustrate these five suggestions for good anecdotal records, the following is a one-week record on Timothy that logs his expressions of humor and the context in which they occur. The record concentrates on his face-to-face interactions with *individual classmates* because he engages in his comical activities more often in that kind of situation.

September 15: Timothy
    Timothy immediately broke into a joking routine as Tomilee came into the room. Refused to get serious about map-making assignment he was sharing with her. Made funny remarks about each suggestion Tomilee made.
    During arithmetic, while working on flash cards with Suzy, managed to remain quite serious while presenting cards to her—but when roles reversed, began making jokes about each flashcard until Suzy gave up.

September 16:
    Building sandbox model of a volcano with Andrew, although many humorous remarks, remained quite serious throughout and project completed.
    Map-making project with Tomilee again disrupted by comedy rather than work. Tomilee finally walked away in apparent frustration. Tim went back to his desk and sat quietly for several minutes.

September 17:
    Math flashcards with Eric went well with good sense of humor but also good flashcard practice.
    Blackboard washing project shared with Andrew and completed with many humorous asides but no disruption of the project.
    Map-making project with Tomilee another disaster. Timothy's constant comedy totally disruptive. Tomilee again gave up. Timothy again very quiet and subdued for a while.

September 18:
    Timothy worked well with Sam on preparing list of materials for science. This time Sam was unable to continue and Tim finished alone. When asked to work on experiment with Suzy, Tim began comedy routine and Suzy asked for someone else. Timothy again subdued and

quiet. (He seems to want to work with Suzy and Tomilee but cannot handle it.) Map-making project with Tomilee now being done by Tomilee alone, who does not want Timothy to help.

September 19:
    Science experiment with Chad very successful. Many humorous asides but not disruptive. Asked Tomilee if she needed help on map, seemed pleased when she said yes, but then was not able to refrain from disruptive comedy.

This would not be an unusual pattern of behavior for a second grade boy, and perhaps his teacher should not make much of it. Most boys at this age would rather not work with girls and might deliberately find ways to avoid it. However, the anecdotal record of Timothy's behavior stems from the teacher's concern that his wonderful sense of humor might be occasionally misdirected. He should keep it but learn when it is appropriate. The evaluation of his behavior by using anecdotal records is a very simple process, one that takes only a few moments each day but that produces a rather definite pattern to analyze. The teacher can help him now by finding ways to make him understand that his humor sometimes gets in the way of his success. This simple observational tool to measure and evaluate Timothy's affective behavior will become a basis for preparing instructional objectives, objectives that will effectively bring about a more appropriate balance between Timothy's sense of humor and his classroom responsibilities.

Anecdotal records, like checklists and rating scales, can take virtually any form that suits a teacher's record-keeping and recording procedures. The record of Suzy's behavior shown in Fig. 4.8 illustrates the ancedotal record format. Suzy's academic performance has declined lately, and she seems reluctant to participate in class activities. Her homework has been poorly done or not done at all for several weeks. She is subdued and moody, behavior very different from her usually friendly manner. By observing her carefully for a while, her teacher may be able to identify those factors in her school environment that might be contributing to her decline in academic performance and personal behavior. Other clues might suggest that she is having difficulties at home or in other nonschool activities.

The anecdotes concerning Suzy's behavior (Fig. 4.8) should be helpful in setting objectives for her during the coming weeks. Her teacher must find ways to help her through this crisis and make her feel comfortable in school so her work will improve. The ongoing record, which accompanies the teacher's attempts to draw her out and give her the constructive attention she needs, will perhaps register Suzy's gradual improvement as she finds her way back to her normally successful behavior.

ANECDOTAL RECORD		
Name: Suzy Grade: Two Teacher: Ms. Adams		

Objective: To determine probable cause of Suzy's decline in academic achievement and work habits by observing her academic and social behavior in social studies discussion period for one week.

Date and Time of Observation	Observation	Reactions and/or Interpretation
March 12 (Monday)	During discussion about courtesy and sharing, Suzy paid little attention. Did not volunteer and shrugged shoulders when asked a direct question.	No interpretation possible yet. Reluctance to participate very unlike Suzy.
March 13 (Tuesday)	Continued lack of involvement during discussion. Definite hostility toward Ned, who tried to question her about sharing with brothers and sisters.	Ned is a close neighbor and his question seemed pointed. Perhaps he knows of problems between Suzy and her sister. (Watch for quiet opportunity to ask about nonschool activities.)
March 14 (Wednesday)	Groups worked together to prepare reports on sharing. Suzy on periphery of her group and unwilling to contribute. When asked for input about family sharing of duties and responsibilities, marked negative reaction in blurted statement, "I do all the work at home, my stupid sister doesn't do anything!"	Wonder if some antagonism has developed between Suzy and older sister (learned that sister in grade 5 often absent this year—her teacher thinks she may be quite ill).
March 15 (Thursday)	Suzy's work in general continues to be poor both in quality and quantity. When asked, during social studies period, to write a list of shared family responsibilities, her list included six items she had to do at home, four items for a brother, and none for older sister. She wrote her list with angry expression on her face and seemed pleased with herself when she handed the list to me.	Called Suzy's mother today after school and asked if she saw evidence of anger or poor motivation. Told me all her time taken up with seriously ill sister in grade 5. *Must* put more responsibility on other two children.

Figure 4.8

March 16 (Friday)	Groups reported to class on their ideas for sharing. Suzy quite agitated while listening to others tell of their shared responsibilities with other members of the family. Read her list with pointed antagonism.	Obvious hurt at extra chores because of sister's illness. Wonder if she has been helped to understand how serious sister is.

Summary: Not certain that all of Suzy's lack of motivation stems from home but quite sure this is important factor. Mother seems willing to talk and school psychologist will be consulted for ideas on how to help Suzy cope. Continue anecdotal record for another week while attempting to find ways to help her.

Fig. 4.8 (Cont.)

The week's record adheres to the five suggestions for good anecdotal record keeping.

1. The teacher determined, in advance, the behavior to observe and record. Since she was quite certain Suzy was feeling anxiety of some kind, she could probably get the best clues from social or group situations such as the unit on sharing and responsibility.

2. The anecdote remains in context. The teacher did not observe isolated behaviors away from the group environment, but rather those activities or assignments that would most likely trigger the specific behavior that would guide her toward the next step, calling Suzy's mother, for instance, or speaking with the fifth grade teacher about Suzy's sister.

3. The anecdotes are specific. The comments are brief but complete enough to remind the teacher of the conditions under which the behaviors were noted.

4. The anecdotes are objective. Although the teacher made note of her reactions and made some tentative interpretations in a separate space, the descriptions of each day's behavior were free of subjective comments.

5. The teacher kept the recording process simple. She did not get bogged down with long lists of behavior or with complicated record folders. The format, though very simple, provides all the space necessary for anecdotes, reactions, and summary.

Whether a teacher uses checklists, rating sheets, anecdotal records, or some combination, systematic observation becomes a valuable means by which to assess children's ongoing progress, particularly in the area of personal growth. It also helps teachers understand how such affective factors interact dynamically with intellectual development to form the child's personality. These simple suggestions for effective observation and recording help to make this process a natural part of teaching and an important addition to the many other techniques for testing, measuring, and evaluating children.

IMPORTANT POINTS TO THINK ABOUT

1. Imagine that you are just beginning the year as a kindergarten teacher. How would you plan to observe each of your children as they arrive?

2. What are some of the affective behaviors you might expect to see as your kindergartners begin to relate and react to their new environment?

3. Can you construct a checklist of "appropriate" kindergarten behaviors for use with your class?

4. Now imagine that you are welcoming a class of ninth graders on the first day of school. What affective behaviors would you include on your checklist?

5. Can you trace the cognitive behavior of a girl in your ninth grade geography class as she struggles to understand the concepts of latitude and longitude? How would you use a checklist, a rating scale, and an anecdotal record to help you evaluate her progress?

NOTES

1. Clinton I. Chase, *Measurement for Educational Evaluation* (Reading, MA: Addison-Wesley, 1978), pp. 157-172.
2. R. L. Thorndike and E. Hagen, *Measurement and Evaluation in Psychology and Education* (New York: Wiley, 1969), pp. 471-490.

ADDITIONAL READING

Bruce Tuckman, *Measuring Educational Outcomes* (New York: Harcourt Brace Jovanovich, 1975).

CHAPTER FIVE

TEACHER ASSESSMENT TOOLS FOR IMPROVING INSTRUCTION
EVALUATING CHILDREN WITH TEACHER-MADE TESTS

IMPORTANT POINTS TO WATCH FOR

Preparing a table of specifications using Bloom's six levels of cognitive behavior will help make the job of test construction easier and more professional.

True-false tests are most effective in evaluating the lower levels of cognitive learning. Although they seem to be quick and easy to write, they require careful attention to wording. The should be kept simple and unambiguous.

Matching tests should be stated with precision and clarity. To avoid test taking by the process of elimination, there should be more response choices than stimulus items.

Completion tests are best used for recall of factual information. Whenever possible, single word answers should be required, and sentences should not be "lifted" directly from the text book.

The multiple-choice test is the most difficult of the objective tests to construct but affords a better opportunity to test the higher cognitive processes. Its main parts are called the *stem* and the *alternatives*.

Essay items afford students an opportunity to demonstrate creative and innovative thinking at the higher levels of Bloom's Taxonomy of Educational Objectives.

Most teachers have their favorite kinds of tests and use them frequently once they become proficient in constructing and administering them. However, whether the favorite test format is true-false, multiple-choice, or essay, they should have knowledge of how good tests are constructed and skill in actually constructing them.

In constructing a test, just as in planning a teaching unit such as one on electricity, objectives play an important role. Instructional objectives for electricity are stated in terms of the content matter children must learn and remember, the skills of scientific investigation they should acquire, and the application of subject matter and skills to higher cognitive processes. These include the abilities to analyze, synthesize, and evaluate what they have learned so that study of electricity does not become simply an exercise in rote memory. It is more difficult to state instructional objectives for the higher cognitive processes because they involve behavior that cannot readily be observed. Unlike memory or the acquisition of skills, the intellectual process of synthesizing information is much more difficult to teach. It is also more difficult to measure. However, since the higher cognitive processes are the most important, teachers must find ways to plan for them in their educational objectives.

USING BLOOM'S TAXONOMY IN PREPARING TESTS

The *Taxonomy of Educational Objectives*[1] discussed in Chapter 3 presents an enlightening discussion of the cognitive processes and how they relate to instruction and evaluation. Bloom's six levels or classes of cognitive functioning provide a helpful guide in planning a teaching unit and in assessing how much and how well children learned the material. Clinton Chase, in *Measurement for Education Evaluation*[2], summarizes Bloom's six cognitive categories and the related behaviors:

Class or Category	Related Behaviors
1. Knowledge—learns specifics, steps in dealing with specifics, stated principles and rules.	Defines common terms, identifies objects, lists, gives sequence of acts, states rule to explain.
2. Comprehension—translates from one symbol system to another, interprets, extrapolates.	States in own words, converts from words to a formula, infers, predicts, explains.
3. Application—in problematic situations draws upon the appropriate facts and principles for solutions.	Explains relation of principles to practical situations, produces objects or procedures, solves problems, organizes for given purpose.
4. Analysis—breaks objects and situations down into their elements, showing basic	Differentiates, recognizes inferences and supporting facts, breaks down objects or

relationships, sees organizational principles.	ideas into components, identifies relevant and irrelevant components.
5. Synthesis—puts together knowledge to produce unique communication, a new plan, or a new set of operations; builds a set of abstract relations.	Develops a creative product, combines elements to produce plans or materials, restructures, reorders ideas or objects to produce unique product.
6. Evaluation—makes judgments on the value of ideas, acts, solutions, and materials in reference to some objective or criterion.	Judges adequacy of a plan of action, appraises product, critically evaluates, justifies organization of ideas or materials, supports a plan of action.

The first two of these classes are closely connected with knowledge acquisition, and associated behaviors are relatively easy to observe and to evaluate. If all testing were done at these levels, evaluation would be quite simple. Even the third level, application, can be taught and evaluated with relative ease. However, the last three suggest higher, more sophisticated learning activities that are more difficult to translate into observable behavior, behavior that must be present before we can say with certainty that a child has learned them.

TABLE OF SPECIFICATIONS

Bloom's six levels of cognitive behavior can simplify test preparation and make the test more professional. By setting the six levels into a table and then listing the content, subject matter, skills, or other learning activities it is designed to measure, teachers can closely tie the evaluation to the instructional objectives. For instance, a unit on electricity might include instructional objectives closely resembling some of the six listed cognitive categories. For younger children, more emphasis would be placed on those cognitive levels requiring simple knowledge acquisition and comprehension. Since the cognitive quality of second graders is still largely associated with concrete manipulation of materials (Piaget's concrete-operational stage), there will be very little evidence of behavior that indicates learning at the upper levels. However, youngsters in the upper elementary and secondary grades can respond to test items that call for higher level cognitive behavior. Figure 5.1 shows how a table of specifications might be set up for the second grade test.

The specifications table lists the major topics that will be included in the test. Since second graders can gain only a fairly primitive knowledge about electricity, the test questions must be concentrated among the lower

Subject	Knowl-edge	Compre-hension	Appli-cation	Anal-ysis	Syn-thesis	Eval-uation	Total
Wiring simple circuit	2	2	1				5
The language of electricity	4	2	1				7
Fuses	2	1	1				4
Electromagnets	2	1	1				4
Safety around electricity	3	1	1				5
	13	7	5				25

Fig. 5.1 A table of specifications for a test on electricity (grade 2).

levels of cognitive behavior. The total of 25 indicates that 25 test items will be included, most of them clustered in the first cognitive level, the acquisition of knowledge. Only one or two exceptionally bright children could be expected to reach the upper cognitive levels.

What purpose does the table of specifications serve? It forces teachers to relate their testing procedures to the material they taught. While it may sound ridiculous that a teacher should use such a crutch to prepare a test, many teachers simply review the unit material and then rapidly assemble a number of test items. This usually indicates that they did not teach the unit according to carefully prepared instructional objectives. Such teaching might be fun but it tends to be haphazard and fails to provide both the teacher and the children with clear evidence of personal and intellectual development.

Instructional objectives are the road maps of teaching, restricting the learning process to a particular route and establishing a territory from which to choose test items. Some teachers, in fact, use the table of specifications to plan a unit in the first place. As the unit proceeds, the table becomes a convenient checklist to help the teacher and the children keep working toward their stated objectives. When they are ready to measure what was learned, the table, with minor modifications, becomes the table of specifications for the test. Since the table actually lists the activities a unit covered, teachers can more easily choose items that assess how much and how well the children have learned. By preparing both a teaching unit and its test around carefully stated instructional objectives, teachers are more likely to construct a valid evaluation instrument.

A table of specifications for a tenth grade unit on electricity is shown in Fig. 5.2. At this age, children should be able to think and learn in varying degrees at all six cognitive levels. Most of them will have learned not only to remember facts and to indicate their understanding of them, but to use them in the application of sophisticated principles to practical experience. In addition, they should be able to analyze information and discover within it important inferences and relationships. The brighter students will be able to synthesize various pieces of information to arrive at new applications. Finally, some will have reached the highest level of cognitive functioning, evaluation, an intellectual process that enables them to critically appraise the material they learned.

Since instructional objectives reflect a teacher's understanding of what children at that cognitive level can do, objectives for a tenth grade unit on electromagnetism will state the behavior expected from the children— behavior that will indicate that they understand electromagnetism at all six levels. When it comes time to formally measure this behavior, the table of specifications will include questions about electromagnets that span the knowledge and the understanding levels.

As a result of their experimentation with electrical equipment, the tenth graders will come to know a variety of applications of electrical principles to everyday life, so the test will include items on application. The experiments should also lead them to contemplate the nature of electricity, and by analyzing what they are absorbing, to begin to understand its organizing principles and fundamental relationships. They should also move beyond the knowledge acquisition level to make new applications as well as tentative judgments about the appropriate use of electricity. To determine whether they have reached these higher levels of cognitive behavior, the table of specifications include test items in the upper three levels.

For the tenth grade, two tables of specifications based on Bloom's six classes of cognitive behavior might be developed. The first will show the major content areas of the unit and how they relate to each of the six levels (see Fig. 5.2). The second will specify the content areas on which the youngsters will be tested and the number of items that will be included from each area (see Fig. 5.3). In addition, each test item will be placed next to the appropriate cognitive class and will indicate the cognitive level of behavior it is designed to elicit. Thus the teaching table closely approximates the testing table.

It takes a little longer to plan a test in this way, but the advantages are clear. Good planning and the use of instructional objectives keep teachers aware of the fact that more than memorization is involved in the learning process. Bloom and other researchers have helped to clarify the hierarchy of cognitive levels through which children move as they develop. The identification of higher levels of learning and thinking has yielded some preliminary insight into the behaviors associated with each level. Understanding these behaviors is the necessary forerunner to effective evaluation. Since the great majority of teacher-made test items are said to require

Subject	Knowledge	Comprehension	Application	Analysis	Synthesis	Evaluation
Alternating and direct current	Knows the parts of AC and DC circuits and related terms.	Understands how current flows in both AC and DC circuits.	Constructs AC and DC circuits from components available in class.	Shows during demonstration ability to recognize electric theory at work in circuits (relationship of watts to to ohms and amps).	Using comprehension of electrical theory and application, designs an original apparatus to do some form of work.	Judges whether direct current (batteries) or alternating current (generator) is more efficient and economical to power a bus.
Electro-magnetism	Knows the parts of electromagnet and related terms.	Understands how magnet and wire coils combine with electric current to produce strong field of force.	Using wire, bar magnets, and batteries, constructs an electromagnet that operates a switch.	While demonstrating, describes a magnetic field and how it relates to the components of the electromagnet.	Designs a circuit to operate a flashing light using the electromagnet principle.	Judges the safety of an electromagnet that uses low voltage to switch on a very high voltage circuit.
Electric generation	Knows parts of electric generator and related terms.	Understands how fossil fuels, water power, and atomic energy are converted to electric power.	Uses own energy to turn crank and generates low voltage with homemade generator.	Describes, during demonstration, how own energy is multiplied many times by using water power and fuels to drive the crank.	Sketches a town and shows how terrain, fuel availability, and placement of generators might provide best combination of power sources.	Evaluates current electric products of a growing community and estimates future generating needs.
Electricity as an energy resource.	Knows several important uses of electricity.	Understands how different geographical areas might use energy resources found close by (water power from streams, and so on).	Applies knowledge of energy resources by describing the probable source of energy for a mountain community, a desert, and an island.	Describes the interrelatedness of all energy resources and the need for conservation.	Designs a delivery system for various energy resources that is balanced and ecologically reasonable.	Examines the growing needs of a developing nation and estimates the availability of various energy sources (coal, water power, and so on.

Fig. 5.2 A table of specifications for a teaching unit on electricity (grade 10).

only rote memorization, it is clear that more attention to advanced intellectual processes is needed. Research in human learning such as Bloom's provides teachers with the much-needed knowledge to teach and evaluate the higher processes.

The table of specifications for constructing a test, then, is simply a plan, or blueprint, to help teachers decide the subject matter on which to test. Instructional objectives specify the actual learning behavior, and test items are then designed to elicit those behaviors. If a test is carefully constructed, children will indicate by their answers (behavior) that the unit has been successful and to what degree. The results of the assessment efforts will then determine future teaching strategies.

Subject	Knowl-edge	Compre-hension	Appli-cation	Anal-ysis	Syn-thesis	Eval-uation	Total
Alternating and direct current	5	2	3	2	1	1	14
Electromagnetism	4	3	2	1	1	1	12
Electric generation	5	3	3	2	1	1	15
Electricity as an energy resource	3	2	1	1	1	1	9
	17	10	9	6	4	4	50

Fig. 5.3 A table of specifications for a test on electricity (grade 10).

TYPES OF TEACHER-MADE TESTS

Despite the seeming endless variety of tests, there are, in general, two major types, objective and essay. We will discuss each category in this section.

Objective Tests

Objective tests are so named because they tend to reduce the opportunity for subjective interpretation by the person taking them. The items are constructed in such a way as to call forth either a single answer as in true-false items or to allow a limited choice of answers as in multiple-choice. Two other types are the matching and completion tests, which also allow a limited choice of responses.

All four of these objective tests are used widely, and all have the same general characteristics.[3] The child:

1. Operates within a completely structured situation.

2. Selects an answer from a limited number of choices.

3. Responds to each of a large sample of items.

4. Receives a score for each answer according to a predetermined key.

As we discuss each type of objective test, we will examine their advantages and disadvantages.

True-False Tests and How to Write Them

The true-false test is one of the most widely used objective tests, perhaps because it seems relatively simple to convert statements from the subject matter to true-false items. However, advantage of quick and easy items has led to the well deserved criticism that teachers use them to take the easy way out. True-false tests, say the critics, are often carelessly constructed. Moreover, they do not evaluate effectively since they demand only rote memorization and neglect the higher levels of the taxonomy. While there is some validity to these criticisms, they are not entirely true. True-false items can be constructed to assess higher cognitive functioning, and they have the advantage of sampling a large amount of subject matter. Since students can answer two or three times as many true-false items as other types in the same amount of time, true-false tests give students a greater opportunity to show what they have learned.

Good true-false test items are written according to the following principles.

Keep them simple Each true-false item should be stated in the simplest, most direct terms. This will reduce the possibility of "reading into" the item more than one meaning or interpretation. Teachers should know exactly what stimulus they wish to present and which response they wish to obtain. If students are unsure of what they are being asked to do because an item is ambiguous, they won't have a clear-cut opportunity to show that they know the answer. The item will have lost its objectivity. For instance, an item from the second grade unit on electricity might read:

T.   F.   A fuse is placed in our home because we want to be safe from the dangers of electricity.

What dangers? Where is it placed in the home? The item is not specific enough to the subject matter and offers the student opportunities to think about extraneous matters. A better way to write the item would be:

T.   F.   Fuses prevent too much electricity from passing through the wires.

Although the improved item does not include the dangers of overloading, the next item will:

T.   F.   Too much electricity in the wires will cause them to get very hot.

From here the test could include a series of simple statements, each referring to a specific bit of knowledge covered in the unit and each presenting a single clue to which the children can respond.

Don't include clues to the answers Words such as "never" or "always" usually signal that the answer is false, while words like "sometimes" or "normally" often indicate a true statement. For instance:

T.   F.   Too much electricity in the wires *usually* causes them to overheat; or

T.   F.   A fuse *always* prevents too much electricity from passing through the wires.

Avoid words that can be interpreted in different ways. Whenever words are included that are indefinite in degree or amount, objectivity is lost and different youngsters will produce different answers. For instance:

T.   F.   It does not take very long for a wire to become overheated.

The phrase "very long" is open to too many interpretations and is thus misleading and confusing.

The tenth grade class can respond to more sophisticated items about fuses, and a true-false test can be designed to measure behavior at the higher cognitive levels, as in the following examples:

T.   F.   A fuse in a television set will prevent lightning damage to the set.

False. Since lightning, if it strikes the electrical wires leading to a TV set, will very likely destroy the set, the important application learning here is to unplug televisions and other such devices during electrical storms.

T.   F.   Wires equipped with fuses are hotter to the touch than those without fuses.

False. In this item, the fuse has nothing to do with how hot the wires might become. Excessive heat indicates electrical overloading. When overloading gets too high, the fuse will merely melt and stop the flow of electricity, thus protecting home and appliances against fire and damage.

If children learn and understand the facts of electricity well enough, they will be able to translate their learning into applied situations such as this. Further, they should be able to analyze the knowledge they have gained and perhaps identify important components of a circuit that must be present to make the system work. To test whether they can, in fact, think and learn at the analysis level, the true-false item will have to be worded appropriately. Two tenth grade true-false questions calling for analysis ability might read as follows:

> T.   F.   When a fuse blows, we know that its resistance to the flow of electricity is less than that of the wire to which it is connected.
>
> T.   F.   If a fuse fails to blow and the wire to which it is connected gets hot enough to cause a fire, we know that excessive power rather than a faulty fuse was the cause.

Both questions call for an analysis of the flow of electricity and of the electrical terms, voltage, resistance, and current, and how these elements combine to produce electricity.

The fifth level of the taxonomy, *synthesis*, calls for behavior that includes the ability to rearrange or recombine learned information about electricity to arrive at a different application of the knowledge than the ones studied. For instance, the class might have conducted a series of experiments showing how fuses protect various parts of a complex circuit. Using this knowledge when they are presented with a new problem, they should be able to synthesize an answer.

> T   F.   A way to protect an entire neighborhood from excessive electrical current is to place fuses in the wires leading from the main power supply to the neighborhood.
>
> T   F.   A way to protect an entire house from excessive electricity is to place a fuse in the main wire between the pole and the house.

Both answers are true and power companies do just this. However, for children to conclude that the statements are true, they will need to be able to think and learn successfully at the *synthesis* level of the taxonomy and at all preceding levels as well.

Finally, teachers may wish to know whether children can operate intellectually at the highest cognitive level, *evaluation*. True-false items will have to be constructed very carefully to call for evidence of this ability. In this case a hypothetical circuit might be presented to the class with an item asking them to evaluate its usefulness, effectiveness, or safety.

> You are building a house and you wish to have five wall outlets in each of the three bedrooms and four overhead light fixtures operated independently of each other. In addition, each room will be equipped with a 4,000 BTU window air conditioner.
>
> T.   F.   One 20-amp fuse will be adequate for all three rooms.

T.   F.   Each room should have its own 15-amp fuse.
T.   F.   Each air conditioner should be provided with a separate circuit and fuse.

The learning process becomes increasingly complex as the level of cognitive ability involved in a problem increases. While true-false tests do not readily lend themselves to the testing of the higher intellectual processes, teachers use them more effectively if they understand what those processes call for.

Writing good true-false items is not to be done a few moments before the test. Good ones require time for reviewing instructional objectives and the material that has been taught. Only then can teachers translate the subject matter into a test that will effectively measure youngsters' learning behavior. Given the difficulty in constructing good true-false items, we would like to go through the process of preparation, beginning with material that appears in a well-known elementary science series, the same book from which we borrowed the checklist in Fig. 4.4. This selection about protists is a small portion of a longer unit called *Tiny Worlds*.[4]

True-false items should be simple, without clues to the answers. They should also be written clearly, without ambiguous terms that might cause misinterpretations. In some cases, the printed material lends itself very directly to good items. The first sentence, for instance, can stand alone as a good true-false statement.

T.   F.   Living things that are neither plants nor animals are called protists.

and another;

T.   F.   Protists have only one cell.

Some of the other material will have to be reworked to achieve the form of true-false items.

T.   F.   A paramecium is one kind of protist.
T.   F.   A paramecium moves by the use of tiny hairlike parts.

The text might also be revised to call for an answer of false:

T.   F.   Protists are nonliving things that look like tiny animals.
T.   F.   Vacuoles help the paramecium move.

Matching Tests and How to Write Them

Most testing experts consider the matching test, despite its longevity, somewhat limited in its effectiveness since it is difficult to prepare items that test the higher cognitive processes. However, when used along with other types of test items (true-false, multiple-choice), the matching test is a useful component of the overall evaluation process because it offers youngsters an additional opportunity to demonstrate what they have learned. In this discussion of the matching test, we will present several examples showing how the test can be used to assess learning at the knowledge, understanding, and application levels of the taxonomy.

As in all test construction, items must be stated with as much precision and clarity as possible to avoid confusion and misinterpretation. To prevent test taking by the "process of elimination," there should be more response choices than stimulus items. Also, each matching exercise should contain information that is at the same taxonomic level.

Knowledge Level

1. ampere
2. ohm
3. volt

a. A measure of electrical resistance
b. A measure of electrical current
c. A measure of electrical power
d. A measure of electrical induction

Understanding Level

1. short circuit
2. electrical overload
3. current surge

a. A condition caused by suddenly decreasing the length of wire through which current is flowing
b. A condition caused by increasing the amperage in a circuit
c. A condition caused by increasing the voltage in a circuit
d. A condition caused by increasing the conducting properties of a circuit

Application Level

Each of the electrical devices in the lefthand column can be built from one of the sets of materials listed in the matching column.

1. A burglar alarm
2. An emergency lighting system
3. A device to demonstrate electrical overloading

a. A 6-volt cell; 20-gauge copper wire in 1", 2", 3", and 10" lengths; a 6-volt flashlight bulb.
b. A 12-volt battery, 50 feet of 20-gauge ignition wire, a 60-watt bulb.
c. A 6-volt cell, a 6-volt buzzer, a switch, 10 feet of 20-gauge copper wire.
d. Two 6-volt cells, 10 feet of 20-gauge copper wire, a 12-volt auto bulb.

The first set of items calls for simple recall of factual material. The second requires recall of facts plus some understanding of their properties.

Observing Protists

Living things that are neither plants nor animals are called **protists.**

Protists have only one cell. Some protists have no color. Some are green. Some swim in water. Some are fastened to other things.

The picture shows one kind of protist. It is a **paramecium.** It is magnified so it looks much bigger than it really is.

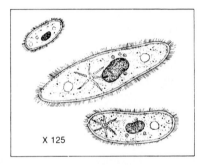

X 125

How are the things you see on your slide like a paramecium? How are they different?

Look at the picture. Does the paramecium have a head or tail? Do you think it is made of one cell or more than one cell? Find the covering and the nucleus.

A paramecium has tiny pockets in its body. These hold food, water, and wastes. The pockets are called **vacuoles.** Find the vacuoles.

Find the tiny hairlike parts that help the paramecium move.

From *Elementary Science—Learning By Investigating* (Brewer, Garland, et al.) 1st edition, © 1972, by Rand-McNally & Co.: pp. 31, 32.

Put a drop of the culture on a slide.
Cover it with a cover glass.
Look at it with the microscope.

THINK AND TALK ABOUT

1. How are the living things you found
    like the paramecium?
2. How are they different?
3. What makes you think
    they may or may not be protists?

Some protists are shown below.

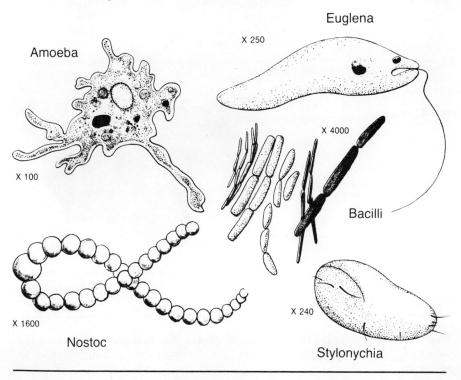

Euglena

X 250

Amoeba

X 4000

X 100

Bacilli

X 1600

X 240

Nostoc

Stylonychia

CONCEPT:

▶ **MANUFACTURING**

Where are the major manufacturing centers in the United States?

What determines location of factories?

Most things used by the people of the United States are produced in factories. Automobiles, clothing, furniture, radios, shoes, telephones, and televisions are factory-made goods that are enjoyed by almost everyone in the nation. Geographers study the reasons why factories are located where they are. They also are interested in the reasons why certain kinds of products are made by factories in particular areas of the United States.

▶ **MANUFACTURING DEVELOPS IN URBAN AREAS**

Most manufacturing is carried on in the large urban areas of the United States. The map below shows the major manufacturing centers of the nation. Study the map key to find out what the different-sized circles represent. Where in the United States are the urban centers in which the largest numbers of people work at manufacturing? Why are most of these centers located in the same part of the United States? Compare this map with the political map of the United States in the *Atlas* to find the names of some of the major manufacturing centers. What reasons can you give for so little manufacturing being located in the western part of the United States?

United States — Major Manufacturing Centers

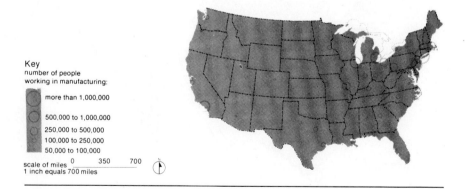

Key
number of people
working in manufacturing:

more than 1,000,000

500,000 to 1,000,000
250,000 to 500,000
100,000 to 250,000
50,000 to 100,000

scale of miles 0   350   700
1 inch equals 700 miles

From *Investigating Man's World: United States Studies* by Paul R. Hanna, Clyde F. Kohn and Clarence L. Ver Steeg. Copyright © 1970 by Scott, Foresman and Company. Reprinted by permission.

The ideal manufacturing center would have certain things available. It would have raw materials nearby. It would have plenty of cheap power. It would have good means of transportation. It would have a plentiful supply of workers. It would have many customers in the area.

It takes a great deal of planning to decide where to locate a factory. Few cities have all of the advantages of an ideal manufacturing center. Men who plan factory locations must decide which advantages are most important to the needs of the particular factory. They must decide where they can manufacture and distribute the products of a factory at the lowest cost and sell them to the largest number of customers.

MANY FACTORS ◄
DETERMINE LOCATION
OF MANUFACTURING

Certain kinds of factories are located near the source of raw materials they use. This is because it is costlier to ship some of the raw materials than the finished or partly finished product. For example, wood pulp is used in making paper. The map below shows the distribution of wood-pulp mills. Most are near forest areas. Why are these mills located here rather than near the eastern urban centers?

Some manufacturing is located ◄
near raw materials

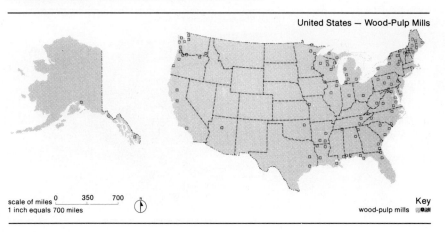

United States — Wood-Pulp Mills

scale of miles 0   350   700
1 inch equals 700 miles

Key
wood-pulp mills

► Some manufacturing is located near sources of power

Certain kinds of factories are located near the source of power they use. Sometimes, it is cheaper to transport the raw materials to the factories and the finished product away from them than to transport power needed to make the product. For example, electric power is used in the manufacturing of aluminum. Aluminum is made from bauxite. Most of the bauxite used in the United States comes from Guyana, Jamaica, and Surinam in Latin America. You would expect that the aluminum mills would be in Latin America. In aluminum-making, the source of raw material is not the reason why the mills are where they are.

The aluminum mills need large amounts of electric power to separate the aluminum from the bauxite. Since so much is needed, it is important that the cost of this power be kept as low as possible. Electric power may be generated by falling water or by heating with coal, oil, or gas. You can see on the map that many aluminum mills are located in Tennessee, Oregon, and Washington. Hydroelectric power in these areas is cheap and abundant because of the dams that have been built across the large rivers. Aluminum mills are located in these areas to take advantage of the cheap power.

United States — Aluminum Mills

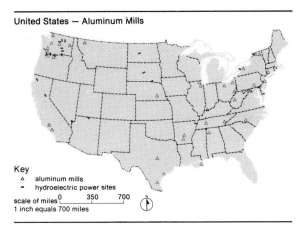

Key
△   aluminum mills
-    hydroelectric power sites
scale of miles   0   350   700
1 inch equals 700 miles

Certain kinds of factories are located close to markets for their products. Sometimes, it is cheaper to transport raw materials and power to the factories than to transport the products away. For example, steel mills built in the United States in recent years have been placed as close as possible to markets. The picture shows a factory at Sparrows Point, Maryland. It was built by the Bethlehem Steel Company. Large markets for steel are nearby in the urban areas of the eastern part of the nation. Other markets along the Atlantic, Gulf, and Pacific coasts are easily reached by water transportation, which is cheap.

Some manufacturing is located ◄ near markets

The third exercise requires that the student both know and understand electrical properties and materials and be able to apply this background to real situations.

Each of the items was written in terms of the instructional objectives built into the table of specifications. When teachers know in advance the material they plan to teach and establish the cognitive levels at which they expect to observe growth, they simplify the task of selecting material and planning test items that will allow children to demonstrate their cognitive growth.

Again, we will demonstrate the process of preparing matching items, this time using material taken from a secondary school textbook on the United States.[5] This brief excerpt about manufacturing is a small sequence among many describing the nation's growth and development.

1. Steel mills	a. are usually located near source of raw material
2. Woodpulp mills	b. are usually located near major steel markets
3. Aluminum mills	c. are usually located near furniture factories
	d. are usually located near water power

1. Western U.S.	a. an area important for its open spaces
2. Eastern U.S. Seaboard	b. an area of relatively little manufacturing
3. Northeast U.S.	c. an area important for its many steel markets
	d. an area important for its skilled labor

Completion Tests and How to Write Them

Completion tests are also very popular among teachers at all levels because they are relatively easy to write. However, the shortcomings discussed in the section on true-false items hold true here. If care is not taken to construct items that reflect the instructional objectives, the tendency will be to simply lift a sentence from the textbook, omitting a word or phrase. Further, completion tests lend themselves primarily to the recall of factual information and not to the higher cognitive levels.

In *Measurement for Educational Evaluation*, Chase[6] lists several suggestions for improving the quality of completion items.

1. Whenever possible, single-word answers should be required.

2. Avoid lifting statements directly from the textbook.

3. Avoid indefinite statements which might logically be answered with several different terms.

4. Delete only key words from completion statements.

5. Do not impair the sense of the statement by deleting too many of its elements.

6. Blanks should be placed at the end of the statement whenever possible.

7. Avoid clues to the correct answer in the structure of the item.

Here are examples of good completion items:

A device for protecting an electrical circuit from an overload of current is called a _____.

It takes one volt to push one ampere through one ohm of _____.

A 60-cycle circuit reverses polarity 60 times each _____.

What mistakes were made in the following completion items and how would you strengthen them?

A _____ is a D.C. power supply made up of several cells.

A fuse will blow whenever the _____ becomes too _____ for the circuit.

A fuse protects a circuit when too much current flows through the _____.

Using Chase's seven suggestions for good completion items, we have prepared several more completion items from the material on U.S. manufacturing.

The availability of hydroelectric power is important to the manufacture of _____.

The proximity of large markets is important in the construction of mills that manufacture_____.

Bauxite is important to the manufacture of _____.

Multiple-choice Tests and How to Write Them

The multiple-choice item is considered somewhat more difficult to construct than the other objective items we have discussed. However, it is a much more effective item for measuring the higher cognitive processes, and a look at its basic elements shows that it is not really difficult to construct as long as teachers pay attention to a few simple rules.

Each multiple-choice item consists of a stem and a series of alternative responses, one of which is the correct response. Alternatives that are incorrect are, for obvious reasons, called distractors.

The stem As in any test question, clarity is the first and most important consideration. The stem in a multiple choice question should present the problem so clearly that students will know *exactly* what is expected of them. It should be constructed in such a way that it leads directly to the alternatives without ambiguity. This can be assured if both the stem and the correct alternative are written as a grammatically complete statement. For instance:

The Connecticut River originates at the Connecticut Lakes in Northern Vermont.

Started this way, the entire item is more likely to have a clearly stated stem and a good set of alternatives. Then, break the sentence in the following way to construct the alternative responses or distractors:

The Connecticut River originates at the Connecticut Lakes in:

a. Southern Canada
b. Northwestern New Hampshire
c. Northern Vermont
d. Northeastern Connecticut

It does not matter very much where the stem is split so long as it makes good sense and contains most of the information. Items at this level should provide clues for *accurate* recall in order for the children to be accurate in their selection of an answer.

It does not matter, either, whether the stem is written as an imcomplete sentence, as above, or whether it is restated as a question. For instance, after the initial statement about the Connecticut River, the multiple-choice item can be written this way:

Where does the Connecticut River originate?

a. In Southern Canada
b. In Northwestern New Hampshire
c. In the Connecticut Lakes of Northern Vermont
d. In Northeastern Connecticut

In either case, the youngsters will have no trouble knowing what is expected of them because the stem is clearly stated.

The alternatives The alternatives (sometimes called *options*) are the "multiple choices" among which students select. Each must be written to flow logically and grammatically from the stem, and each alternative should seem *plausible*; that is, a youngster who does not recall the exact origins of the Connecticut River might choose any one of the alternatives. Thus, multiple-choice items with plausible alternatives demand more intensive "remembering" to avoid guessing.

Since the alternatives are as plausible as the correct response, they are called "distractors." They are designed to force students to think by making their choices more difficult. The distractors, although plausible, must have no element of correctness about them. They must be clearly and unequivocally wrong responses so that students will not be misled by choices in which they can see partially correct elements. Such elements make the question ambiguous for the student and unreliable as a means of evaluating learning.

Good multiple-choice items, then, must contain a clearly stated stem that contains enough information for children to know exactly what is expected of them. They must also contain a correct alternative and several incorrect distractors; all of which must flow logically and grammatically from the stem. The distractors must be plausible but completely wrong. Moreover, experts on test construction say keeping the responses as short as possible also helps to avoid ambiguity, Finally, all choices should be homogeneous in content to avoid any that are obviously wrong.

Here is an item that is poorly written.

The rich alluvial soil of the Connecticut Valley has produced one of the most productive tobacco-growing regions of the nation, and it was formed by:

a. the creation of soil by the erosion of the surrounding mountains
b. the depositing, by the river, of silt along its banks
c. annual flooding
d. the construction of dams and waterfalls

The stem is too long and is poorly written. Students do not know whether they are being asked to say how the alluvial soil was formed or how the Connecticut Valley was formed. Although both are part of the process of river valley formation, the first is a single factor within the second. In addition, the alternatives are too long and each one is not only plausible but partially correct depending on how the student decides to interpret the stem.

This example shows how a carelessly worded item can lead to confusion and poor testing procedures. Although it is just as easy to construct a good item by incorporating the suggestions that have been mentioned, there probably is no way to build a good multiple-choice item around this particular topic. Instead, the teacher should select significant portions of the subject of river valleys or soil formation from the instructional objectives and write several items. For instance:

The soil along the banks of the Connecticut River at Hadley was deposited mostly by:

a. erosion
b. weathering
c. flooding

All three alternatives create some soil formation but students should know from studying the Connecticut River that in this portion of the valley topsoil was deposited because of constant flooding leaving new layers of silt each time the water receded.

What is the present geographic configuration of the Connecticut River bed?

a. V-shaped
b. U-shaped
c. meandering

The children should know that the river changes its river bed configuration over millions of years from a fast-flowing and narrow V-shaped bed to one that is broad and U-shaped. Although the river meanders in some places, these are the exceptions.

Multiple-choice items can also be written at each level of the taxonomy.

Knowledge Level

Where is the mouth of the Connecticut River Valley located?

a. New Haven
b. New London
c. Saybrook
d. Essex

Simple recall of information is all that is asked.

Understanding Level

Which term most accurately describes the soil deposited at the base of a canyon?

a. volcanic rock
b. alluvial fan
c. sedimentary deposit
d. conglomerate

Children need to recall information about erosion and soil formation accurately and understand how these phenomena build specific geographic formations.

Application Level

To help retain the valuable farm lands along a river, man often builds:

a. dikes
b. underwater dams
c. waterfalls
d. flood gates

Children must *apply* their knowledge and understanding of rivers and flooding to know that dikes will prevent rampaging floods from carrying away the soil.

Analysis Level

A river that flows between steep mountains for a hundred miles and then suddenly into a broad plain will require that people who live in the plain build dams:

a. at the head of the canyon
b. at the mouth of the canyon
c. two miles below the mouth of the canyon
d. at several points along the canyon

In analyzing the flow of such a river children should understand how water from the mountain streams will swell the water level in the river and cause it to flow faster and in dangerous amounts. They should conclude, if they can perform at this cognitive level, that a series of dams will likely afford the best protection.

Synthesis Level

In addition to providing drinking water, a reservoir high in the mountains can be an important source for which of the following needs of man?

a. transportation
b. irrigation
c. electricity

Children now will have to analyze the information they have gained about the flow of water in order to synthesize a new way to make use of the reservoir. Writing good items at this cognitive level is the most difficult because children do not have the opportunity to test and try out various theories. Items most nearly elicit the behavior of synthesis when they include several alternatives that *might* be possible and that are all *plausible*. In this case, children should use their ability to synthesize to see that electricity is the best answer. As the water plunges from the upper levels, it can be diverted temporarily through tunnels and against the blades of electric generating turbines. By examining the alternatives, children must visualize how each might be accomplished. When they consistently select the correct alternative in a series of such multiple-choice items, the teacher can get a fair estimate that they are learning to think at the systhesis level of the taxonomy.

Evaluation Level

Which of the following strategies would be the most equitable solution to the perennial drought problems of a large population living in a dry plain below a well-watered upland area?

a. divert the water from the upland lakes by aqueducts
b. change the course of a major river that serves the upland region
c. drill deep wells in the plains area
d. build a series of dams in the upland region to store water for the plains area

Each response is plausible and each poses economic and emotional problems. Making a thoughtful judgment in terms of available information is called for. This kind of thinking transcends the other five levels but is also dependent upon them. Much like Piaget's formal-operational level of cognitive behavior, the evaluation level of Bloom's Taxonomy is the highest order of intellectual response.

We can demonstrate the process of preparing good multiple-choice test items by returning to the excerpt on manufacturing. First, find a statement such as the following that is grammatically correct and that sets forth clearly one of the facts in the material:

Most manufacturing is carried on in the large urban areas of the United States.

If the sentence is split after the word "on," it will have a logical stem and the correct alternative response. Set up as a multiple-choice item with the correct alternative included as one of four choices, the statement looks like this:

Most manufacturing in the United States is carried on:

a.
b.
c. in the large urban areas
d.

The three additional alternatives must be both plausible and absolutely wrong. A number of possibilities suggest themselves immediately, including such topographical areas as the Great Plains or the Rocky Mountains. Or they might include geographic areas described in compass terms, the

Far West, for instance, or the South Central States. Another possibility is to include areas that have special characteristics like waterfalls or navigable rivers or abundant natural resources.

The important thing to remember is that each alternative, or distractor, must clearly be wrong, or the children may see in them enough truth to make them partly correct. For instance, the alternative, "in the Eastern half of the United States," would encompass most of the large urban areas and there would be two alternatives that were essentially correct. The following three alternatives, taken from the maps in the textbook pages, meet the criteria for a good multiple-choice question:

Most manufacturing in the United States is carried on:

a. in the Southwestern states
b. near the nation's large waterfalls
c. in the large urban areas
d. where natural resources are most abundant

Here is another item taken from the same material.

The best location for an aluminum plant is near abundant sources of hydroelectric power.

This time, instead of splitting the sentence into a stem and the correct alternative response, we have restated the stem portion in the form of a question.

What is the best location for an aluminum plant?

a.
b. Near abundant sources of hydroelectric power
c.
d.

Three distractors to complete the item could include:

What is the best location for an aluminum plant?

a. Near heavy population areas
b. Near abundant sources of hydroelectric power
c. Near major seaports
d. Near the bauxite mines

These two items call for several kinds of cognitive functioning. Since they ask for the recall of facts, the items test at the *knowledge* level of Bloom's Taxonomy. They also call for some understanding of the factors that help decide the placement of different manufacturing processes; therefore, thinking at the *understanding* level is necessary. Thinking at the *application* level is also evident since youngsters would have to think through what they know about the appropriate placement of factories and then *apply* this information to the specific demands of the item.

If a teacher's objectives call for learning at the analysis level, additional items must reflect that stage of cognitive development. As in the previous items, the process begins with a complete statement, but this time the statement must indicate that analysis of available information is necessary for a decision. For instance

> An ideal site for a steel mill would include plentiful labor, cheap power, good transportation, proximity to markets, and abundant resources.
>
> Since all of these conditions are not available, the manufacturer must select the site that has the most important of these conditions.
>
> A logical site for a steel mill would be:
>
> a. Chicago
> b. Denver
> c. Kansas City
> d. Salt Lake City

Chicago has four of the five conditions, and the absence of the fifth, abundance of natural resources, is minimized by the cheapest available transportation. There is a large labor force in the Chicago area, abundant hydroelectric power, and water resources for shipment of raw materials to the mills. Chicago also has important markets for steel products.

To determine whether children are able to think at the *synthesis* level, multiple-choice items must demand that children combine their knowledge, understanding, and application skills with their analytic abilities and apply them to a new situation, such as deciding how a woodpulp mill might be economically feasible when built *away* from its raw material, the forests. Here is the statement that includes the stem and correct alternative.

> A woodpulp mill cannot be built near a large forest because of environmental damage that would be done to the adjacent terrain and wildlife. It should be built where the logs can be transported to the mill in the cheapest and cleanest way and with the least disruption of the environment.

Rephrased, the stem should look something like this:

> You must choose the best site for a woodpulp mill to process lumber from Northeast Wisconsin. Environmental controls prevent building the mill near the forest. The most realistic site for the plant will be:
>
> a. in Western Wisconsin where trains can carry the logs from the forest
> b. in Western Michigan where ships can carry the logs from the forest

   c. in Northern Minnesota where population is sparse and people won't be
      bothered
   d. in Buffalo where abundant waterpower exists to run the mill

Youngsters should be able to analyze the map and determine that "b"
would be the best answer.

    Finally, for those students who are beginning to solve problems at the
evaluation level, a question might ask for a value judgment about the best
site for a steel mill, one that would be economically feasible for the
company while protecting the best interests of the population. Here is one
such question.

A steel mill should be located with full consideration of the need for its
products, of the health and safety of people, and of the ecological and
environmental impact it will have on the area. Which of the following would be
the most favorable site for a steel mill?

   a. The Northern Great Lakes
   b. New Mexico
   c. Eastern Massachusetts
   d. The Florida Everglades

Although a question like this will be subject to much discussion, on the
face of it at least, the Northern Great Lakes would seem to be a logical if not
perfect location. However, since children must learn to analyze the impact
of a huge, noisy, dirty, and unsightly factory, the job of setting objectives
and teaching children to think and learn at the highest level of the
taxonomy is clearly the most complex.

    Each of the foregoing test items—true-false, matching, completion,
and multiple-choice—is an example of structured response items in which
students are limited in the answers they can give. The essay test, another
well-known test form, is an open response test that often allows students a
broader range in their answers.

Essay Tests

Ranging broadly in their answers is just what children should not be
allowed to do. If the purpose of testing is to call forth specific behavior that
will clearly indicate how much and how well youngsters have learned,
questions that do not call for specific responses will pose difficulties in
assessing the level of children's cognitive functioning. Essay questions, in
other words, regardless of their open-choice nature, must be constructed
according to the same rules that apply to all test items.

    The advantage of the essay question is that it affords the student a
better opportunity to demonstrate creative and innovative thinking and to
arrive independently at alternative solutions to problems. These are
aspects of the higher cognitive levels, and because they are difficult to

evaluate, essay questions must be constructed to call for the specific behaviors associated with them. It is not enough to ask a loose essay question such as, "How is a river formed?"

Such a question will produce a broad variety of responses depending upon which aspects of river formation each youngster remembers and at which cognitive level each is functioning. Instead, a teacher should determine the intellectual process to be evaluated and then call for that process in the question. For instance, if children merely need to *recall* facts, the objectives will be for first level thinking, and the essay question might read this way:

> Describe the geographic origins and endings of four major rivers of New England.

If the objectives call for second level thinking, understanding as well as remembering, the essay question might read this way:

> Name two major geographic conditions associated with river formation and describe how each contributes to the formation of a river.

To discover whether they can *apply* information at the third level, the question might read:

> Describe how an underwater dam can solve the navigation problem caused by low water in the river.

They should be able to tell how raising the water level above the shallows can feed water into a set of locks and canals by which boats can bypass the shallows.

A question calling for fourth level responses might look like this:

> Explain how a system of dams along a river can prevent flooding, provide needed irrigation, and produce electricity.

The question calls for good memory, understanding, and application skills. To answer it well, youngsters will have to analyze the components of flood control, irrigation, and hydroelectric generation to know how each can be accomplished in such a system of dams.

Here is a question calling for behavior at level five:

> Illustrate at least one major benefit man can gain from a reservoir high in the mountains, in addition to that of drinking water.

This is the same question that appeared in the multiple-choice section of this chapter, but now the youngsters have an opportunity to be more original and creative. From their knowledge of water flow and geography, they might well synthesize a response relating to hydroelectric generation, or they might come up with others such as the cooling of atomic energy plants or the operation of water wheels.

Finally, the essay question is an excellent vehicle by which to assess thinking at the *evaluation* level.

> Discuss the economic and emotional problems that might inhibit or delay the building of a large dam to provide water for people in another state.

To do well on this question, youngsters will have to consider everything they have learned about rivers and their impact in order to project themselves into hypothetical situations and roles.

Guidelines for writing essay items The guidelines for writing good essay type items are essentially the same as for other types of test items. Here are some suggestions for effective essay items and tests:

1. Use essay tests particularly to measure the higher order mental processes.

2. Be sure to include sufficient questions to adequately sample the material.

3. Make the language in the questions clear. Avoid words or phrases that are open to a variety of interpretations, and keep sentence structure clean and simple.

4. Be sure to use items that are pertinent to the subject.

5. Be sure that the directions are clear and understandable, and tell the students in advance that the test will be an essay examination.

Even with clear and sound instructional objectives, a table of specifications, and quality construction of the essay items, the essay test raises other problems. Correcting essay items is difficult, time-consuming, and, on occasion, too subjective. The difficulties in achieving reliability and consistency in correcting answers to essay items is well known to teachers and test makers alike. The same person correcting the same answers, with a time lag in between, will grade them differently. In addition, the grades of the same students, whose exams were corrected by different people, can range from A to E.

Essay questions are frequently used apparently because they seem easier to construct. While it is true that an essay exam requires less time to construct because there are fewer items as compared to an objective exam, the essays need to constructed carefully. Once the items are constructed effectively, these guidelines should increase the objectivity and reliability of scoring:

Guidelines for correcting essay items

1. If possible, ignore the student's name when correcting answers. Don't allow personal preferences for particular students to influence the grade.

2. If there are five questions, correct all answers to the first one, then to the second, and so on. It is more difficult to go entirely through one student's paper, then another. Instead, gear up for one question and correct it.

3. Prepare a model answer to which to compare the students' answers. Correcting essays without a model is sloppy and will dramatically reduce fairness.

4. If there are to be any weighting factors, such as one question counting more than others, make that decision in advance and inform students prior to the test.

5. Correct the answers on the basis of how their content relates to the model answer. Handwriting, spelling, and grammar can be dealt with separately but such mechanical considerations should not influence judgments about the quality of an answer. While this isn't easy, it is the best procedure by which to achieve objectivity.

In addition to the construction and evaluation of essay tests, two other questions are frequently asked. First, should students have options on an essay exam such as answering three out of five? Although it sounds humane, this approach defeats the purpose of testing. Since the essay measures and evaluates students' ability to attain the instructional objectives, all the students should answer the same questions. This allows the teacher to measure, evaluate, and plan future instructional experiences.

Second, should the students know the type of exam in advance? Knowing what type the exam will be influences students' studying. Moreover, this question suggests a related question: whether or not items should be mixed on a test. Switching from one type of item to another is difficult for the student. It is not good procedure to mix essay and objective items on one test. The test can include more than one type of objective item, but if it does, the items should be classified with all true-false together, all multiple-choice together, and so forth. Expecting the student to jump from one to the other type is not considered good testing procedure because it creates confusion and detracts from what should be a comfortable test environment.

LIMITATIONS AND PITFALLS OF TEACHER-MADE TESTS

We would like to conclude this chapter with a few words of caution concerning the use of teacher-made tests. We repeat that the most important testing, measuring, and evaluating is the kind that goes on daily in classrooms. Thus daily observation and teacher-made tests are invaluable tools for watching children progress. However, they must be used with the same attention to planning that accompanies actual teaching. Teachers have a tendency to casually run off ditto sheets filled with poorly worded questions when they rely upon their own tests. There is also a tendency to become careless in observational techniques. In the day-to-day action of the classroom, it is easy to procrastinate with this phase of the evaluation process and then to rush it.

Evaluation is not an activity that comes last in the learning process. It is ongoing, beginning the moment teachers face their class and continuing as the basis for daily plans and instructional objectives. If there is a single most common pitfall of teacher-made evaluation tools, it is that teachers tend to be haphazard in planning and administering them.

We would also like to caution you that teacher-made tests have certain limitations. Regardless of the most painstaking construction, they will reflect only the progress and learning activities of the children for whom they are made. They cannot be used to compare these children with those in other parts of the country or even in other parts of town. Moreover, they cannot be constructed with the same degree of reliability and validity of standardized tests. Although this limitation may seem to be a weakness, it is also a great strength of teacher-made tests. Despite the value of comparing one group of children with others around the country, the most immediate and important reason for testing is to evaluate *individual children* and the *individual progress* of each one. Evaluation tools and instructional objectives prepared with this in mind will avoid the pitfalls of haphazard testing, and the test results will yield the information needed for good diagnostic teaching.

IMPORTANT POINTS TO THINK ABOUT

1. You are now the professor in this course in tests and measurements. Using this chapter, prepare a table of specifications for a test of 25 items.

2. If you were teaching a first grade class and you wished to make up some simple true-false items about living things, what cognitive level or levels would you probably be testing?

3. For your fifth grade social studies unit on the Eskimos, can you write two good true-false items? two good matching items? two good completion items?

4. Imagine that you are constructing a test on climate and weather for your ninth grade. Can you write a good multiple-choice item that tests thinking at the synthesis level of cognitive thinking? another for the evaluation level?

5. Using the section on essay questions in this chapter, write an essay
   question that calls for a description of the principle of writing essay
   questions.

NOTES

1. B. S. Bloom *et al.*, eds. *Taxonomy of Educational Objectives: Handbook I, Cognitive Domain* (New York: McKay, 1964).
2. Clinton I. Chase, *Measurement for Educational Evaluation* (Reading, MA: Addison-Wesley, 1978).
3. R. L. Thorndike and E. Hagen, *Measurement and Evaluation in Psychology and Education*, Ch. 3, 4 (New York: Wiley, 1969).
4. A. Brewer, N. Garland and A. Marshall, *Elementary Science—Learning by Investigating*, Level 3 (Chicago: Rand McNally, 1974), pp. 18-19.
5. P. Hanna, C. Kohn, and C. Ver Steeg, *Investigating Man's World. United States Studies* (Glenview, IL: Scott, Foresman, 1970), pp. 282-285
6. C. Chase, *Measurement for Education Evaluation*, pp. 117-119.

CHAPTER SIX

CHARACTERISTICS OF STANDARDIZED TESTS

IMPORTANT POINTS TO WATCH FOR

Two extremely important characteristics of tests are validity and reliability.

A test can be said to be valid if it measures whatever it is supposed to measure. Since no instrument is completely valid or totally invalid, we must concern ourselves with the degree of validity.

There are three major types of validity: content, construct and criterion-related validity.

Reliability is an essential ingredient of a good test and refers to the level of consistency attained by the test. Reliability is expressed in quantitative terms.

Correlation refers to the degree of relationship between two variables. The relationship can be expressed numerically and is called the coefficient of correlation.

In Chapter 1, we said that a bewildering array of tests is available to teachers. Literally hundreds of instruments have been developed to test almost every conceivable aspect of child growth and development. Some are very good and fulfill the claims of their publishers. Others, despite their authors' grandiose claims, are not so good.

WHAT ARE THE CHARACTERISTICS OF A GOOD TEST?

What is it about one test that makes it better or worse than another? Perhaps the characteristics of a good test can be understood more easily if we set out to construct an imaginary one. Suppose we have decided to construct and publish a test of map and globe skills. We must ask ourselves a number of questions to begin. First, who will take the test? Published tests must be designed to reach a large population, in this case youngsters who need to be tested on map and globe skills. Many thousands of youngsters at the upper elementary and secondary school levels study maps and globes in conjunction with geography, history, and economics. For a full understanding of these and other subjects, a good working knowledge of maps and globes is necessary.

Second, what will be the content of the test? It might include questions on latitude and longitude, on great circle routes, or on the various types of map projections. Given the enormous amount of information available on the subject, the test must be made appropriate to the youngsters who will be tested. This requires an assessment of how much children at different grade levels have already learned about maps and globes. In other words, we must become familiar with the curricula of schools throughout the country in order to write a single question.

Armed with this information and a thorough knowledge of the map and globe skills taught at different grade levels, we can begin to think about the test items. They might be objective items such as true-false items, fill-ins, or multiple-choice questions. Or they might be subjective, providing an opportunity for students to express themselves in detail. Since the test will be a group test taken by many children at the same time, grading will be most reliable if the test uses objective items predominantly.

VALIDITY

One extremely important characteristic of a good test is *validity*. Simply stated, a test is valid if it measures what it is supposed to measure. If a test of intelligence is purported to have high validity it will include items that require children to make intelligent decisions. If the test maker says that the test is valid for measuring chemistry knowledge, the questions must require the children to recall facts about chemistry. A test of chemistry that includes items about biology will not accurately measure what it claims to, and it will *not* be valid. The test on maps and globes, then, in order to be valid, must be constructed of items that measure children's knowledge of the subject. Furthermore even if all the questions are about maps and globes but cover material beyond the ability level of the children who are to be tested, the test will not be valid and will, therefore, be inappropriate to the group.

Consequently, validity is an important concept in testing. Teachers who understand how this characteristic is built into a test are more capable of making sound professional choices in the selection of tests they use. There are three types of validity: *content validity*, *construct validity*, and *criterion-related validity*.

Content Validity

A test of map and globe skills for seventh graders must present test items directly related to the material studied by those children. The appropriateness of a test to the content of the curriculum being studied has to do with a type of validity known as *content validity*. A test map and globe skills for seventh graders, then, is a *valid* instrument as long as the questions on the test are truly representative of the material the students have studied in school. This type of validity is especially important in tests of achievement.

Construct Validity

If the test were to include only items that ask children to recall facts about maps and globes, its content validity alone might be sufficient to describe the test as valid, that is, one appropriate for seventh graders. However, thorough knowledge of map and globe skills requires more than the simple storing of terms and definitions to be given back to the teacher at testing time. It requires the use of other, more subtle behavior including judgment and the ability to solve problems by applying the information learned about maps and globes. For instance, children may memorize the names and positions of the lines of latitude and longitude and be able to repeat them. Although an important activity in which children should become proficient, this is simply assimilation of content. The facts themselves are more critical as the tools by which problems are solved later on.

Suppose the following problem is included on the test: "On February 10th at 9 a.m., a westbound jetliner reported crossing the International Date Line at 44° north latitude at a speed of 450 knots. Two hours and fifteen minutes later, the pilot radioed a distress signal and nothing more was heard. At approximately what longitude would you begin your search?"

No matter how many facts about latitude and longitude a child knows, they will be of no use unless the child can use them to locate the plane. A successful answer will require the use of intelligence and judgment. These are aspects of cognitive power that play vital roles in the learning process. However, neither intelligence nor judgment can be measured directly, largely because they are not, in themselves, immediately observable. Nevertheless, they are important enough to build the test around them since they must be part of a thorough understanding of map and globe skills. Therefore, decisions about questions calling for intelligence and judgment must be made in order to ensure the test's construct validity.

We measure constructs by observing behavior Human qualities are variables known as *constructs*. Their existence is inferred from observable behavior. For instance, when children use information they have already learned to solve problems, their problem-solving *behavior* indicates that they are using what has come to be called intelligence and judgment. We infer, in other words, from their behavior both the existence and the quality of these cognitive powers.

The test on maps and globes, then, will not only measure the children's recall of facts, but will also include items that test the intelligence and judgment appropriate to their ages. The approximate cognitive levels of children in each grade provide one indication of their ability to use these constructs. The cognitive levels described in Chapter 2, for instance, are identified by behaviors that indicate whether children are behaving at the concrete-operational or formal-operational level of intellectual ability. In addition, the results of many thousands of intelligence tests specify the cognitive behavior to expect from children at various ages. The questions on the test must be constructed so that they demand the full range of cognitive behavior appropriate to children's developmental levels. If the test demands too much or too little, it will be lacking in construct validity.

Sources of construct validity There are several ways to measure construct validity, all derived from the behavior of the group to be tested. For instance, children known to be more intelligent should do better on questions that call for intelligence and judgment than children of lesser ability. If this happens, we have one indication that the test has construct validity.

Second, development in cognitive quality or in the use of judgment will be reflected in the way children answer questions. As children increase their cognitive levels, they will improve their performance each time they take the test. This aspect of construct validity can be tested experimentally. If half the children in a class receive intensive training in the deliberate use of judgment and then do better on the test than the half that remained in the regular curriculum, we have a second indication that the test has construct validity.

Furthermore, if we compare the results of this test with the results the same youngsters show on other kinds of tests that are known to have good construct validity, the results on both should correlate quite well. In other words, the children who do well on items that require judgment in one test should do about as well on a test of intelligence. Those who do less well will probably do less well on the intelligence test. Such similarity or correlation between different tests, both of which require judgment, provides a third bit of evidence that the items are valid for the testing of constructs. By the same token, if we compare the test with one that has little known construct validity, a test of basic skills for instance, there will be little correlation since the two tests are measuring two different things, judgment and simple performance.

Finally, all the items must be constructed with such care that each will call forth the same degree of cognitive power. Each will adequately sample the behavior so that roughly the same number of youngsters will get each item correct. If the items do bring about such a consistent pattern of responses, the test is said to have *internal consistency*. This is yet another way of determining construct validity.

Many human traits or qualities in addition to judgment and intelligence cannot be measured directly. Such human traits as verbal reasoning, musical ability, spatial abilities, mechanical aptitude, motivation, and many others are properly called constructs; they can be measured only with instruments that have *construct validity*. The ability to measure constructs is important in all testing, but especially so in psychologically oriented tests and personality tests.

Criterion-related Validity

Very often, tests are used to identify specific abilities. For instance, part of the test on map and globe skills might be designed to determine whether youngsters are able to perform the kinds of tasks necessary for using maps and globes. Such questions might not include much information about maps and globes, but rather will ask children to do such things as measure distances, locate directions, and identify symbols that represent various geographic features. Children who do well on such tasks might be identified as capable of working successfully with maps and globes because the same kinds of skills apply. If the children who indicate such ability go on to perform well with maps and globes, the test is said to be valid for predicting specific behavior. A prediction of what a child will do is an assessment of the child's probable ability, called a criterion. Subsequent behavior is measured against this criterion. Tests that accurately predict behavior in this way are said to have *criterion-related validity* and may be of two types, those having *concurrent validity* and those having *predictive validity*.

Concurrent validity A comparison of the youngsters' actual map and globe skills with their test performance reveals the test's *concurrent validity*. In other words, the test scores are compared with actual concurrent performance, and the degree of relationship between the two gives an indication of validity. The relationship of test scores to a predetermined *criterion*, that of the teacher's ratings of actual classroom behavior, is called *criterion-related validity*. The measurement of actual classroom performance concurrently with or immediately following the test describes the process of establishing a test's *concurrent validity*.

Predictive validity The test might also be used as a longer-range predictor of map and globe skills such as predicting children's ability to solve complex navigational problems requiring judgment and intelligence. Such questions ask children to use judgment similar to the kind they will be called upon to use later. If those who do well on such questions later do well on the actual navigational problems, the test can be said to have *predictive validity*. Once the test establishes predictions about children's subsequent classroom performance, these predictions become the criterion to which subsequent behavior is related. This is another example of *criterion-related validity*.

TO DETERMINE VALIDITY, TEACHERS MUST OBSERVE BEHAVIOR

Validity, no matter how it is determined, is based upon some measure of behavior. Before the validity of the test can be ascertained, the relationship between the behavior to be evaluated and the purposes for the test must be determined. This relationship applies to each form of validity.

Content Behavior

The test will have content validity if its questions call for responses that closely relate to the subject matter the children have studied and the learning objectives of the teacher. Only the responses to the test will indicate how closely the content of the questions relates to the content of the curriculum. Responses are forms of behavior that indicate whether or not the test is valid.

Construct Behavior

The test will have construct validity if its questions call for responses that clearly indicate that human traits or qualities such as judgment are at work. Since their apparent influences on learning and not the constructs themselves are subject to measurement, the test must be oriented toward the *behavior* that the constructs control. The use of intelligence to solve a new problem or the use of judgment and reasoning to locate a missing jetliner are examples of such behavior. Behavior substantiates the inference that constructs are at work and that questions are indeed testing and measuring their quality and power.

Criterion-related Behavior

The test will have criterion-related validity when its questions call for responses that relate closely to actual performance. If those children who perform well on the test also perform well as they begin their actual classroom work on maps and globes, the teacher's grades (criterion) will relate closely to the test grades, and the test will have concurrent validity. If children whose test scores indicate the ability to solve problems requiring judgment learn to solve such problems after several weeks or months of study, the teacher's grades (criterion) will again relate closely to the test scores, and the test will have predictive validity. One test widely used for its *predictive qualities* is the Scholastic Aptitude Test, used to predict a student's ability to succeed in college-level studies. High verbal scores predict good performance in such "verbal" subjects as English and sociology. High math scores predict good performance in quantitative subjects.

Validity, then, must be built into a test. Makers of tests must determine beyond any reasonable doubt what they plan to test. Whether they wish to measure what subject matter (content) children have learned, or how well they use problem-solving ability (construct), or the degree to which they will probably succeed (criterion-related) in actual classroom work, testers must be certain that their test actually measures what they claim it will measure. The test must then be administered to a great many children of upper elementary and secondary school age to be certain that the test makers and the educators agree that the test is valid for most of the children who will be taking it.

TESTS CANNOT BE VALID FOR ALL CHILDREN AT ALL TIMES

Two final and very important words about validity. No matter how universally appropriate a test may need to be, there are probably groups of children who simply have not studied the subject or who have approached it from some innovative or unique direction. Such children will either do very poorly on the test or perhaps will be so advanced that the test will be too easy for them. In either case, the test will not be valid for them. Teachers who must choose and interpret the standardized tests to be used for individual classes or for the entire school are familiar with this problem. However, knowing something of the way validity is built into a test helps them determine whether their children are able to behave in the ways demanded of them by the test.

Second, no matter what the publisher claims about a test's validity for a certain group of children, there will always be individual children for whom the test is not appropriate. Tests are built on the assumption that all children grow and develop at approximately the same rate, and, in the broadest of terms, this may be so. However, Piaget himself cautioned against rigidly categorizing children in given cognitive levels just because their age indicates that this is where they should be. A child of 10, for instance, might be functioning far beyond the concrete-operational stage while the other students in the class lag a year or two behind in cognitive ability. No child should be forced to fit the conditions of a test or a rigid curriculum that has been developed for all children of that age. The new knowledge of the developmental ways in which children grow and learn is a constant reminder of the individuality of each child. Both the materials that are taught and the questions that are asked are appropriate for most children at any given time, but rarely for all. Tests, therefore, are not *entirely* valid or invalid. The *degree* of validity at a given time and for a given group of students determines whether or not particular tests are used.

RELIABILITY

A second essential ingredient of a good test is reliability. Simply stated, reliability is the degree to which measurements of content knowledge or of cognitive ability are consistent each time the test is given. If questions consistently call for approximately the same behavior from each child each time the test is given, the test is consistent, or reliable. For instance, if 25 eighth graders take a test on Monday and again on Thursday, the student who ranked first on Monday's test should retain first place on Thursday; the student who placed fifth on Monday should be fifth on Thursday, and so on. In fact, if all 25 children retained their original ranks, the test would have excellent reliability. However, children's behavior varies enough from test to test that there will nearly always be some shifting in rank from the first to the second testing.

There are two ways to build consistency into a test. One has to do with the test environment, the other with the test's construction. The physical conditions under which each test is taken must be as equal as possible. If the temperature of the room, for instance, is ten degrees higher on the second occasion, certain children may well become very uncomfortable, and this will affect their performance. Other physical aspects of the test situation including lighting, seating, the attitude of the person giving the test, and so on are important conditions to which children are sensitive and responsive. Any one of these conditions can inhibit children's performance on a test or cause them to perform differently during the second session, particularly if the testing situation changes dramatically from the first session to the second.

While such physical conditions of the testing environment are relatively easy to keep constant, psychological factors are more difficult to control, and these will often create reliability problems. Emotional stress, for instance, that did not exist on Monday but that is there on Thursday will almost certainly cause a child to perform differently on the test. There is little a teacher can do to stabilize the anxiety level of a child who comes to school on Thursday filled with anger against another child. Physical illness can also affect the second testing.

In spite of such threats to a test's reliability, teachers must do what they can to control the testing environment. Surprisingly, most good standardized tests prove to have quite high reliability in spite of such emotional and environmental factors.

By far the more critical condition that determines reliability is the nature of the test itself. It must be constructed in such a way that it assures, as far as possible, that children will rank about the same each time it is given. The length of the test and the quality of the individual questions or test items are the two most critical considerations in developing a test.

The Importance of Test Length

The length of a test usually refers to the number of questions. Generally speaking, the longer the test, the more reliable it will be. Since a test is really a sampling of all the material the children have studied on a particular topic, the more samples the test includes, the more accurately it will reflect what the children have studied. In turn, children will have more opportunities to show what they have learned. The more responses they are allowed to make, the more likely they are to perform to their particular level of knowledge and the more likely they are to achieve the appropriate rank. In sampling the knowledge children have gained, the more samples there are, the more reliable the evaluation.

However there are limits to the number of items that should be included. The general rule that the longer the test the more reliable it will be holds true only up to the point of diminishing returns. A test that included every item of information studied in an entire year would be ridiculous both to construct and to take. Instead, test makers determine when they have an adequate sampling of material and then try out the test to discover whether they have to add to it. An analogy helps to explain the situation: A soil expert hired to test land for the installation of a concrete foundation is expected to sample the area thoroughly enough to prove that the soil conditions are adequate. If he takes but one sample core from the northeast corner and approves the soil, the builder would be negligent in accepting this judgment. By the same token, the builder is equally irresponsible to allow the expert to spend ten days at 200 dollars a day digging up every square inch of the land. There is a happy medium, in other words, both for the soil tester and the test builder; both take as many samples as they need to make an adequate and reliable judgment, either about the material on which the children will be tested or the land on which the foundation will be installed.

The Importance of Item Quality

The second important factor in a test's reliability is the quality of the items themselves. Those who make their living at constructing tests know how difficult it is to make each question as precise and as understandable as possible. They know that a vague question, one that might be interpreted differently by a child on two separate occasions, will seriously affect reliability. The child's answer on each occasion must be the same or the test maker will have to conclude that the item is not producing consistent measurements. Each question that tends to be unreliable in this way detracts from the test's overall reliability. The more items that are vague or ambiguous, the less likely the children will be to maintain their ranks from one testing to the next. Ambiguous items contribute to unreliability in another way as well. If children read more than one meaning into a question, their answers will reflect this, and teachers correcting the test may not agree on which answer is correct. Even the same teacher correcting both sets of answers sometimes interprets them differently each time. Such human characteristics as fatigue or tension can cause teachers to vary their interpretation of the same answer from one day to the next. It is obvious, then, that the less ambiguous the question, the more likely a child will answer it exactly the same way on two different occasions and the more likely a teacher will grade it the same way each time.

Reliability, then, is the degree to which a group of children will achieve the same ranks on a test each time they take it. Reliability can never be perfect because it is affected by human behavior, a trait difficult to keep constant under the best of circumstances. However, an acceptable reliability can be achieved if the conditions of the testing environment are kept as consistent as possible so that children will perform in the same way on each test occasion. In addition to the testing environment, questions must be clear to the children and must have only one answer acceptable to those who will correct them.

TESTING THE TEST TO ESTABLISH RELIABILITY

Once the test is complete, including carefully developed questions based on an adequate sample of the available material, the test maker is ready to test, so to speak, to discover how reliable it really is. If ten children take the test on two different occasions, it will be an easy matter to glance at the ranks achieved each time and make a statement about reliability. In Fig. 6.1, it is obvious that nearly all children maintained their ranks each time, and those who shifted ranks did so only slightly. Thus the degree of relationship between the two test situations was high, and the test has good reliability. If the shifting of ranks is much more significant, as in Fig. 6.2, the test maker must conclude that the degree of relationship between the two test situations is very low. Since children were not consistent in maintaining their ranks, the test is inconsistent or unreliable. These results indicate that the test will not reliably yield the same relative rank each time it is given.

There are several ways to establish a test's reliability. The three most commonly used are *test-retest, equivalent forms*, and *split halves*.

Test-Retest Reliability

Perhaps the simplest method is to give the entire test on two different occasions. This *test-retest* method, although quite simple, presents several problems. First, some children memorize better than others and, if the time

	1st Test Session	2nd Test Session
Pupil	*Rank*	*Rank*
John	1	1
Bill	2	2
Sam	3	4
Mary	4	3
Tom	5	5
Andrew	6	6
Larry	7	7
Brian	8	9
Paul	9	8
Alice	10	10

Figure 6.1

	1st Test Session	2nd Test Session
Pupil	*Rank*	*Rank*
John	1	3
Bill	2	2
Sam	3	5
Mary	4	4
Tom	5	1
Andrew	6	10
Larry	7	6
Brian	8	9
Paul	9	8
Alice	10	7

Figure 6.2

lapse between sessions is too short, memory can cause considerable shifting in ranks. Second, if the time lapse is too long, the dynamic nature of human behavior can cause the same shifting. Given the developmental nature of growth, children vary from each other and from their own performance from one testing to another. Several children who did not do well on the first testing might have a growth spurt in cognitive ability or emotional development. They might do quite differently the second time as a result of these changes. Testers must take care then, to avoid both problems by establishing what seems to be an optimum length of time between the two sessions.

Equivalent Forms Reliability

A second method of establishing reliability is that of *equivilent forms.* This method requires two completely different tests, each consisting of an adequate sample of the material that was studied and each equally valid or appropriate to the subject. By giving both tests and comparing ranks the tester can determine reliability. Moreover, since memory, or test wisdom, is not a factor in this method because of the entirely different questions, both forms can be given at the ame time. The major problem with this method is obvious. The test maker must do twice as much work to develop the test. Despite this inconvenience to the test maker, many standardized tests, particularly in the areas of intelligence, achievement, and basic skills, include equivalent test forms.

Split-Halves Reliability

A third way to determine the reliability of a test is to divide the items into two equal groups and grade each half as a separate test. This is known as the *split-halves* method of determining reliability. Care must be taken when using this method to divide the test into halves that are equal, not only in length but in the degree to which each half samples the material to be tested. In a sense, the test is made into two equivalent forms, each of which contains items of the same difficulty and tests the same things. If the test is made of reliable questions that will be answered the same way by the same children on separate occasions, all the even numbered questions can be considered as Test A and all the odd numbered items as Test B. The split-halves method is generally used when equivalent forms of a test are not available or when time does not allow for the test-retest method.

All three methods of determining reliability are widely used to determine a test's reliability by comparing the ranks of a group of children on two separate test occasions. Despite the method of determining reliability, each one uses essentially the same test both times. In summary, if youngsters achieve the same relative ranks each time, the test is reliable. This means that the subject matter has been adequately sampled and the questions well written. In addition, the physical conditions of the test situation and the physical and emotional status of the children were similar each time.

CORRELATION

The term *correlation* describes the way two sets of ranks relate to each other and reflects the degree of a test's reliability. Correlation, in fact, means relationship; it is a statistical term used to describe the relationship between two traits or characteristics that change or vary. Most human traits vary from one time to another or under differing sets of conditions and are called variables. Test results are really evidence of such human variables. They show how such variables as memory or intelligence or basic skills are manifested in human behavior. The behavior in this case is the behavior of test performance, and we infer, from the test results, the quality or quantity of the variables tested.

Whenever one variable is compared to another, then, we are describing how one correlates with the other. In the case of the test-retest method of reliability, one measure of achievement is related or correlated with a second. In convincing someone that performance on one test relates well to performance on another, one needs to describe that relationship in terms other than "good." The statistical term for doing this is *correlation*. When the relationship, or association, between the two sets of results is strong, the correlation is said to be high. When the association is weak, the correlation is low. If no relationship exists at all between the two sets of results, there is no correlation.

Coefficient of Correlation

Actually, the association between any two variables, such as the two sets of results in Fig. 6.1 and 6.2, may be expressed as a coefficient of correlation, a statistical device with a great many applications in the analysis of human behavior. For our purposes, we ask only that you understand how the coefficient is stated and what it means. Coefficient of correlation is simply a method of expressing relationship in a quantitative or mathematical way in order to introduce a greater degree of precision and clarity into statements about how variables relate to each other.

If two sets of test results were exactly alike and each youngster exhibited exactly the same cognitive ability on each test, the correlation would be perfect. This would be expressed by the coefficient +1.00. If something less than a perfect relationship existed, the coefficient would be something lower than 1.00, perhaps +.80. If no relationship at all seemed to exist and children answered each set of test questions in completely different ways, the coefficient of correlation would be 0. Correlation is as elusive and tenuous as human traits themselves. A coefficient of +.70, for instance, would be a good indication of construct validity for relating the test on maps and globes to the Lorge Thorndike Test of Intelligence. The same procedure is used in all measures of correlation. Whenever two variables are being compared, they are compared in terms of the strength of the association between them; this degree of strength is the coefficient of correlation. We can apply this concept to the criterion-related validity in the test on map and globe skills. One variable will be the children's behavior on the test before they begin to study maps and globes. Another will be the predicted behavior of the children after three months of study. If the children accurately perform all of the behavior about maps and globes that the test predicted they would, there would be a high coefficient of correlation, which would indicate to a reader that the test has high predictive or criterion-related validity.

Correlation, then, is a tool for measuring the relationship or strength of association between variables. It is expressed as a mathematical coefficient to indicate its position along a continuum of correlation, from no correlation at all to perfect correlation. Later we will discuss how correlation can be expressed as a negative relationship. For now, you should understand that measures of validity and reliability are expressed as coefficients in order to indicate clearly the degree of relationship that exists between the two variables being measured. A coefficient of validity would indicate how closely one test relates to another that tests essentially the same things, or how closely children's actual behavior relates to the behavior predicted by the teacher (criterion-related validity). A coefficient of reliability would express, mathematically, the degree to which a test produced consistent behavior on two different occasions (test-retest), or on two equal halves of the same test (split halves), or on two separate tests of the same material (equivalent forms).

IMPORTANT POINTS TO THINK ABOUT

1. The three major types of validity are content, construct, and criterion-related validity. Can you describe each one and pinpoint the importance of each for standardized tests?

2. Concurrent validity and predictive validity are important aspects of standardized instruments. What do these two validities mean, and how can they be important to the potential user of a test?

3. The second essential ingredient of a test is reliability. Describe this concept and be able to tell why it is an important ingredient of a test.

4. Name and describe some conditions of the testing environment and the individual taking the test that could adversely affect test reliability.

5. The coefficient of correlation is the quantitative expression of the degree of relationship between two variables. Describe how the co-efficient of correlation is useful in helping teachers determine the degree of validity and the reliability of a test instrument.

ADDITIONAL READINGS

R. L. Thorndike and E. Hagen, *Measurement and Evaluation in Psychology and Education*, 3rd ed. (New York: Wiley, 1969).

A. Anastasi, *Psychological Testing*, 4th ed. Ch. 6 (New York: Macmillan, 1976).

American Psychological Association, *Standards for Educational and Psychological Tests* (Washington, D.C.: APA 1974), pp. 25-48.

L. J. Cronbach, *Essentials of Psychological Testing*, 3rd ed. Ch. 6 (New York: Harper & Row, 1970).

CHAPTER SEVEN

STANDARDIZING TESTS AND INTERPRETING RESULTS

IMPORTANT POINTS TO WATCH FOR

Standardized tests are designed in the same way as scientific experiments. They are important tools to assist in providing meaningful experiences for students.

Statistics are immensely useful in understanding tests and interpreting test results competently. Statistical processes are the ways and means of dealing with numbers that are used to describe test behavior and performance.

Three major types of measurement are (a) measures of central tendency, (b) measures of variability, and (c) measures of relationship.

The three major types of measures of central tendency are the mean, median, and mode. The range and standard deviation are measures of variability, and correlation is the primary measure of relationship.

The standardization process of a testing tool is critical for the final value of the instrument to potential users. Careful sampling techniques, item construction, and other processes must be accomplished effectively to build confidence in an assessment tool.

Test norms are the ways that test results are reported. Their interpretation is critical, and a sound knowledge of their meanings is important to all test users. Some of the test norms are percentiles, grade equivalents, age equivalents, and standard scores.

In our discussion of teacher-made tests we pointed out that continuous daily observation is a vital component of the teaching process. Continuous observation, well planned and systematic, keeps teachers aware of the progress of each child and provides the information necessary to meet the intellectual and personal needs of each. For the most part, the techniques of observation and testing help teachers discover where each child stands in relation to their instructional goals and expectations. Although a teacher may be interested to know how one child's progress in arithmetic relates to the progress of the other children, the individual's unique and very personal behavior is of much greater concern. In a general way, the teacher will compare the child's behavior with that of Erikson's *juvenile period* or perhaps ask to what degree the child is behaving successfully at Piaget's *concrete-operational* stage of cognitive development. Teacher-made testing procedures, in other words, are not designed to measure children's progress or standing against some defined standard, but simply to keep teachers close to them and to help them grow and learn at their own best rate.

However, there are times when teachers will want to know how one child stacks up against others of the same age throughout the school, the state, or even the nation. To get this information teachers must turn to assessment instruments that are called "standardized tests."

WHAT DO WE MEAN BY STANDARDIZED?

Any scientific study requires standardized procedures by which each experiment or observation is conducted. Standardized procedures are *controlled* procedures that do not vary from one experiment to the next. By keeping all of the conditions surrounding the experiment standard, scientists can be more certain of the outcomes and pronouncements they make following their experiments. If five different scientists in five different laboratories decided to perform systematic experiments to determine the effects of nicotine on rats, they would all have to administer exactly the same amounts of nicotine at precisely the same intervals. They would also have to administer the nicotine in exactly the same way and then take measurements with the same careful attention to precision and agreed-upon procedures. If they ignored the standardized procedures, their findings would vary, and their individual conclusions would not have the force of a combined effort.

Standardized tests are designed in the same way as scientific experiments. They provide teachers with the tools necessary to make accurate scientific observations. They include detailed instructions for administering them and reporting the results. They also provide suggestions for keeping the testing environment as uniform as possible so that teachers giving the test in widely different locations will keep their "laboratory" conditions scientifically the same. Such uniformity of procedure allows teachers throughout the nation to give exactly the same test in exactly the same way. When all second grade teachers report their test results or "scientific observations," there should be a relatively high degree of uniformity about their findings. Similarly, if children around the country take the same standardized test under the same conditions, a teacher will have a fairly good idea of how one child stands in comparison with others of the same age.

A standardized test, then, is one that calls for uniformity of administration and interpretation in order to allow comparisons among children of the same age or grade level. In spite of critics who say that such comparison is unfair and unnecessary, ours is a world of comparison. A person cannot seek a new position without being evaluated by prospective employers on some scale or standard of performance. Secretaries are hired for their typing and shorthand skills and are almost always asked to take a standardized test. Prospective employers could care less that they can type much better today than they could yesterday. Instead, they want to know how well a job applicant can perform compared with norms or standards that have been established for secretarial skills. If the applicant does not compare well with thousands of others who have taken the test, someone else will be hired.

Similarly, the testing process for admission to college involves standardized tests that predict students' ability to do college work. Until fairly recently, at least, most colleges have not been concerned with individual improvement. Admissions officials compare one student's score on the SAT or the CEEB with thousands of others. The test scores determine whether the individual is accepted.

Some states still require standardized achievement tests of their secondary students, and the results become important means by which promotions are made and by which courses and curricula are chosen. Moreover some nations operate national testing programs, and performance on these standardized examinations is the basis for acceptance to certain kinds of secondary schools and colleges. To say that such state and national testing programs are competitive is quite an understatement. The point here is not to evaluate the criticism or the values of standardized tests but to become aware of their widespread use and to learn how they are constructed and used. In this way, teachers will become more knowledgeable about this important evaluation task and more professional in using the results.

STATISTICS NEEDED TO INTERPRET TEST RESULTS

The very word statistics can and sometimes does raise phantoms in some minds of a confusing and incomprehensible chaos of numbers. Nevertheless, the mathematical skill necessary to deal with statistics, at least at the level of skillful interpretation of test results, is no more than that of a seventh grade. The emphasis here is on understanding and interpreting test results. In the absence of this competence, too many injustices have been perpetrated on children. Perhaps the most prevalent mistake made by teachers and others who work with children in the realm of testing and interpreting is the tendency to overinterpret. This involves drawing a conclusion, making a decision, prescribing instructional plans, or even allowing an attitude to begin to develop toward a student on the basis of a single test result. It results from the test interpreter placing too much faith, emphasis, or confidence on one test score. These frequent occurrences have added to the criticism of testing. Conversely, in some school systems batteries of standardized tests are administered annually because it has always been that way. In April or May, a week is designated for testing and all students at designated grade levels take the subtests that make up the battery. The tests are scored either manually or by machine, and the necessary data for each child are reported. Perhaps some teachers or administrators give the results a cursory study before filing them. The results are placed in each child's cumulative folder; the principal files the school results; and the system totals are filed in the central office. There may be a newspaper article if the results of a particular subtest are substantially higher than the national norm, but little else occurs with the results. These two descriptions of overinterpretation and underuse of test results point out the two extremes of what should not happen.

The professional who incompetently uses test results by consistently overinterpreting can and probably does hurt children. This situation refers not only to the individual classroom teacher or specialist but can refer to a school or school system. The grouping of children in high, middle, or low groups on the basis of one test result or on the basis of a less than strong test is an example of overreliance on tests. In the other case, unless there is an objective for administering tests and plans to use the results to improve instructional experiences for students, it is unproductive to administer them. The best way to avoid both pitfalls is to select the best available instruments and be able to interpret test results competently and cautiously.

Standardized tests quantify behavior in order to be briefer and more precise. Saying that Jim did pretty well on the test opens his performance to many and varied interpretations. Did Jim get all the answers correct? Did Jim get half of he answers correct and still score highest in the class? It would be better to be able to state that Jim has 23 right out of 30 questions with a class average of 19 right. The more quantitative information teachers have the more precise they can be in describing and interpreting test results.

Obviously, statistics do not solve all testing problems. Moreover, a lack of skill in dealing with statistics can cause the same problems that ambiguous narrative descriptions cause. Statistical processes are merely the ways and means of dealing with numbers used to describe test behavior and performance. The purpose for statistics in testing is to describe an individual score or sets of scores and their relationships to each other.

One of our colleagues uses the following technique early in his course on testing. He asks the members of the class to get the names and telephone numbers of five of their classmates. He then instructs them to add the telephone numbers and divide by the number five. The result, he explains, is the average or the mean, an important concept in testing. Then he instructs the students to try dialing the number they computed as the mean. If they actually did dial the number representing the mean they computed, then whomever they reached would be contacted totally by chance. The point is that the averaged telephone numbers were relatively worthless. The same with test scores and numbers. They are relatively worthless unless teachers use the appropriate statistics in the proper manner at the proper time, and interpret them with skill. The example of the average of the telephone numbers is extreme. The result obtained by averaging the numbers would not, we hope, cause anyone to believe that the result meant something. Here is a more realistic example that shows that caution in interpretation is good procedure.

The development office of a college wished to obtain some descriptive data concerning alumni donations and thus decided to compute the mean of the donations received. We will use a small number of givers for illustration. Thirty members donated to the development fund as follows: one gave $100,000.00; one gave $1,000.00 and 28 gave $10.00 each for a total of $280.00. You can already see what is going to happen. The total of all donations was $101,280.00, and when we divide this figure by the number of donors (30), the mean is $3,376.00. Most development officers would be quite thrilled if this meant what it apparently says. Thus, a properly computed statistic can be quite misleading unless additional information and good judgment are brought to bear on the all-important interpretation of the computed results.

This example is an exception to the familiar concept of normal distribution or the bell-shaped curve. When a sufficient number of people are tested on a specific trait or skill, it is theorized that the distribution of scores will approximate a normal distribution. Think of a physical trait such as height or weight or an aptitude such as musical or artistic talent. Assuming these traits or aptitudes could be accurately measured in a large number of people, their distribution would appear as it does in Fig. 7.1. There would be some very tall and short people or some very talented and not so talented people at the extremes, but most of the people would tend to cluster toward the middle.

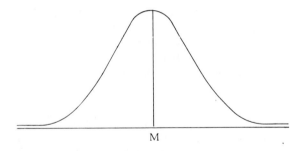

M

Fig. 7.1 A normal curve.

Howard Lyman states in *Test Scores and What They Mean*[1] that the normal curve is important for four reasons

1. It is a mathematical model whose properties are known completely;

2. it is a model which is approached by the distributions of many human characteristics and most test scores;

3. it is relevant to the understanding of certain inferential statistics, and

4. it gives a basis for understanding the relationship between different types of test scores.

All reasons are important, but the fourth is especially relevant. There are two characteristics of the normal curve that should be remembered: (a) the curve is perfectly symmetrical and the same number of cases will be situated to the left as to the right; (b) the tails of the curve do not touch the base line, since theoretically the curve goes on and on into what we might call plus and minus infinity.

Due to these and other characteristics of the normal curve, we know the percentages of cases that fall at given points. The practical range of the curve is said to be from −3SD to +3SD. The SD stands for units of standard deviation on the normal curve which we will discuss later in this chapter.

If the percentages in Fig. 7.2 were rounded off, we could say that:

Between +1.0 and −1.0, 68% of the cases fall
Between +2.0 and −2.0, 95% of the cases fall
Between +3.0 and −3.0, 99% of the cases fall

Test makers and publishers use these characteristics of the normal curve in a variety of ways to report individual scores. The ways of reporting the scores are frequently referred to as norms and come in a variety of packages such as percentiles, stanines, grade equivalents, and others—terms that will be explained later in this section. To explain these, we must first discuss the three main types of measurement: measures of central tendency, measures of variability, and measures of relationship.

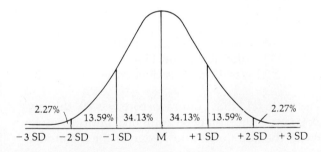

Figure 7.2

Measures of Central Tendency

The three measures of central tendency are the mean, median, and mode.

The mean The mean is the arithmetical average and is the most frequently used statistic. The symbol for the mean is $\overline{X}$ or M ($\overline{X}$ is most frequently). The sum of the scores is divided by the number of scores, and the result is the mean. The formula for computing the mean looks like this:

$$\overline{X} = \frac{\Sigma X}{N}$$

when Σ means to add or to sum, $\overline{X}$ stands for raw score, and N is the number of scores.

The median The median, since it is the midpoint of the distribution of scores, has the same number of scores abouve and below it. It is an actual score when there is an odd number of scores, and it is interpolated between the two middle scores when there is an even number. For example, if we had four scores of 30, 29, 28, and 27, the median would be 28.5, with 2 scores above it and two below it.

The mode The most frequent score to appear in a distribution is the mode.
    The following distribution of scores is presented in ranked order from high to low score. Compute the mean and state the median and the mode. (We have used small numbers and only a few scores to simplify our illustrations.)

95	68	55
93	67	54
90	67	51
90	64	49
89	63	48
75	61	46
73	61	46
70	60	45
70	58	42
70	55	41

The mode is 70 and the median is 62. The score of 70 appears three times, and the median of 62 has 15 scores above and 15 scores below it. The summation of the raw scores (ΣX) was 1916. This divided by the N of 30 equalled a mean of 63.87.
    If you took this test and were told that your raw score was 89, the raw score by itself would tell you very little. You need additional information to interpret the raw score. With the additional knowledge of the mean and

median of distribution, you know that your raw score of 89 was well above the rounded mean of 64 and also well above the median of 62. In addition, because the scores were ranked, the 89 was the fifth score from the top.

These three measures of central tendency, and in particular the mean and median, are most useful to teachers and have utility for both teacher-made and standardized tests. They provide teachers with a point by which scores can be compared and contrasted. And, although the publishers and authors of standardized tests, with the assistance of computers and other technical advantages, deal in hundreds or thousands of scores in their test sample population, the processes for computing the measures of central tendency are basically the same.

Measures of Variability

In a normal distribution, over two-thirds of the cases fall between locations −1SD and +1SD. The two important measures of variance are the range and standard deviation of a distribution. Deviation is an important concept in testing and usually refers to the difference between a score and some fixed point such as the mean. Thus, the deviation for a score of 75 in a distribution with a mean of 85 would be −10.

The range The range is the difference between the highest and lowest score. The range in the previous distribution is 95 − 41 or 54. The range indicates the gap between the highest and lowest scores. A small range suggests more homogeneity in the distribution than a large range. However it remains for the standard deviation to give more information concerning the variance of a given distribution.

The standard deviation The standard deviation is difficult to define. Nevertheless, it can be considered as the "average" deviation or variance from a fixed point with the mean as the fixed point. The best way to understand it is to calculate one.*The symbols used for standard deviation are S.D. and s or Sigma. All of these should be used in specific situations but are frequently used interchangeably. We will use the sigma symbol, s.

Consider a distribution containing these raw scores:

$$15, 13, 13, 10, 9, 8, 7, 6, 5, \text{ and } 4$$

The formula for computing the standard deviation is

$$s = \sqrt{\frac{\Sigma x^2}{N}}$$

*Additional examples and exercises for the statistical procedures in this section may be found in Appendix C.

The x stands for the deviation of a raw score from the mean or $X - \overline{X}$. Since we need to know the mean to calculate standard deviation, compute it, and for practice identify the median and mode.

The mean is 9, the median is 8.5, and the mode is 13.

The computation would look like this:

$X - \overline{X}$	$=$	x	x^2
15 − 9		+6	36
13 − 9		+4	16
13 − 9		+4	16
10 − 9		1	1
9 − 9		0	0
8 − 9		−1	1
7 − 9		−2	4
6 − 9		−3	9
5 − 9		−4	16
4 − 9		−9	25
			124 $= \Sigma x^2$

The raw score minus the mean from each raw score yields the individual deviations, x. Following the formula, each deviation is squared. The sum of the figures in the x^2 column yields 124.

Therefore,

$$s = \sqrt{124/10} = \sqrt{12.4} = 3.52$$

Despite the small numbers and amounts we have used for illustration, the example and the method show that variability is a key factor in understanding distributions. Although there are different ways to compute standard deviation, all methods arrive at the same important finding. To take another example, imagine that thousands of scores have a mean of 100 and a standard deviation of 15. Such large samples, if randomly drawn, usually approximate closely the normal distribution. Refer now to Fig. 7.2, where the normal curve is shown with the percentages between the standard deviations points of the curve and the mean. Fifteen, *the standard deviation* in the sample, refers to the raw score units pertinent to the distribution. The standard deviation of a distribution is stated in raw score units.

Percentiles A score of 115 falls exactly at +1SD on the curve. At this point, we know that 34% of the cases fall between that point of +1SD and the mean. Also, because the curve is symmetrical, 50% of the cases fall to the left or below the mean. Adding these two percentages, we see that the score of 115 is higher than 84% of the cases in this distribution. This is a percentile; the symbol is P. The percentile is defined as that raw score point value at or below which a specified percent of the cases fall. Thus the 40th percentile is the raw score value below which 40 percent of the cases fall. What would be the percentile score for a raw score of 85 in our distribution? This score falls at −1SD on the curve. Thirty-four percent of the cases fall between this point and the mean, which leaves 16% to the left of this point. Therefore in this distribution the raw score of 85 has a percentile rank of sixteen, P16.

Percentile bands In recent tests a percentile band or range has been reported. Rather than state the specific percentile such as 14 or 86, test publishers will present them in bands such as 10-18 or 84-88. This innovation is an excellent reminder that a score is not a fixed point but can vary as a normal function of testing.

It is important to know what these various ways of reporting scores on a standardized test mean and how they are derived.

Between what two raw scores would 68% of our distribution fall? If you said between 85 and 115 you are right. It takes 15 raw score points to move to +1SD or −1SD on the normal curve. To include 95% of the cases, the raw score extremes would be between 70 and 130, and to include 99% of the cases the raw score limits would be 55 and 145 in this distribution with a standard deviation of 15 and mean of 100.

To further clarify this concept, use Fig. 7.2 and try the following example:

Our distribution has a mean of 80 ($\overline{X}$) and standard deviation (s) of 8. What are the raw score limits to include 68, 95, and 99% of our cases, respectfully?

If you answered 72 and 88, 64 and 96, 56 and 104 you are correct.

Standard scores Now consider a distribution where $\overline{X} = 100$ and $s = 15$. The specific raw scores of 85, 115, 70, 130, 55, and 145 fall exactly on the points at ±1SD, ±2SD, and ±3SD. Because these can be located precisely and because the percentages of cases between these points and the mean are standard, those raw scores can be converted to percentile norms. Fortunately the percentages between any given location and the mean that fall between +3SD and −3SD are fixed. However, the standard deviation for two raw scores that do not fall exactly on 1, 2, or 3 standard deviations on the curve, such as 80 and 120, must be computed.

z-scores First, these raw scores are converted into standard scores called z scores. The z score is the expression of a raw score in standard deviation units. The formula for computing the z score is:

$$z = \frac{X - \overline{X}}{s}$$

Our new scores of 80 and 120 would compute as follows:

$$\frac{80 - 100}{15} = \frac{-20}{15} = -1.3 \quad \text{and} \quad \frac{120 - 100}{15} = \frac{+20}{15} = +1.3$$

The z score must have a plus or minus sign to indicate the direction from the mean. The ±.3 for raw scores 80 and 120 are expressions of raw scores in standard deviations units. The advantage of standard scores is that they have comparison potential between distributions assuming the distributions approximate a normal frequency distribution. If we had a score of 59 in one distribution and 86 in another distribution, and both raw score values computed to a z score of + .8, then the raw scores would both be exactly the same distance from the means in their respective distributions.

Column 1 in Table 7.1 (the complete table appears in Appendix B) refers to the z scores, and Column 2 refers to the percentages of cases that fall between given z score locations and the mean. In the previous distribution, which had an $\overline{X}$ of 100 and an s of 15, we computed the z scores for raw scores of 80 and 120.

The raw score of 80 computed to a z score of −1.3 with the minus sign indicating that it was to the left of the mean, and the number of 1.3 indicating that it was one and three-tenths standard deviations from the mean. The raw score of 120 computed to a z score of +1.3; thus the interpretation is similar to the previous z score with one *major* difference:

Table 7.1

(1) Z	(2) Area between the Mean and Z	(1) Z	(2) Area between the Mean and Z	(1) Z	(2) Area between the Mean and Z
1.05	.3531	1.20	.3849	1.35	.4115
1.06	.3554	1.21	.3869	1.36	.4131
1.07	.3577	1.22	.3888	1.37	.4147
1.08	.3599	1.23	.3907	1.38	.4162
1.09	.3621	1.24	.3925	1.39	.4177
1.10	.3643	1.25	.3944		
1.11	.3665	1.26	.3962		
1.12	.3686	1.27	.3980		
1.13	.3708	1.28	.3997		
1.14	.3729	1.29	.4015		
1.15	.3749	1.30	.4032		
1.16	.3770	1.31	.4049		
1.17	.3790	1.32	.4066		
1.18	.3810	1.33	.4082		
1.19	.3830	1.34	.4099		

the plus sign shows that it is above the mean or to the right of the mean on the normal curve. The two z scores of ±1.3 are exactly the same distance from the mean but in opposite directions.

Find the z score of 1.3 in Column 1 of Table 7.1. The corresponding percentage between the z of ±1.3 locations and the mean is 0.4032 or 40% rounded. You have to remember the plus or minus sign to interpret appropriately. The raw score of 120 has 40% of the cases between its z location and the mean. Since one-half or 50% of the cases fall to the left or below the mean, this score is higher than 90% of the cases, thus it has a percentile of 90 or P90. The raw score of 80 has a z score of --1.3. What would the corresponding percentile be? A percentile of 10 is correct. The z score is a standard score that translates a raw score into units of standard deviation and indicates the direction and the distance from the mean.

Two disadvantages of the z score are the plus and minus signs and the decimals. Both can cause difficulties when there are many z scores to work with. Erroneously transposing a plus to a minus or vice versa could cause rather dramatic results.

T scores To get rid of the signs and decimals of the z score, we can designate a convenient standard deviation and mean and then convert the z score. The most frequently converted z score is called a T score and shows exactly what the z score shows. It has a mean of 50 and standard deviation of 10. T scores are determined by multiplying the z score by 10 and adding 50, so $T = 10z + 50$. The conversion of our raw scores of 80 and 120 would look like this:

$$T = 10 \ (+1.3) + 50 = 13 + 50 = 63$$
$$T = 10 \ (-1.3) + 50 = -13 + 50 = 37$$

Remember that the T score has a $\overline{X}$ of 50 and s of 10; therefore the 63 is 1.3 standard deviations above the mean and T of 37 is 1.3 standard deviations below the mean. Other standard score conversions can be used such as, $\overline{X} = 500$ and $s = 100$ and $s = 20$. Though they serve quite well, the most frequently used standard score norm in school standardized testing is the T score.

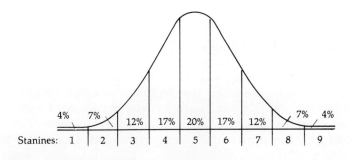

Figure 7.3

Authors and publishers of standardized tests use several other norms to describe test results. One statistic developed by the Air Force is called the stanine. A stanine is a single digit standard score with a mean of 5 and a standard deviation of 2. The curve in Fig. 7.3 shows the stanines and percentages within each stanine.

The stanine distribution includes in stanine 5 20% of the middle scores, 10% to the left and 10% to the right of the mean. Stanine 1 contains the lowest 4% of the distribution, and stanine 9 contains the highest 4%.

Deviation I.Q. Another norm has been introduced into intelligence testing. The ratio I.Q., which reads I.Q. = M.A. ÷ C.A. × 100 (where M.A. is Mental Age and C.A. is Chronological Age), is being replaced by what is called the deviation I.Q. The concept is the same as that of the T score except the mean is 100 and standard deviation is usually 16 and occasionally 15. Thus, if $\overline{X} = 100$ and s = 16, scores 84 and 116 are at locations −1SD and +1SD, respectively. A T score could legitimately be used as a standard score for a test of mental ability. However, the 100 I.Q. has historically been considered average. The number has become so fixed in our minds that trying to convince a parent that the score of 50 is right on the mean would be futile. Figure 7.4 shows the relationships between some of these standard score norms.

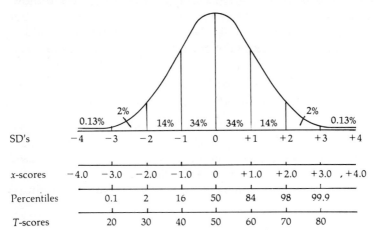

Figure 7.4

Measures of Relationships

Chapter 6 introduced the concept of correlation; we will explore it more thoroughly at this point. The primary measure of relationship is correlation. There is a mistaken tendency to believe that when two variables are strongly related, one causes the other. The fact that scores on a reading test and on a math test are strongly and positively related does not mean that one caused the other. To know that there is a strong correlation can be helpful in devising a curriculum and planning meaningful experiences for children, but teachers cannot assume causality from a correlation expression.

Cofficient of correlation Correlation is the degree of relationship between two variables and is expressed quantitatively by the coefficient. The coefficients of correlation for validity or reliability use the symbol, r. The range of possible coefficients of correlation is from +1.0 to −1.0. Figure 7.5 graphically shows the coefficients' dimensions:

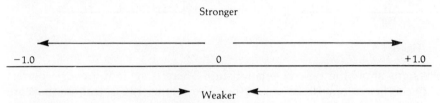

Figure 7.5

The lines with arrows above the base line show that the correlation becomes stronger as the coefficient moves away from 0 towards either +1.0 or −1.0. The lines with arrows below the base line indicate that the correlation is becoming weaker as the coefficient approaches 0. A 0 correlation means that there is independence between the variables, so no relationship exists. The higher the coefficient, either plus or minus, the stronger the expression of correlation. The coefficient shows the strength of the correlation and the sign, either plus or minus, shows the kind of correlation. For example, −0.78 and +0.78 are equally strong but mean different things. The test results presented in Table 7.2 will illustrate.

In a perfect positive correlation (+1.0), the ranks on both variables are exactly the same. High on one variable and high on the other or low on one variable and low on the other depicts a + 1.0 coefficient.

In a perfect negative correlation (−1.0) the exact opposite is the case. The variables are in reverse relationship so that high on one variable and low on the other, or low on one variable and high on the other indicates a perfect negative correlation. Correlations of 1.0 have the same strength but

Table 7.2

Case	Perfect Positive Reading Rank	(+1.0) Math Rank	Perfect Negative Reading Rank	(−1.0) Math Rank
A	1	1	1	5
B	2	2	2	4
C	3	3	3	3
D	4	4	4	2
E	5	5	5	1

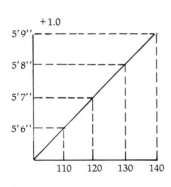

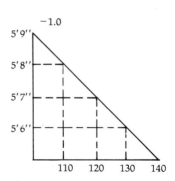

Figure 7.6   **Figure 7.7**

the signs show the type of relationship. There is seldom if ever a perfect (1.0) coefficient of correlation: further, the coefficients in test manuals are positive correlations far more than negative ones.

Another way of looking at correlations is to see them plotted on a graph. The two variables, height and weight, show a +1.0 and −1.0 correlation in Fig. 7.6 and 7.7.

A question frequently asked is what is a "good" or "strong" correlation. This is a difficult question because the quality or strength of the correlation is relative to the test or to the test characteristics being studied. The validity coefficient for a personality test might be acceptable at a lower degree of strength than the coefficient for an achievement test. However, this guide can generally be used to assess correlations:

±0.70 to ±1.00	High to very high
±0.40 to ±0.70	Average to fairly high
±0.20 to ±0.40	Present, but low
0 to ±0.20	Neglible to very low

Using Correlation to Assess Validity and Reliability

An understanding of correlation helps teachers assess the validity and reliability of a standardized instrument.

The types of validity were discussed in Chapter 6. Criterion-related validity is expressed as a correlation coefficient. The important factor here is to identify the criteria and then observe the expression of relationship or correlation. If we were constructing a test to measure reading comprehension in the upper middle grades, we would find another instrument that has been well reviewed, been around long enough to establish a reputation, and is measuring the same learning as the test under construction. We would administer both tests to a sample population, and we would have two variables or scores on each case. A high positive coefficient of correlation would indicate that the reading test has as high a validity as the established test.* Similarly, if a group test of intelligence were on the drawing board, then we could pair this test with the Stanford Binet or W.I.S.C. (both well-known tests) and observe the results of the correlation study.

The criterion does not have to be another test. It can be the marks given by teachers or the ratings of supervisors in a vocational setting. However, controlling the criteria and the *reliability* of the criteria is a most critical task. In addition, the coefficient of correlation for criterion-related validity tells the predictive power of a test.

The more clearly defined the criteria and the stronger the correlation, the more confidence we can have in the predictive power of a given test.

Finally, if a school were selecting a test for math computation, it would wish to look at many instruments. One of the factors in deciding would be the validity coefficients. While there is no cutoff point or passing grade for the coefficient, the higher the coefficient the better, other factors being equal.

Reliability refers to test consistency, whether the same or similar results will occur upon repeated administrations of the test to the same populations. First, instruments should be valid; that is they must measure what they purport to measure, and second, the results should be consistent. To summarize, reliability is a statistical concept stated with a coefficient of correlation or r. Whether the method of estimating reliability is test-retest, odd-even, equivalent form, or other ways, the process will generate a reliability coefficient. Although a definite fixed point cannot be generalized for a good or bad reliability coefficient, it should be high (+0.70 or above).

Tests that claim to have equivalent forms should always state an equivalent or alternate form reliability. Since either form A or B can be given with the same or similar results, the equivalent form reliability coefficient will indicate the degree of reliability. This is an important factor in the assessment of a test that has equivalent forms.

Standard Error of Measurement

There is one additional function of reliability called the standard error of measurement or SE.† It is not an error in the sense of a mistake but rather an expression that no test is perfectly precise. The higher the reliability coefficient, the lower the SE, while a lower reliability coefficient will result in a higher SE. The standard error states the dimensions that a given score may vary due to test reliability. The SE may be stated in raw

---

*Samples and exercises for computing the coefficient of correlation will be found in Appendix C.

†The formula for computing the standard error of measurement is $s_m = s\sqrt{1-r}$, where s is the standard deviation of the distribution and r is the reliability coefficient.

scores, percentiles, or other norms and is really an expression of the standard deviation of an individual score.

A standard error, for instance, could be stated as ±4. If Jimmy scored 105 on a mental abilities test (I.Q.) with an S.E. of 4, he could take the test repeatedly and we would expect his score to fall between the raw score points listed below:

101-109	68% of the time
97-113	95% of the time
93-117	99% of the time

The concept of standard error emphasizes the fact that no score is a rigid, fixed point. Better, safer, and in the best interests of students is thinking of possible bands or ranges of scores for the individual.

NORMS

We have already dealt with two kinds of norms, percentile norms and standard score norms. Of course the norms provided on any test are only as good as the quality of the test construction process and the efficacy of the sample test population. More will be said on these topics in following sections of this chapter.

Age and Grade Equivalents

Two additional norms are used frequently in educational and psychological tests: age norms based on groups of children of the same age, and grade norms, based on groups in the same grade. Generally, tests of mental ability use age norms, called age equivalents, and achievement tests use grade norms, called grade equivalents.

Norms are derived from computations of the performances of cases from the sample population. If a sample group of students aged 9 years and 8 months score an average of 55 on a test of mental ability, then this raw score of 55 is stated as 9-8 in age equivalents. If this same group were in Grade 4 and the test were administered in October, then the grade equivalent would be 4.2, which represents the 2nd month of Grade 4. Age equivalents are stated in years and months, such as 10-2, 13-11, or 6-3. Grade equivalents are reported as the years and months in school, such as 4.2, 6.9, or 11.1. Table 7.3 shows how a chart might look for converting raw scores to both age and grade equivalents.

Both types of norms have utility but also built-in hazards. The major danger is the misunderstanding that can occur for age and grade equivalents above the average. For instance, Tony is 9-8 and in Grade 4. The results of his test in math concepts is well above the mean for his grade and age, with an age equivalent of 11-5 and a grade equivalent of 6.9. Yet if Tony were placed in a group receiving math instruction with students aged 11-5 and at Grade 6, he probably could not keep up or truly comprehend

Table 7.3
Reading comprehension

Raw Score	Reading Grade Equivalent	Reading Age Equivalent
10	11-0	6.2
11	11-1	6.3
12	11-3	6.4
13	11-4	6.6
14	11-6	6.7

and understand because age and grade norms are in relation to the age and grade level of the student being tested. Although Tony has mastered the math concepts for his age and grade level and is above average for his age and grade level, this does not mean that he is performing at age 11-5 and grade 6.9. If teachers took the time to explain this to parents, they would prevent many misunderstandings.

As these various kinds of standard score norms make clear, different tests can present their tables of norms differently. It takes careful attention to ensure that the proper tables are used in order to convert raw scores correctly to the various norms. Tables 7.4 and 7.5 are from the Gates-MacGinite Reading Tests— Primary C.[2] This level is designed for Grade 3 and has two subtests, vocabulary and comprehension. The tables show the norms for comprehension. Note that norms are provided for the beginning, middle, and end of the school year. These tables show how raw scores are converted to other norms such as grade equivalents and percentiles.

Many tests provide student profile sheets. These profiles allow us to see all the pertinent norm information data per child in one location. The profile can also be used to graph the performance of a student to show performances on various subtests. The profiles also allow teachers to follow the growth patterns of an individual student from year to year. The student profile sheet from the Comprehensive Tests of Basic Skills is reproduced in Fig. 7.8.[3] This profile relates to Level 1, which spans the grade levels 2.5 to 4.9. It shows one way to present conversions clearly.

HOW ARE STANDARDS OR NORMS DETERMINED FOR INTELLIGENCE TESTS?

When Sam takes an intelligence test, his score is expressed as an I.Q. which is derived in much the same way that scores are derived for all standardized tests. Standardized tests are carefully put together according to known and accepted principles of test construction in order to make them both valid and reliable. In addition, the test makers have spelled out the precise conditions under which the tests should be given and how they

Table 7.4

GRADE LEVEL 3.1 (OCT.)			GRADE LEVEL 3.5 (FEB.)			GRADE LEVEL 3.8 (MAY)		
Raw Score	Standard Score	Per-centile	Raw Score	Standard Score	Per-centile	Raw Score	Standard Score	Per-centile
1	—	—	1	—	—	1	—	—
2	—	—	2	—	—	2	—	—
3	—	—	3	—	—	3	—	—
4	—	—	4	—	—	4	—	—
5	—	—	5	—	—	5	—	—
6	30	2	6	—	--	6	—	—
7	31	3	7	—	—	7	—	—
8	32	4	8	29	2	8	—	—
9	34	5	9	31	3	9	—	—
10	36	8	10	33	4	10	30	2
11	38	12	11	34	5	11	32	4
12	39	14	12	36	8	12	33	4
13	41	18	13	37	10	13	35	7
14	42	21	14	39	14	14	36	8
15	43	24	15	40	16	15	37	10
16	44	27	16	41	18	16	38	12
17	45	31	17	42	21	17	39	14
18	46	34	18	43	24	18	40	16
19	47	38	19	44	27	19	41	18
20	48	42	20	44	27	20	42	21
21	48	42	21	45	31	21	43	24
22	49	46	22	46	34	22	43	24
23	50	50	23	47	38	23	44	27
24	51	54	24	47	38	24	45	31
25	51	54	25	48	42	25	46	34
26	52	58	26	49	46	26	46	34
27	53	62	27	50	50	27	47	38
28	54	66	28	50	50	28	48	42
29	54	66	29	51	54	29	48	42
30	55	69	30	51	54	30	49	46
31	56	73	31	52	58	31	50	50
32	56	73	32	53	62	32	50	50
33	57	76	33	53	62	33	51	54
34	58	79	34	54	66	34	52	58
35	58	79	35	55	69	35	53	62
36	59	82	36	56	73	36	53	62
37	60	84	37	57	76	37	54	66
38	61	86	38	58	79	38	55	69
39	62	88	39	59	82	39	56	73
40	63	90	40	60	84	40	57	76
41	64	92	41	61	86	41	58	79
42	66	95	42	62	88	42	60	84
43	67	96	43	64	92	43	61	86
44	69	97	44	66	95	44	63	90
45	71	98	45	68	96	45	65	93
46	73	99	46	71	98	46	70	98
47	75	99	47	73	99	47	71	98
48	—	—	48	75	99	48	74	99

Table 7.5

Raw Score	Grade Score	Raw Score	Grade Score
1	1.3	26	3.3
2	1.3	27	3.4
3	1.4	28	3.5
4	1.4	29	3.6
5	1.4	30	3.7
6	1.5	31	3.9
7	1.5	32	4.1
8	1.5	33	4.3
9	1.6	34	4.5
10	1.6	35	4.6
11	1.7	36	4.7
12	1.8	37	4.9
13	1.9	38	5.0
14	2.0	39	5.2
15	2.2	40	5.4
16	2.3	41	5.6
17	2.4	42	5.8
18	2.5	43	6.0
19	2.6	44	6.2
20	2.7	45	6.6
21	2.8	46	7.0
22	2.9	47	—
23	3.0	48	—
24	3.1		
25	3.2		

should be scored. These procedures help assure the "uniformity" we spoke of earlier in the chapter.

Before any test is administered officially by any school system, it is given to selected groups of children throughout the country. This sampling process, as we have explained, affords the test makers an opportunity to "test their test" on a wide variety of groups. Many hundreds of children of the same age are given the test, and their scores are carefully analyzed, not only their overall score, but their answers to each item as well. By this process, the test makers are able to tell if their items and the test in general produced uniform results regardless of the cultural nature of each sample group or of the part of the country in which they lived.

COMPREHENSIVE TESTS OF BASIC SKILLS

EXPANDED EDITION

Level 1 Form S

Student's Name _____

Grade _____

Teacher _____

Test Date _____

School _____

STUDENT PROFILE SHEET

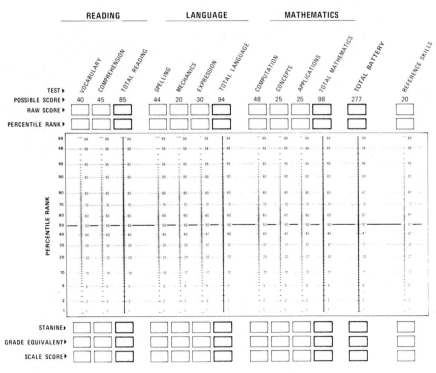

For instructions for completing this chart and for tables to convert raw scores to other scores, see *Comprehensive Tests of Basic Skills, Expanded Edition, Examiner's Manual*, Level 1, Form S.

Figure 7.8 (From Comprehensive Tests of Basic Skills, Form S. Reprinted by permission of the publisher, CBT/McGraw-Hill, Del Monte Research Park, Monterey, CA 93940. Copyright © 1973 by McGraw-Hill, Inc. All Rights Reserved. Printed in the U.S.A.

Perhaps the most important aspect of this standardization process is determining how many items a child should be able to answer correctly in order to be considered normally intelligent for that age. For example, test makers carefully analyze the responses of all 7 year olds. If they answered 20 items correctly out of a possible 80, then the average 7 year old should normally score 20. This, of course, is a "raw score" and must be converted to an expression of intelligence called the "intelligence quotient" or I.Q. If Sam's score was 20, we would say that he had an I.Q. of 100, the expression of average intelligence. Obviously, if his score were higher or lower, his intelligence quotient would change accordingly, and his intelligence would be described as above or below normal.

In determining that the average 7 year old should be expected to score 20 on this intelligence test, the test makers have established a norm for children of that age. In addition to the norm for 7 year olds, of course, norms are also established for children of all ages. Special tables in the testing manual provide this information. Timothy, for example, who is 6 years and 4 months of age, will have a different norm than Sam. He will be expected to answer fewer than 20 questions correctly. Thus, for any child of any age, normative scores are listed in a table in the test manual. Since the table also gives the I.Q. readings for all scores above or below the norm, it is a simple process to match Timothy's raw score of 27 with his chronological age and see that he has answered more questions correctly than the norm group of children of age 6 years and 4 months.

The Concept of Mental Age

I.Q. scores are expressions of a human characteristic known as "mental age." For Sam, whose score on the intelligence test was exactly the same as the norm for 7 year olds, his mental age is exactly the same as his chronological age. To compute the I.Q., the test makers simply divide Sam's mental age (in months) by his chronological age and then multiply that figure by 100. In Sam's case, 84 divided by 84 is 1, and 1 multiplied by 100 is 100. Multiplying by 100 is an arbitrary procedure that makes the I.Q. score easier to handle. For instance, Timothy's chronological age is 6 years and 4 months, expressed as 6-4, while his mental age is 7-1, much higher than his chronological age because he answered more questions correctly than the average child of his age. His mental age (85 months) divided by his chronological age (76 months) yields 1.11. Multiplying by 100 eliminates the decimal point and the I.Q. score is around 111, eleven points above the average I.Q. of children his age. Timothy's mental age of 7-1 indicates that he is as intelligent as an average child 7 months older. Finally, in the case of Ted, whose mental age (6-5) is somewhat lower than his chronological age (7-0), the division (77 months + 84 months) yields a figure of less than one, or 0.92. With an I.Q. of 92, Ted has the mental age of an average child 5 months younger than himself and an I.Q. 8 points lower than that of his norm group.

Understanding the concept of mental age and knowing the way I.Q. is computed (M.A. ÷ C.A. × 100) are useful bits of information that keep teachers from becoming careless is describing the intellectual ability of their youngsters and help them understand how test makers arrive at mathematical expressions of intelligence. To supplement this general discussion of how intelligence tests are standardized, we will examine a well-known intelligence test and see how its publishers conducted the task of building it.

STANDARDIZING THE HENMON-NELSON TEST OF MENTAL ABILITY

The Henmon-Nelson Test of Mental Ability[4] is a widely used general intelligence test and one thought by most testing experts to be well constructed.

In the examiner's manual, the test authors describe the necessity of sampling the total population of children to be tested in order to obtain representative samples of behavior. Since it is impossible to test millions of children, a careful selection, or sample, of these youngsters must be tested instead. Since the performance of this small, representative group will provide the normative scores, or norms, to which teachers compare the scores of their own children, it becomes clear why it is essential to sample *all* unique groups of the population. For instance, if the test makers were to include a number of items calling for knowledge of farm practices, a sample of 10,000 children from the New York City school system would not provide an appropriate normal response that is representative of the entire population. The same problem would exist if the authors were to use 10,000 rural youngsters to obtain representative responses about city life. They know that rural children perform differently on many test situations than do city children. Children who grow up in certain geographic areas also perform differently than those of other areas, and so do youngsters of different cultural and ethnic backgrounds. Even within a city, there are important human differences among the total population, and samples from each unique group must be included in order to obtain good representative responses.

The authors point out that a random selection must be made from the entire population. Without this, the test might well be biased against certain children who will take it. An important example of such bias was the inadequate sampling of Black students who for many years performed poorly on standardized tests, not because they were less intelligent but because their population had never been included in the standardization process. Since responses representative of Black socioeconomic, cultural, and geographic backgrounds did not appear on the test they were required to take in the schools, Black children had to respond to items requiring behavior many of them had never learned. Although we will discuss this aspect of testing in another chapter, it is appropriate here to point out this important reason for examining carefully the sampling process of the tests that are broadly administered.

To avoid bias on their test, the authors of the Henmon-Nelson began with the total population of children in grades three through twelve in regular attendance at public elementary and secondary schools throughout the United States. Since they could not reasonably be expected to "test their test" on all 30 million of these youngsters, they devised criteria and procedures for sampling all important aspects of this huge population.

First, they acquired a listing from the United States Bureau of the Census of all public school systems in the country. They grouped the systems into 8 strata according to enrollment size and into 48 states, one for each of the continental states. Samples of school systems, then schools, then individual classrooms are randomly selected so that every state, every unique geographic area, every socioeconomic area, every cultural and ethnic area were represented.

The Henmon-Nelson consists of three levels, designed to test children in grades 3 through 6, 6 through 9, and 9 through 12. It was determined that 250 classrooms from each level would be an adequate sample size on which to try out the new test. Tables and other data in the test manual indicate that, in the course of a year, over 96% of the selected sample actually took the test, a total of over 20,000 youngsters.

Deciding How Good the Test Is

The process of determining whether a test is usable is quite complex and involves considerable statistical analysis. Item analysis, validity, and reliability, part of the processes of test construction, were then applied in the standardization of the Henmon Nelson.

Item analysis The strength or usability of any test is determined by the strength or usability of its individual items. When the authors began to assemble their test, they first determined the kinds of behavior they wished to elicit from children. Since theirs is a test of general intelligence, they had to include a broad array of test items that would allow a wide variety of response opportunities. The objective was not to examine children on what they remember or on how much they know, but to see to what degree they can use information to think, make judgments, and arrive at intelligent decisions. The enormous amount of knowledge and information from which test items might be selected thus calls for great care in selecting and constructing each item. Each child, regardless of geographic, socioeconomic, or cultural environment must have an equal opportunity to respond successfully to the test items. This means that city children inexperienced in the language of the farm must have enough items containing familiar information to which they can respond. Thus both city children and farm children will miss some of each other's items but will have enough others on which to apply the behavior of intelligent decision making.

Each item, then, is carefully worded in much the same way as items in teacher-made tests. Then the original 297 items were shown to experienced teachers for their criticism. Two hundred and fifty of these were administered in two separate forms to children who were divided into three ability groups—inferior, average, and superior. These classifications were determined by their scores on three other well-known group tests of intelligence. Any item that did not show a significant increase in correct responses from the inferior to the average or from the average to the superior group was discarded. When a given item is answered correctly by a significantly larger group of bright children than by slower children, the item is said to "discriminate" and is a good test item.

Of the 250 items administered on the first trial test, 101 were retained as "discriminating." A second trial test eliminated another 11 items, and the final version of the test was published with two equivalent forms.

Validity In this case, validity means the degree to which the Henmon-Nelson really tests a child's ability to make intelligent judgments. The care taken in selecting, constructing, and analyzing each item contributes a great deal to the validity of the test but construct validity, concurrent validity, and predictive validity are important as well. On construct validity, comparing the results of this test with those of others considered to be good, the Henmon-Nelson manual shows a strong correlation with three other well-known tests of intelligence.

On concurrent validity, checking the test scores against other criteria such as current school grades or scores on achievement tests, the manual shows that the Henmon-Nelson correlated quite well with well-known standardized achievement tests. This means that children who did well on achievement tests also did well on the Henmon-Nelson, something one would expect to happen since children usually perform in academic work in direct relation to their intelligence.

The Henmon-Nelson's predictive validity is less well established. When this revision of the test was published, not enough time had elapsed to compare the school grades children achieved some time following the test with the test results themselves. However, the authors state that they believe the long range predictive abilities of the Henmon-Nelson will be at least as good as that of other well-known intelligence tests.

Reliability The Henmon-Nelson authors used the split-halves method of determining the test's reliability by considering the odd numbered items as one version and the even numbered items as another. When compared, the two versions showed a high degree of reliability as shown by the coefficients of correlation in the manual.

Determining the Norms for the Test

We described norms earlier in the chapter as the average performances obtained by the sample group that took the test during its standardization period, in this case approximately 7000 children for each of the three levels of the test. For each age, then, the average (or mean) scores became the normative scores (or norms) to which all other children who subsequently take the test are compared. Norms are usually expressed in terms other than the raw scores obtained by the sample group. A raw score of 74, for instance, is a normative score for children of a certain age, but it tells the classroom teacher little. To be useful, the raw score must be converted to some other standard by which children are judged and which can be universally understood to mean the same thing to every teacher who gives that particular test.

The Henmon-Nelson provides four different norms to which any given child can be compared: percentile ranks, grade equivalents, mental age, and I.Q.

Percentile norms Tables in the test manual show the percentile rank for each raw score obtained on the test by children in the sample group. For instance, a child who achieved a score of 45 for grade three has a percentile rank of 79. This means that, of the several thousand third grade children who took the test during the standardization period, 79% of them scored below the child who got a 45. Teachers who give the test in their classes can use these percentile ranks to determine those of their own students. If Bill, for example, achieved a raw score of 25, the table would show his percentile rank as 46, indicating that he did better than only 46% of the sample population. Since the sample group accurately represents all third graders in the nation, Bill's position is somewhat low.

Grade equivalents Raw scores have also been converted to grade equivalents. Bill's raw score of 25 indicates that he has performed about as well as those children in the sample group who were in the third month (November) of grade three when they took the test. The assumption is that the third grade children who take the test nationally and whose raw scores are 25 have the mental ability (or intelligence) equivalent to a child in November of the third grade. The authors of the Henmon-Nelson, as well as other test experts, caution against using grade equivalents to compare mental ability with achievement. This should be done only if both tests are given at nearly the same time during the year and only if both tests were standardized with the same population.

Mental age norms The Henmon-Nelson's table for mental age shows that Bill's raw score of 25 places him at the mental age of 8 years and 6 months (8-6), the same as for those third graders in the sample group who achieved that raw score. Since Bill's chronological age is 9 years and 1 month (9-1) we see that he performs mentally at a lower level than the average child of his age.

I.Q. norms For a number of reasons, the familiar process of computing I.Q. by the formula M.A. $\div$ C.A. $\times$ 100 is not adequate for accurately computing I.Q.'s at various ages. A more uniform method is the "deviation I.Q." described earlier in this chapter. A table in the Henmon-Nelson manual shows a child's deviation I.Q. Bill, for instance, with a chronological age of 9-1 and a raw score of 25, is shown to have a deviation I.Q. of approximately 94, somewhat lower than that of the average child of his age. Each of the four norms we have described were obtained from the original sample group of 20,000 or so children who first took the Henmon-Nelson. For every single raw score, from 5 to 90, a percentile rank, a grade equivalent, a mental age, and an intelligence quotient were derived. These become the norms with which teachers compare the children in their classes.

Administering the Test

Earlier in this chapter, we emphasized that good standardized tests, like any good scientific research tool, must be administered uniformly to obtain consistent and usable data. Standardized tests such as the Henmon-Nelson were originally administered and standardized under precise and carefully controlled conditions. In order to make this test as useful as possible, teachers must adhere to the same uniformity of procedure with which it was originally given. Only in this way can they be certain that the results are consistent with those of the original. Only in this way can a teacher say with any degree of certainty that Bill seems to have the mental ability of a child considerably younger than himself, a finding which becomes extremely important in planning Bill's learning activities.

Uniformity of procedure is made easy on the Henmon-Nelson, and any teacher who follows the simple and brief instructions for sound testing procedures will have no trouble securing good results.

GENERAL INTELLIGENCE TESTS ARE SCREENING TESTS

The Henmon-Nelson and others like it are called tests of general intelligence. They usually yield a single I.Q. score, although some yield separate scores on verbal and nonverbal reasoning along with a composite I.Q. Such tests of general intelligence are designed to predict, from a very small sample of behavior, the individual's probable ability to behave intelligently in other situations. The behavior a child exhibits on the test is not important in itself but only as it relates to some broader form of behavior. For instance, a vocabulary portion of the test is important, not to determine how many words children may know, but because it demonstrates children's probable ability to use vocabulary in wider applications of language skills. If items call for an adequate sample of children's current language behavior, their potential for intelligent language behavior in the future can be predicted. Similarly, in the nonverbal area, an intelligence test calling for computational skills will provide clues to children's ability to make a wider variety of mathematical applications in the future.

Essentially, general intelligence tests are used as initial screening devices to provide important first clues to children's general ability to make judgments and intelligent decisions. Often the test will indicate more apparent ability in one area than another. It is not uncommon, for instance, for a child to achieve a much higher I.Q. score on computation than on verbal ability. This initial screening indicates that some conditions exist that make the child better able to perform certain kinds of tasks than others. Teachers who examine the results of the test must consider the possible reasons for the difference in scores. There may be a true difference in the child's potential between nonverbal and verbal ability. The higher score on computation may indicate more interest in nonverbal activities, or less adequate experience in verbal development.

Sometimes teachers can point to a significant difference in the quality of teaching as the reason for such score differences. However, if a test is being used primarily as an assessment of current ability, a teacher can simply say that the child is more capable in one area than another. On the other hand, if a test is being used as a diagnostic screening device, the results can help teachers think about enriching the child's experiences in the verbal area or developing the nonverbal area as a means to personal success. In either case, the general intelligence test provides a first assessment of children's probable intellectual ability.

TESTS OF SPECIAL APTITUDE

To further probe potential initially indicated on a general intelligence test, more specific tests of special aptitude are available. Such tests measure special aptitude in music, mathematics, science, engineering, medicine, law—literally every academic and vocational endeavor. All are standardized in much the same way as the Henmon-Nelson except that the behavior sampled is narrower in scope and the tests are designed to yield evidence of intelligent behavior in specific areas. The phenomenal growth of special aptitude tests arises from an ongoing theoretical controversy about the nature of intelligence, which will be discussed in detail in the next chapter. Briefly, the controversy arose at the beginning of the testing movement and concerns itself with the question of whether intelligence is a "unitary" or "general" factor or whether it consists of a variety of separate and identifiable "special" factors.

If intelligence is a general quality inherent in a child, all academic and vocational endeavors should have the same potential for fulfillment. If the quality and quantity of experiences in each area is equal, each should be equally exhibited in the child's behavior. An I.Q. of 120 on a general intelligence test, then, would mean that for all practical purposes the child has the potential to do well above average in *all* areas of intellectual endeavor.

However, if we understand intelligence to be composed of a number of separate factors, these can be better identified through specific testing in the areas of indicated strength. For instance, a child who does much better on the computational sections of a general intelligence test than on the verbal sections, might be given intensive tests of nonverbal behavior. If such tests indicate that high potential seems to exist in this area, the child should look to mathematics, science, or engineering as possible career choices.

Teachers who understand this controversy can make more knowledgeable decisions about the evaluation instruments they use. As for the argument itself, time and continued experimentation influence each side. We believe that children and teachers can benefit from wise use of both kinds of intelligence tests. General or unitary intelligence tests are best used as screening devices for further diagnosis. If the test performance indicates weakness or strength in specific areas, many special aptitude tests as well as test batteries that include a variety of factors are available.

One well-known example of a special aptitude test is the *Seashore Measures of Musical Talent*.[5] This widely used tool for predicting musical ability calls for behavior very specific to that involved in music. Its six subtests show how narrowly such a special aptitude test samples behavior to predict success:

1. Discrimination of Pitch: Judging which of two tones is higher.

2. Discrimination of Loudness: Judging which of two sounds is louder.

3. Discrimination of Time: Judging which of two intervals is longer.

4. Judgment of Rhythm: Judging whether two rhythms are the same or different.

5. Judgment of Timbre: Judging which of two qualities is more pleasing.

6. Tonal Memory: Judging whether two melodies are the same or different.

Another well-known test battery, designed to measure a variety of intellectual traits, is the Differential Aptitude Test,[6] an instrument that clearly reflects the multifactor theory of intelligence in the titles of its subtests: Verbal Reasoning, Numerical Ability, Abstract Reasoning, Space Relations, Language Usage (spelling and grammar), Mechanical Reasoning, and Clerical Speed and Accuracy.

The need for special aptitude tests such as the Seashore Test of Musical Talent and multiple aptitude tests such as the DAT arose when psychologists began to recognize that general tests of intelligence were too general and did not probe effectively into aptitude in specific traits of intelligence. The theory of multiple traits was developed early in this century when it was thought that Binet's concept of a single general trait called "judgment" was not descriptive enough of the nature of intelligence. He believed that this single trait could be assessed by examining the individual's ability to use judgment (1) to maintain consistency in direction (stay on the track), (2) to choose appropriate means of solving problems, and (3) to evaluate one's actions objectively.

The multifactor theory was developed by E. L. Thorndike, who said that intelligence consisted of many "specific" factors but no "general" factor. Thurstone developed a theory that seemed to be a compromise between the ideas of Binet and Thorndike. He stated that intelligence probably consisted of neither a general factor nor a large number of specifics but, rather, of six to ten primary or "group" factors. These included number, verbal, space, word fluency, reasoning, and rote memory. Note how closely they resemble the titles of the Differential Aptitude Test mentioned above.

The group-factor theory has gained considerable acceptance among psychologists even though general intelligence tests are still widely used. Many believe this is a more practical theory as a measure of assessing individual traits that are important to vocational or academic success. Most, however, feel that both kinds of tests are valuable when used with skill and precision, the general test to be used as an initial screening instrument and the multifactor or multiple aptitude batteries to be used to explore in greater depth individuals' specific intellectual strengths and weaknesses.

The controversy over the nature of intelligence points up the need for caution and discretion in the selection, administration, and interpretation of intelligence tests. Teachers must avoid accepting blindly what ambitious promoters of tests might suggest as the best way to test intelligence. Instead, the continuing study of human behavior and the learning process are the best defenses against the claims of any single "expert" in the testing field. Finally, since teachers typically assess children's general abilities to learn and solve problems as well as attempt to determine their abilities to perform these functions in narrow fields of behavior such as mathematics or music, they must discriminate carefully among the many standardized tests available.

THE STANDARDIZATION OF ACHIEVEMENT TESTS

Achievement tests, more than any other type, are given most frequently. Most teacher-made testing materials, for instance, are achievement tests and are normally prepared to measure progress in specific curriculum areas such as tenth grade science or sixth grade reading. Unlike intelligence or aptitude tests, which measure a child's *potential* for learning, achievement tests measure how much and how well children have learned. While intelligence tests are largely a means of assessing a child's ability to solve problems, achievement tests are based solely on the experiences the child has had up to a particular point. For instance, an intelligence test given to Tomilee in grade two might indicate the intellectual capacity to learn more than the average child of her age. Her mental age of 8 and I.Q. of 124 predict that she should be doing better than average work, not only in second grade but all the way through school. Further, her high score on an arithmetic aptitude test predicts that she will do particularly well in that subject. On the other hand, an achievement test in arithmetic in grade five will assess her cumulative ability to solve math problems. Standardized achievement tests provide a more scientific and objective opportunity for assessing growth than do teacher-made tests. Because of the rigorous standardization procedures involved in the development of a good test, teachers can be more objective in interpreting scores. Since good standardized tests require uniformity of testing and scoring procedures, a test administered in strict accordance with the test maker's instructions will provide a fairly good estimate of how well students live up to their potential in a given subject, and how each student stands with reference to other children of the same grade who have taken the same test. Finally, analysis of the items students miss provides important clues to their weaknesses and to the developmental teaching strategies to strengthen them.

Before we examine a well-known standardized achievement test, we would like to make some important points about intelligence and achievement tests.

Intelligence tests *cannot* measure innate intellectual ability directly. Potential for learning must be observed in the current *behavior* of the individual, behavior that is the result of experience. From current behavior, teachers can infer or predict the potential for future learning. For this reason, we cannot assume, as early testing researchers did, that intelligence tests ignore the role experience plays in performance.

This may seem confusing since items on both intelligence and achievement tests depend upon experience with the test's objects or concepts. Items, for example, that test verbal ability require knowledge and experience with content as well as vocabulary and the skills to speak and write vocabulary words in meaningful combinations. Nonverbal items for younger children and those unable to read and write also require sufficient life experience in order to recognize and identify information. The difference lies in the use each test makes of experiences and learning. Intelligence tests are less dependent upon specific experiences. They use test responses as the basis for abstract inferences about behavior. In order to show whether a child can think in a particular way, intelligence tests present a variety of items to reveal how the child uses information to solve problems. The use of experience to solve new or unique problems is an accepted definition of intelligent behavior, and this is the kind of behavior called for on intelligence tests. Moreover, the ability to solve problems by using both experience and innate potential is indicative of success in life. Therefore, the major function of intelligence tests is to evaluate children's *current* behavior to determine their potential for *future* success.

Achievement tests, on the other hand, are generally heavily dependent upon specific curriculum content and are considered to be tests of *terminal* rather than *future* behavior. They demonstrate how *current* behavior indicates the quality of *past* learnings.

One well-known and widely used standardized achievement test is the Stanford Achievement Test.[7] Actually a series of tests, the Stanford consists of a set of test batteries for evaluating achievement from the primary grades through high school. Our discussion of the Stanford's standardization will be somewhat briefer than that for Henmon-Nelson since all major tests are standardized along the same lines.

STANDARDIZING THE STANFORD ACHIEVEMENT TEST

Sampling

Two separate standardization programs were carried out for the 1973 edition, one near the beginning and one at the end of each grade. Most school systems administer the Stanford during one of these periods to ensure accurate comparison between their children and the sample group.

As was done in the Henmon-Nelson, the test authors attempted to sample the total population of youngsters in American schools. Youngsters were selected who were representative of various important geographic regions, of different socioeconomic groups, of school systems of different sizes, and of both public and private schools. Over 275,000 children from 109 school systems and 43 states were included in the sample group upon which the test was tested.

Item Analysis

To prepare the test items, the authors explored the instructional objectives of the nation's schools; analyzed the most widely used textbook series in various subject areas, as well as a wide variety of courses of study; and reviewed the latest research pertaining to child behavior and learning at successive grade levels and ages.

After this research was completed, the authors prepared tables of specifications like the ones discussed in the last chapter. These "blueprints" were prepared with the assistance of curriculum experts from each subject area who helped in identifying the appropriate instructional objectives to which the test items would relate. Each author then wrote the test items and tried them out on subject matter specialists and in selected classrooms. The completed sets of items were turned over to the editorial board of the publisher (Harcourt Brace Jovanovich), who meticulously refined each item in terms of corrections of content, sound principles of item construction, and overall grammatical structure and readability. (This process is similar to the procedure we discussed in the section on teacher-made tests.) In addition, a special group edited the items to assure that they would be appropriate for each special cultural group in order to avoid test bias that might penalize certain children. Finally, selected teachers were asked to criticize each item and recommend changes. In all, five groups of specialists participated in the important process of writing, analyzing, refining, and editing the items.

Validity

The process of item construction and analysis described above was a first step in constructing a valid test. As we said before, the strength of individual items determines the strength of the total test. Since this is an achievement test, the most relevant type of validity is content validity. The Stanford is said to have good content validity because the test is considered to constitute a sound representative sample of the skills, knowledge, and understanding that are the goals of instruction in a contemporary school.

Reliability

The reliability, or consistency, of the Stanford was determined both by using the split-halves method and by a statistical process known as the Kuder-Richardson Formula. A table in the manual shows high reliability coefficients for all of the eleven subtests in this particular test level. Thus, a child who takes the test a second time will score very nearly the same each time.

DETERMINING NORMS FOR THE TEST

As for the Henmon-Nelson or any other standardized test, the authors of the Stanford were interested in establishing accurate norms. The norms established on this test are described in terms of percentile ranks, grade equivalents, stanines, item difficulty values, and scaled scores.

Percentile Norms

The test manual includes tables that show the percentile rank for any raw score from 1 to 99. Sixth graders, for instance, who obtain a raw score of 29 on the math concepts subtest would have a percentile rank of 92, indicating that they did better than 92% of the sample group upon which the test was standardized. It also means that they probably would do better than 92%

of all of the thousands of sixth grade youngsters who have taken or will take this test throughout the nation.

Grade Equivalents

The sixth graders' raw scores of 29 on the math concepts subtest place them at a grade equivalent of 9-1. This means that all sixth grade children in the standardized sample who took this test and earned this raw score were said to have learned math concepts equivalent to those of the average child in the first month of grade nine. This corresponds well to the high percentile rank and would be expected.

The test authors caution against misinterpretation of grade equivalents, just as the authors of the Henmon-Nelson did. For instance, although a score of 29 indicates progress in math concepts three years above the norm for sixth grade, it does not mean that the student is just as advanced in other subjects. Moreover, the same grade equivalents in two different subtests are not equivalent because of the different nature of each subject. Also, a year of growth in mathematics concepts in grade four will represent much more learning than it will in grade eight. Such cautions are good indicators that test writers and publishers are aware of the limitations of even the best of standardized tests. The growing criticism of testing has practically eliminated the generous claims of excellence made by test makers of a few years ago.

Stanines

The term stanine, a contraction for the words "standard nines," indicates that all the scores obtained by the standardizing sample were spread over a scale of nine points. Most of the scores fall within the middle, or fifth, stanine since this is where the average scores cluster. Stanines above and below represent progressively fewer scores with only 4% falling in stanines 1 and 9.

Stanines yield much the same information as percentile ranks and are helpful in indicating a student's relative standing compared to a norm group. Thus, a sixth grader with a percentile rank of 92 places well above the average stanine, in stanine 8.

Item Difficulty Values

This norm indicates the degree of difficulty posed by specific items, allowing comparisons between a classroom group and the sample group. Item difficulty values are expressed as percentiles, and each item in each of the eleven subtests of the grade 6 Stanford Achievement Test was assigned a rank when the standardizing test was completed. For instance, 70% of the children who took the Math Concepts subtest during the standardizing process got item number ten wrong. If in another group of children 95%

missed number ten, we would assume that the item was more difficult for them than for the sample group. If only 20% failed item ten, we would assume that they were better prepared on that topic than was the sample group. Perhaps the danger in this kind of comparison of local to standardizing groups is that teachers might tailor their teaching to the content in the tests. Teaching to pass the test is one of the major criticisms leveled at teachers and test makers alike. If the goal of teaching is to help children develop good learning and thinking habits as well as to acquire knowledge, when the test controls what and how teachers teach, children lose much of the creativity and excitement of the learning process.

Scaled Scores

Another norm developed for the Stanford is the scaled score. Derived through a statistical procedure, the scaled score permits the translation of raw scores at each test level into "standard scores" that can be compared directly between various test levels of the same subtest.

The sixth graders who correctly answered 29 items on the Math Concepts subtest have scaled scores for math concepts of 194. That scaled score will have the same meaning when they take the test again in grade seven and again in grade eight. Significant changes in the score from year to year will indicate either more or less growth in math concepts and will provide a relatively simple way to observe children's progress over a period of time, progress not only in terms of their own learning rate but as compared with a national norm.

All of the five norms provided by the authors of the Stanford Achievement Tests are designed to help teachers better understand each child's progress. Each is helpful in its own way in showing how children stack up against the sample population upon which the test was tested and standardized. They provide the standards against which all children who subsequently take the test are compared, and, theoretically at least, they indicate that the sixth graders, whose scores far exceed the five norms for the children in grade six, are considerably more advanced in math concepts than the average sixth grader in the nation.

ADMINISTERING THE TEST

The directions for administering the Stanford must be followed to the letter. If testing procedures vary to any significant degree from those of the population sample, the test loses its usefulness and the scores cannot be compared with the norm scores. It would be like comparing apples and oranges, and the results would not be valid.

SUMMARY

We have described only two of the many types of standardized tests on the market. In addition to general intelligence and achievement tests, there are standardized tests of special aptitude, vocational skill, personality assessment, mechanical ability, clerical speed, spelling, reading, and so on. The list is impressive and teachers must choose carefully in order to make maximum use of them.

A standardized test samples the total population and tests it using carefully constructed items administered under carefully controlled conditions. The sample population is theoretically representative of the total population of children of that particular age or grade level. The scores of the children in the sample group are converted into various "normative scores" or norms—intelligence quotient, percentile rank, grade equivalent, stanine score, scaled score, and mental age, among others—and these are set into tables in the test manual. Tests given under the same conditions as existed for the sample group and in exactly the same manner duplicate the original standardizing process. The classroom group, and individual children within it, can thus be compared directly with those of the sample to allow conclusions about a child's intelligence, achievement, aptitude, or emotional development as they compare with others of the same age or grade.

Norms have become a way of life for teachers, and standardized tests are merely a precise way of applying them to specific groups of children or a specific child. With normal professional caution and attention to good testing practice, teachers can determine children's progress and plan for their continued growth.

There are various sources to assist teachers in evaluating tests and in deciding which test is more appropriate for a particular situation. The manual of the test, additional information provided by the publishers in their technical supplements, and the *Mental Measurement Yearbooks** are among the most helpful. The test manual should contain sufficient information to allow a teacher to make a judgment concerning the instrument. Information on the sample population used in the construction of the test, item construction and analysis, validity and reliability data, and norms should be clearly presented. When sufficient information is not provided, teachers should not assume it has been done and that the test is acceptable. A lack of information is a serious matter, and a test should not be used until a teacher is satisfied that it has been constructed with skill in a professional, competent manner.

*An invaluable reference is the *Mental Measurements Yearbooks*. These yearbooks, edited by Oscar K. Buros, provide critiques on recently published tests or critiques on revisions of existing tests. Most frequently the critiques provided are from two or more sources, and thus the reader can get two or more perspectives. The first yearbook was published in 1938 and the seventh in 1972. For any professional who needs to make judgments concerning testing instruments the yearbooks will be of great assistance.

IMPORTANT POINTS TO THINK ABOUT

1. Standardized tests are important tools in testing, measuring, and evaluating student performance. What aspects of a test make it "standardized" as contrasted with teacher-made tests?

2. Define the three measures of central tendency: the mean, median, and mode. Identify or compute these three in the following distribution: 28, 26, 20, 20, 18, 15, 11, 10, and 8.

3. The standard deviation of a distribution is the square root of the summation of the squared deviations divided by the number. Review the formula for the standard deviation and compare the formula with the verbal definition. What is the symbol that represents variance in the formula?

4. Assume a distribution with an $\overline{X}$ of 90 and s of 8. What raw scores would be located two standard deviations above the mean and one standard deviation below the mean on the normal curve?

5. A student achieves a raw score of 52 on a standardized test that translates to a percentile of 55. Interpret the meaning of the percentile to this imaginary high school student.

6. The z score is a standard score that states a raw score in units of standard deviation. Describe a standard score and its advantages.

7. Correlation deals with relationship, and the coefficient expresses the degree of the relationship between two variables. Describe the characteristics of a positive and negative correlation.

8. Norms are ways of reporting the results of test performance. Describe the following norms: age equivalent, grade equivalent, and stanines.

NOTES

1. Howard B. Lyman, *Test Scores and What They Mean* (Englewood Cliffs, NJ: Prentice-Hall, 1963).
2. Gates-MacGinite Reading Tests, Primary C, (New York: Teachers College Press, Columbia University, 1965).
3. Comprehensive Tests of Basic Skills (Monterey, CA: CTB/McGraw-Hill, 1973).
4. Henmon-Nelson Test of Mental Ability (Boston: Houghton Mifflin, 1959).
5. Seashore Measure of Musical Talent (New York: The Psychological Corporation, 1942).
6. Differential Aptitude Test (New York: The Psychological Corporation, 1961).
7. Stanford Achievement Tests (New York: Harcourt Brace Jovanovich, 1972).

ADDITIONAL READINGS

Oscar K. Buros, ed., *Mental Measurements Yearbooks,* 2 vol. (Highland Park, NJ: Guyphon Press, 1972).

Clinton I. Chase, *Measurement for Educational Evaluation,* 2nd ed. (Reading, MA: Addison-Wesley, 1978).

Louis J. Karmel and Marylin O. Karmel, *Measurement and Evaluation in the Schools,* 2nd ed. (New York: Macmillan, 1978).

Arnold J. Lien, *Measurement and Evaluation of Learning,* 3rd ed. (Dubuque, IA: William C. Brown, 1976).

Gilbert Sax, *Principles of Educational Measurement and Evaluation* (Belmont, CA: Wadsworth, 1974).

Fred M. Smith and Sam Adams, *Educational Measurement for the Classroom Teacher* 2nd ed. (New York: Harper & Row, 1972).

CHAPTER EIGHT

ASSESSING INTELLIGENCE TO IMPROVE INSTRUCTION

IMPORTANT POINTS TO WATCH FOR

Multiple aptitude tests were developed to refine the assessment of intelligence by calling for a variety of "special" behaviors such as verbal reasoning, numerical ability, and mechanical reasoning.

Special aptitude tests help to assess specific intellectual behavior more thoroughly.

Individual intelligence tests are considered powerful tests of intellectual potential *and* instruments to assess the interaction of intelligence with personality factors.

Intelligence test results are often used along with results on achievement tests to compare *potential* for achievement with *actual* achievement.

Intelligence test results can help teachers set realistic expectations and determine the most effective learning strategies for children.

Intelligence tests can help teachers identify specific interests and activities and provide special curriculum activities to foster them.

General intelligence tests can give teachers important clues about children's emotional problems. Individual intelligence tests can then be used to further diagnose the specific problems.

Intelligence tests are valuable tools for predicting success and for educational and vocational guidance.

Observing and measuring intellectual behavior is essential to researchers as they continue to probe the nature and function of intelligence.

...we must come to an understanding of what meaning to give to that word so vague and so comprehensive, "the intelligence."[1]

—Binet, 1905

I look upon intelligence as an effect rather than a cause, that is, as a resultant of interacting abilities, nonintellective included. The problem confronting psychologists today is how these abilities interact to give the resultant effect we call intelligence.[2]

—Wechsler, 1958

It seems to us that in intelligence there is a fundamental faculty, the alteration or the lack of which, is of the utmost importance for practical life. This faculty is judgment, otherwise called good sense, practical sense, initiative, the faculty of adapting one's self to circumstances. To judge well, to comprehend well, to reason well, these are the essential activities of intelligence.[3]

—Binet, 1905

Intelligence, as a hypothetical construct, is the aggregate or global capacity of the individual to act purposefully, to think rationally, and to deal effectively with his environment.[4]

—Wechsler, 1939

These statements, made by two of the most important and productive contributors to our understanding of human behavior, point out dramatically the dilemma teachers face as they go about the task of assessing children's intelligence. The first and third statements were made by Alfred Binet and the second and fourth by David Wechsler. The statements are important because they span the years in which modern psychology has researched this vital human characteristic. They are important, also, because they express the dilemma each of these researchers faced as he went about the monumental search for the meaning of intelligence. The dilemma is this: how can we measure something we cannot even define? And if we can't define it, how can we be so presumptuous as to go blithely about the business of administering tests that supposedly reveal children's intelligence?

Binet devoted nearly all his professional life to studying the elusive concept of intelligence, and his first test, developed in 1905, was the pioneering instrument from which all subsequent intelligence testing arose. Wechsler has spent an equal number of years developing and refining his theories of intelligence, and he is still very much an active researcher and writer. His Wechsler-Bellevue Scale, published in 1939, is also a pioneering instrument, and his subsequent tests of intelligence for children and adults are undoubtedly among the most widely used individual intelligence tests in the world.

We have already briefly discussed intelligence in previous sections of this book. In Chapter 2, we described Piaget's developmental theory of cognitive growth, and in Chapter 7 we saw how one well-known intelligence test was standardized. We wish to begin this chapter with an emphatic reminder that the concept of intelligence, after all of the research and theorizing that has been done, is still just a hypothetical construct that we know (or think we know) exists, but about which we have no direct knowledge. After we finish this discussion of a human characteristic we know so little about, we will talk about the results of intelligence tests and how they can help teachers improve their teaching.

INTELLIGENCE AS A HYPOTHETICAL CONSTRUCT

Scientists have a way of explaining things they cannot define directly. Electricity, for instance, is a familiar phenomenon for which there is no direct definition. Instead, electricity must be described in terms of what it does. As scientists observe it in action, they build descriptions of it by applying terms such as current, negative, positive, electron, proton, and so forth. By using these words to describe the activity, or behavior, of electricity, scientists form verbal *constructs* by which they attempt to understand its nature. The constructs, in time, help them form *hypotheses* about electricity—tentative conclusions based on the electrical activity observed and described. As knowledge about electricity grows, through observation and experimentation, the hypotheses also change, and new information makes the previous description obsolete. Until scientists acquire conclusive evidence as to the exact nature of electricity, its definition will remain tentative and subject to change—a *hypothetical construct*. Other phenomena such as nerve conduction and many of the functions of the brain are defined as hypothetical constructs, so conclusions about the nature of these functions must remain tentative until more is known about them. Although such a dearth of precise definitions may seem discouraging, practically all well-defined phenomena were once hypotheses that were constructed from evidence available at the time. The shape of the earth, the existence of other galaxies, the theory of flight, radio, and television were painstakingly constructed as hypothetical constructs and were the subjects of intensive research and experimentation before tentative conclusions gave way to factual understanding and definitions.

Intelligence, too, is a hypothetical construct defined not as a thing with clearly describable parts but in terms of the current understanding of its function. From observations of behavior, psychologists have inferred the presence of the human quality or characteristic they have named intelligence. Often, the behaviors, too, are hypothetical constructs invented for a better understanding and description of the process of intelligence. Binet, for instance, considered that intelligence was composed of a variety of mental functions including judgment, comprehension, and reasoning. Each of these functions is also a hypothetical construct—each described or defined in terms of what its role is understood to be in human behavior. A half-century later, David Wechsler described intelligence as the individual's capacity for purposeful action and rational thinking, two intellectual activities also defined in operational rather than direct terms.

It would seem, then, that the most intriguing and vital characteristic in human nature is perhaps the most difficult to understand. Throughout the life of modern psychology, this elusive construct has challenged the most determined researchers—and won. However, this does not mean that the continuing attempts to assess and measure intelligence are misled or misguided. Much as scientists have come to agree about and to master the properties of electricity, psychologists and researchers, despite their differences, have produced a body of language and common understanding about intelligence that is shared by most individuals working with the concept. Already, the large body of operational definitions that has evolved in the study of intelligence has laid a reasonably firm foundation for statements about a child's better-than-average or less-than-average ability.

THE LANGUAGE OF INTELLIGENCE

Teachers use the language of intelligence almost constantly as they discuss children's progress and as they work to find ways to help children grow and learn. The pioneers in the search for the meaning of intelligence are largely responsible for its language. A review of their contributions is essential to an understanding of the concept.

Binet and Simon — The First Intelligence Scale and the Concept of Mental Age

Binet thought of intelligence as a global concept by which individuals received thousands of stimuli from the environment and by sifting and sorting, organizing, and reorganizing, accepting and rejecting these stimuli, individuals could adapt and direct them. Although he wondered, as the quotation at the beginning of this chapter indicates, "what meaning to give to that word so vague and so comprehensive . . .," he was pragmatic enough not to get bogged down by years of theoretical research. Instead, he went ahead on the assumption that something called intelligence existed, and he began to experiment with ways to measure it.

Just as Freud did much of his pioneering work in the field of mental health by studying mental patients, so did Binet begin his study of intelligence. At first, he was concerned not with discovering a way to quantitatively measure intelligence, but with finding some way to classify the degrees of abnormality he observed in his patients. His 1905 scale, developed with his partner Simon, was an attempt to do just that, and it yielded the now famous classification of mentally retarded children as idiots, imbeciles, and morons. The scale consisted of 30 tests in ascending order of difficulty. Items at the beginning were simple tests of physical response to stimuli such as following a moving object with the eyes, grasping a small object that is touched, and grasping a small object that is seen. The scale became progressively more difficult, and the concluding items required the definitions of abstract terms, a cognitive task of high order by today's standards.

The 1905 scale was a sort of standardizing effort somewhat like that described in Chapter 7, based on a sample population of 100 normal

Culver Pictures

ALFRED BINET

Alfred Binet was born in Nice, France, in 1857. He later went to school in Paris and received a law degree in 1878. Practicing law did not appeal to Binet, and he soon decided to go back to school. In 1890 he recevied a degree in the natural sciences, and in 1894 he earned his Ph.D. in science. His doctoral thesis was on the nervous system of insects. During the time he was working on his doctorate, Binet became deeply interested in hypnosis, and in 1886 he published a book on the subject, showing the effect of different suggestions on subjects in both the hypnotic and waking states. He published another book in 1886 on the general topic of reasoning and intelligence. Later he would devote all his time to the pursuit of knowledge in this field.

In 1902 Binet wrote another book on intelligence, using as his basic data the thinking processes displayed by his two teen-age daughters. He would give a reasoning problem to his daughters and analyze the steps they took to reach a solution. Though he found that they attacked and solved some problems in the same way, he noted marked differences in their approach to other problems. In his own immediate family Binet thus observed the pervasiveness and importance of individual differences.

When in 1904 the French minister of public instruction announced his wish to identify and place in special schools those children who were mentally retarded, it was no wonder that Binet took on the challenge. This was a situation made to order for a student of individual differences. He asked for and was granted an appointment to the special committee being set up for this purpose. If children who could not seem to profit from regular schooling were to be placed in special classes, a device or technique had to be developed to identify these children. Binet argued that the diagnostic technique should be intellectual, not medical. It had been the practice in France to use physicians to diagnose mental retardation, since retardation was believed to be a physical condition. Binet pointed to the errors and inconsistencies which occurred in these medical diagnoses. If a child were seen by three different physicians on three successive days, three completely different medical diagnoses would result from these examinations.

Thus in 1905 Binet, with a collaborator named Theodore Simon, published the first real intelligence scale. For their test, Binet and Simon assembled a series of intellectual tasks, rather than the sensory-motor tasks that Galton had used. Binet felt that

Adapted and used with permission of Norman and Richard Sprinthall, authors of *Educational Psychology: A Developmental Approach* 2nd ed. (Reading, MA: Addison-Wesley, 1977).

intelligence was displayed in one's ability to make sound judgments, rather than in one's ability to react quickly to a physical stimulus. Binet thus took intelligence out of the medical-physiological realm and placed it in the intellectual-psychological area.

In 1908 Binet revised his original test, retaining the best items from the 1905 scale and adding a number of new tasks. In scoring this 1908 test, Binet utilized a new term, *mental age*. The test would not be scored simply on the basis of the number of items a child passed, but rather in reference to age standards. Binet's scoring technique thus defined intelligence as a *developmental* rather than a *static* concept.

In 1911, shortly before Binet's untimely passing, a second and final revision of the Binet-Simon test was published. This test was a further re-finement of the original scale, again substituting new items for previous items that had failed to predict which children would or would not profit from the school experience.

Binet's death in 1911 shortened a career just reaching full bloom. It is certain that many of the controversies that erupted in the field of intelligence would have been lessened had Binet lived long enough to complete his work. For example, Binet believed that intelligence was not just a fixed, immutable individual trait, but rather a developing, trainable, dynamic cluster of abilities that could be nourished or stifled as a result of environmental inputs.

Binet's contribution to educational psychology was enormous. If a man's work can be measured by the amount of research his work has generated, Binet must stand near the very top in psychology.

---

children and an unknown number of retarded youngsters. Three years later, a revised test of 58 items was published, and this 1908 scale generated the concept we know as mental age. Binet and Simon noted that certain groups of questions could typically be answered correctly by a majority of children of certain ages. A child of three who could answer a specified number of questions from the first section of the scale was said to have a mental age of 3. Children who answered fewer were assigned a lower mental age, and those who answered more were assigned a higher one. This concept is still very much with us in contemporary testing.

Binet and Simon, then, contributed the extremely important concepts of objective intelligence testing and mental age. In addition, their description of the functions of intelligence, particularly those of reasoning, judgment, and comprehension, became the foundation language to which so many later theorists added their own theoretical definitions. Their description of intelligence as a global process using a variety of cognitive functions was the first of a series of operational definitions by a long line of researchers, some very dogmatic and some very thoughtful and tentative, who laid claim to adequate definitions.

Charles Spearman—The Two-factor Theory of Intelligence

Charles Spearman[6] made his contribution to the search for the meaning and nature of intelligence mostly during the 1920s. His statistical analysis of the ways in which various cognitive functions seem to relate to each other led him to perceive what he thought to be a "general" factor of intelligence. He called this "g" and theorized that it was an underlying *general intelligence* common and necessary to all intellectual functioning. He also noted that other, less important factors of intelligence seemed to be present and were specific to the particular function being measured. A test of reasoning, for instance, was seen to require some intellectual activity very specific to the process of reasoning while also requiring a much larger portion of general intelligence. In the same way, a test of memory was thought to require an intelligence factor specifically related to the process of memory, along with the all-important general factor.

Spearman's theoretical description of intelligence, then, posits two factors, one, the vital general intelligence (g) and the other, the less important specific factors (s) for each of the specific intellectual activities thought to make up the intelligent process. The higher mental functions were thought to require more of the universal g, and individuals who functioned well at high levels were thought to be more intelligent than those who had to rely on many s's.

Spearman was really searching for what he thought was a "unitary" theory of intelligence, one that would prove that *only* g was present in all intellectual functioning. His admission that many s's also seemed to be present led to his contribution of the two-factor theory, one that provided yet another theoretical construct of intelligence along with new language and the use of statistical procedures for discovering the presence of cognitive ability.

L. L. Thurstone — The Theory of Primary Mental Abilities

Where Spearman theorized and then experimented to prove his theory, Thurstone[7] went the other way and built his theory on the basis of intensive study of the correlations worked out by Spearman. Although Spearman's use of correlation procedures to discover the relationship of intelligence to various kinds of intellectual functioning was a major contribution to the mathematical study of intelligence, Thurstone went much further and developed the process of multiple-factor analysis. This was a more rigorous way of examining how various mental activities related to each other, and it led to his conclusion that at least eight separate factors were involved in intelligent functioning. He thus took Spearman's universal, g, and found within it a number of factors he called Primary Mental Abilities (PMA). These included spatial visualization, perceptual ability, verbal comprehension, numerical ability, memory, word fluency, and reasoning.

One researcher often takes the findings of a predecessor and brings to bear more sophisticated procedures to prove, disprove, or modify them. Binet and Simon made their major contributions during the first decade of this century; Spearman made his in the 1920s and Thurstone in the 1930s. Each built upon the one before and each significantly changed our understanding of the nature of intelligence. As the explanation of intelligence became more complex, so did the language and the procedure for examining it. From Binet's global theory to Thurstone's multifactor theory, in less than 30 years, many new terms and extremely sophisticated mathematical formulas evolved for discovering more factors of intelligence.

Raymond Cattell—The Theory of Crystallized and Fluid Intelligence

Not all researchers were caught up in the race to discover multiple factors of intelligence. Raymond Cattell[8] was a student of Spearman's, and his research led him to theorize that his teacher's universal, g, was, in reality, two universal g's. He called the first *fluid intelligence* and considered this essentially are inherited potential. The second he called *crystallized intelligence*, a function of educational and cultural opportunity working to modify or to fulfill the potential of fluid intelligence.

Crystallized intelligence, since it is largely formed by experience, contributes to the acquisition of skills and abilities important to problem solving and educational success. These include good verbal facility, a wide range and selection of memories, mathematical ability, and, in short, an abundance of cultural experiences that are the heart and substance of intelligence tests.

Fluid intelligence, since it seems to be inherited, is relatively free of cultural influence, and undergirds activities that do not require specific, educationally acquired experiences or skills. For instance, the solution of problems calling for spatial perception or for speed of perception would be heavily dependent on fluid intelligence.

A significant assumption underlies Cattell's construct of intelligence: intelligence is a product both of inheritance and environment. This is an important point since these were the peak years of the nature-nurture controversy, and hereditarians and environmentalists fought for acceptance of their respective theories of the origins of intelligence.

Cattell's contribution was his challenge to the unitary factor of general intelligence. He contended that no matter how many individual factors of intelligence are finally discovered, they will all be seen to derive from one of two very broad group factors, that which is inherited and that which is a product of the environment.

J. P. Guilford — The Structure of Intellect

It seems that the more the function of intelligence was examined the more factors seemed to be present. Thurstone's eight or ten traits of Primary Mental Ability is one example of this. Subsequent researchers, particularly J. P. Guilford,[9] subdivided Thurstone's traits even further and developed a construct of intelligence composed of no fewer than 120 traits.

Previously, the structure of intelligence was thought to be in the nature of a hierarchy, with the higher, broader functions (abstract reasoning for instance) encompassing the lower such as verbal or mathematical ability. The lower functions were eventually thought to encompass even lesser abilities such as word memory and computation skills. The hierarchy was originally derived by mathematically relating the results of specific aptitude tests with tests that were thought to measure the higher mental processes. If a correlation was found between general verbal intelligence and word fluency, the latter, as a function of intelligence, might be considered to be contained in the former. It can readily be seen how each trait might contain traits of ever decreasing order.

Guilford theorized that each measurable trait of intelligence was important and unique, and those that seemed, on the surface, to be narrower in function than others were not necessarily contained in the latter. Rather, each should be considered as a full partner in the overall functioning of intellect.

His "structure of intellect" is complex and is constructed from his own hypothetical assumption that the growing list of mental factors discovered by Thurstone and his successors could be made to yield a large but manageable list of traits. He began by asking what sort of *operation* was involved in each factor, and he arbitrarily determined that five such operations could be considered. They were cognition, memory, divergent thinking, convergent thinking, and evaluation.

After deciding which *operation* a given factor, such as memory, was performing, he asked a second question. What are the *contents* that are acquired by the *operation* considered in the first question? For instance, what kind of information is processed or stored away or acted upon as we use the operation called memory in the learning process? Guilford estimated that four kinds of *contents* could be involved: figural, symbolic, semantical, and behavioral.

After determining which *content* was associated with which *operation*, Guilford asked a third question. What are the mental products that are the result of the *operations* that were performed on the *contents*? In other words, what do we learn from the process of applying our various factors of intelligence? The outcomes, or products, are thought to be the following six: units, classes, relations, transformations, and implications.

The three questions asked by Guilford resulted in five *operations* performed by the intellect, four *contents* upon which the intellectual operations may be performed, and six intellectual *products* that combine to form the three-dimensional "structure of intellect" shown in Fig. 8.1. Multiplying the five operations by the four contents and then multiplying that result by the six products yields the 120 separate traits of intelligence that Guilford thought made up the total function of the intellect. His contribution to our understanding of the nature of intelligence is based on his rejection of the unitary theory of Thurstone and on his sophisticated statistical analysis of the relationships among the traits. After developing his theory of 120 traits, he went about the process of verifying their existence by the statistical procedure of factor analysis. At this writing, all but about 20 traits have been verified.

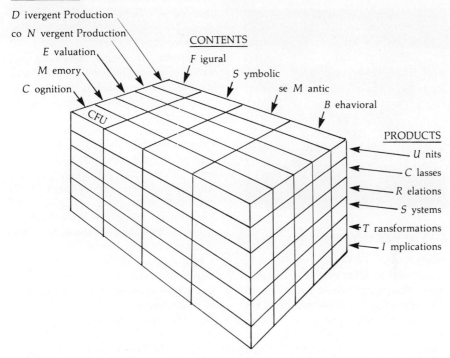

OPERATIONS

D ivergent Production
co *N* vergent Production
 E valuation
  M emory
  C ognition

CONTENTS

F igural
 S ymbolic
  se *M* antic
   B ehavioral

CFU

PRODUCTS
U nits
C lasses
R elations
S ystems
T ransformations
I mplications

Fig. 8.1 Structure of intellect cube. (Reprinted from *Psychological Bulletin*, No. 52, 1956, by J. P. Guilford.)

David Wechsler — Nonintellective Factors in Intelligence

We quoted David Wechsler in the beginning of this chapter as saying that intelligence was the global capacity of individuals to deal effectively with their environment. In part, he was echoing Binet, whose own global definition at the turn of the century made clear his view that measured intelligence was only one of three components necessary to an adequate assessment of intelligence. Only when the educational and medical components were integrated with the results of the psychological tests could a complete and global assessment be made.

The inclusion of personality and other nonintellective traits such as motivation and drive in describing intelligence was not accepted by most theorists who followed Binet. Not until the 1930s did David Wechsler conclude that intelligence could not be considered as separate and distinct from the total personality. His extensive clinical work at New York's Bellevue Hospital afforded him the opportunity to observe and test individual patients for whom relatively complete psychological assessments had been made. This led him to think that test scores alone could not be adequate to a full understanding of intelligence. In 1940, he said, "As soon as one attempts to define general intelligence in terms other than test

DAVID WECHSLER

Wechsler was born in Lespedi, Roumania, in 1896, one of seven children. His family moved to New York City when David was six years old. He attended the New York public schools and in 1916 graduated from the College of the City of New York. Following college, he immediately enrolled in the graduate psychology program at Columbia, doing his M.A. thesis under R. S. Woodworth in 1917. With America's entry into World War I, Wechsler was drafted into the army. While awaiting his induction he joined the great Harvard psychologist E. G. Boring at Camp Yaphank in Long Island and helped to administer and score the recently developed Army Alpha intelligence test. Because of his training in psychology, and especially because of his work with Boring on the Alpha test, Weschsler, after his own induction, was sent by the army for basic training in the School of Military Psychology at Camp Greenleaf in Georgia. He was then assigned to Fort Logan, Texas, where his duties included testing thousands of recruits on

the Army Individual Performance Scales, the Yerkes Point Scale, and the Stanford-Binet IQ test.

During this time, Wechsler became increasingly impressed by the disparity often shown between a man's tested intelligence and the quality of his previous work record. Often a man would test at a very low level on the various assessment devices, yet his past history indicated that he had been quite successful on his civilian job. The same man often proved later to be extremely competent in performing his military duties. Wechsler began to question the validity of the tests, especially the Stanford-Binet with its high verbal content. Perhaps the Binet test did predict success or failure in school, but it was proving to be less effective in predicting performance in the military. Wechsler concluded that perhaps by emphasizing the intellectual component, the Stanford-Binet was missing other aspects of a person's makeup which may contribute to one's overall intelligent behavior. These ideas, however, were not fully solidified, nor did they result in public expression until 1939, with the publication of Wechsler's own intelligence test.

In 1919 the Army sent Wechsler to France and later to England, where, at the University of London, he had the rare opportunity of working with both Spearman and Pearson. From Spearman, Wechsler learned of the two-factor theory of intelligence, "g" and "s", and from Pearson he was schooled in statistical techniques, especially the techniques of correlation.

Wechsler was discharged from the army in August 1919 and then applied

Adapted and used with permission of Norman and Richard Sprinthall, authors of *Educational Psychology: A Developmental Approach* 2nd ed. (Reading, MA: Addison-Wesley, 1977).

for and won a fellowship for study in France. From 1920 to 1922, he studied at the University of Paris and at the Laboratory of Psychology at the Sorbonne. During this time he met both Theodore Simon and Pierre Janet.

In 1922 Wechsler returned to the United States, where he became both a part-time graduate student in psychology at Columbia and a staff psychologist at the Bureau of Child Guidance. In 1925 he received his Ph.D. degree from Columbia.

From 1925 to 1932 Wechsler worked in private practice as a psychologist. During this period he also worked part-time for the Psychological Corporation, the company which was later to publish the tests that bear his name.

In 1932 he became chief psychologist at New York's Bellevue Psychiatric Hospital, and in 1933 he also joined the faculty at New York University's College of Medicine. From this point on, Wechsler devoted much of his energy to the creation of a new intelligence test, a test that would be suitable for adults (which the Stanford-Binet wasn't), and a test that would tap performance as well as verbal factors. After trying out many items from previous tests, and also creating new items of his own, Wechsler produced in 1939 the now-famous Wechsler-Bellevue Intelligence Scale. Concurrently, he published *The*

Measurement of Adult Intelligence, a book in which he brought together all his ideas on the question of intelligence and how it should be measured. He defined intelligence as "the global capacity of an individual to think rationally, to act purposefully, and to deal effectively with his environment." He saw intelligence, thus, not as a narrow capacity but as a global capacity that includes emotional and motivational as well as intellectual components. Wechsler did not separate intelligence from other personality factors.

In 1949 he developed the Wechsler Intelligence Scale for Children (WISC), and in 1955 he revised his adult test, calling it the Wechsler Adult Intelligence Scale (WAIS). In 1963 he introduced the Wechsler Preschool and Primary Scale of Intelligence (WPPSI), a test designed for children of ages four through six-and-a-half. Recently, Wechsler introduced a new version of the WISC, called the WISC-R. The WISC-R was standardized on a sample group of 2200 children, including whites and nonwhites in approximately the same proportions as they are represented n the population.

Wechsler's name has become synonymous with intelligence testing in America. He is truly one of the great psychologists of our time.

---

scores, one is forced to conclude that intelligent behavior must involve something more than sheer intellectual ability." and a few years later, in 1943, he added, "As soon as one attempts to appraise intelligence—test ratings in terms of global capacity, that is, the ability or abilities to deal effectively with any and all rather than specific situations, it becomes strikingly evident that even our best tests of intelligence give only incomplete measures of the individual's capacity for intelligent behavior."[10]

Wechsler's first intelligence test the Wechsler-Bellevue Scale, was published in 1939 and was followed later by revised versions for both children and adults. These individually administered tests reflected the recognition that more than verbal ability was involved in intelligence. A nonverbal section was included that assessed the individual's ability to perform such nonverbal tasks as picture completion, block design, picture arrangement, and object assembly. Thus separate I.Q. scores could be obtained for both verbal and nonverbal intelligence. Although the two were thought to be separable, they were also thought to interact with each other, and a composite I.Q. was computed that reflected this interaction of intelligence factors.

Wechsler's contributions to our understanding of the nature of intelligence can best be described as a verification and refinement of Binet's original concept of intelligence as a global process, one that consists not only of cognitive or intellectual factors but also of affective ingredients such as personality, attitudes, motivation, and drive. Further, the intellectual and nonintellective factors interacted dynamically to produce the global behavior described as "intelligent."

It is interesting to note that Binet, one of the very first, and Wechsler, one of the very current giants in the study of the nature and assessment of intelligence, both spoke of its global nature. Both were sensitive to the need for describing intelligence in the context of the total personality and both considered the single I.Q. score as inadequate for a full assessment of general intelligence. Binet's and Wechsler's careers span nearly a century, virtually the entire history of modern psychology, and their monumental efforts are the cornerstones of our understanding of the nature and function of intelligence. Although intelligence cannot yet be defined in precise and quantitative terms, Binet and Wechsler have clarified many assumptions about the existence of this capacity to learn. The functional definition of intelligence as the capacity for intellectual work and social and emotional adaptation provides a firm base from which to assess, understand, and describe the intelligent behavior of children.

USING INTELLIGENCE TESTS TO IMPROVE INSTRUCTION

We hope that with an understanding of the operational definitions of intelligence and their evolution, teachers will approach the assessment of intelligence with both caution and optimism. The knowledge that intelligence cannot be defined in concrete terms or observed directly should help teachers realize that statements and judgments about a child's I.Q. or general ability must be made with that knowledge in mind. In a later chapter, we will show how unfortunate and, perhaps, unprofessional judgments have led to some rather strident criticisms of testing in general.

On the other hand, the contributions of the individuals we have just discussed have provided very useful ways of determining both general and special abilities. In spite of their theoretical nature, the findings of these researchers have proved to be of great practical value in looking for ways to assess intelligence and improve teaching strategies. Understanding the nature of intelligence, as it is currently defined, along with some knowledge of how it is measured and interpreted, provides teachers with important tools for helping children make the most of their intellectual potential.

Tests of General Intelligence (Group)

In Chapter 7 we discussed at length one test of general intelligence (the Henmon-Nelson), and we described the process by which tests are standardized. Such tests are useful in gaining some understanding of a child's overall ability to succeed in academic work. The discussion of Binet and others suggests that such tests were designed by psychologists who feel strongly about the role played by some universal factor of intelligence that they think is present (to one degree or another) in all cognitive activities. Most psychologists, whether or not they completely accept this concept, agree that such tests can be used effectively as screening instruments.

Since most tests of general intelligence cover a wide range of activities, from simple recall to high-level abstract thinking, they give an indication of the *kinds* of cognitive ability youngsters have. For instance, Tomilee, who has an excellent vocabulary and who is also interested in literature, may do very well on certain sections of the test requiring verbal memory and usage. Her answers will verify this impression of her verbal abilities, but they might also reveal that she does not do well in mathematical reasoning. This initial picture of Tomilee's general ability should prompt her teacher to look more deeply into the possible reasons for the difference between her language and mathematics performance. A typical mistake teachers make at this point is to accept the I.Q. score as a final description of her ability.

A more professional approach would be to begin asking some questions. Is Tomilee's relatively low score in arithmetic reasoning the result of lesser aptitude in that area? Or is it the result of fewer or weaker experiences in arithmetic than in language areas? Does it have to do with motivation or perhaps some emotional rejection of mathematical activity? Whatever the reasons, her teacher must try to determine the causes for the discrepancy, particularly if the difference is a significant one. If the teacher can decide, on the basis of this single screening device, that Tomilee's problem with arithmetic reasoning can be solved by specific kinds of arithmetic enrichment such as tutoring, the general intelligence test has been valuable. It has pointed out an area of apparent weakness in which the teacher can intervene by tutoring her, encouraging her, giving her more homework, trying innovative approaches to teaching arithmetic, or signing a contract with her calling for more arithmetic production. The strategies for improving her behavior in arithmetic are limited only by the imagination of a creative teacher.

Whatever action is taken, it will not include the acceptance of her arithmetic reasoning I.Q. as final, even though future evaluation might prove that to be the case. There is too much evidence about the effects of experience on current learning to justify the assumption that a single I.Q. score tells the whole story.

Of the many tests of general intelligence, most are group tests designed to save time, and all have been carefully standardized to test a general ability to solve intellectual problems in light of experience. Although they have grown directly out of the theory that a unifying factor of general intelligence is important to all cognitive functioning, most reflect the recognition that language and nonlanguage ability need to be assessed separately. Thus, general intelligence usually include items stressing both language and nonlanguage material.

Multiple Aptitude Tests

Our brief history of the search for the meaning of intelligence pointed out the gradual shift away from the single-factor theory to a theory of intelligence as a many-faceted construct. When Spearman postulated his unifying g while recognizing the presence of many related s's, he was paving the way for further research into the multifactor theory of intelligence. Currently, the most prevalent view of intelligence in America recognizes the presence of several so-called "group factors." Thurstone led the way toward this concept with his listing of eight or ten "primary mental abilities," each permitting the individual to perform certain rather broad categories of behavior. For instance, one of the original primary mental abilities, "verbal comprehension," seemingly plays an important role in such activities as reading comprehension, verbal analogies, and verbal reasoning. Predictably, this factor is assessed by vocabulary tests. Another factor, called "number," seems to be necessary to the accurate and speedy solution of simple arithmetic problems. Thurstone thought a third, "perceptual speed," played an important role in perceiving visual similarities and differences.

Thurstone's "primary mental abilities" have been expanded in number by later psychologists, such as Guilford with his theory of 120 separate traits of intelligence. The work of such researchers has led not only to the multifactor theories of intelligence but also to the development of tests of multiple aptitude to assess the factors themselves. The Differential Aptitude Test mentioned earlier is one example of such an instrument currently in wide use to measure the facets of verbal reasoning, numerical ability, abstract reasoning, clerical speed and accuracy, mechanical reasoning, space relations, spelling, and language usage.

While a test of general intelligence might be a preliminary indication of specific strengths or weaknesses, it will do so in only a general way. A multiple aptitude battery such as the DAT will further refine this initial assessment. (Depending on the school system, the DAT or some other multiple aptitude test might well be used *instead of* a general intelligence test.) The results of children's performance on the subtests will yield a more precise picture of their abilities in specific areas, clearly separated from other areas. Test batteries such as the Differential Aptitude Test (DAT), the Primary Mental Abilities (PMA), and the Guilford-Zimmerman Aptitude Survey are examples of the many multiple aptitude batteries available for group testing. All were designed to implement the multifactor theory of intelligence, and all have been carefully standardized in the same way as the Henmon-Nelson.

Special Aptitude Tests

If the information about Tomilee's arithmetic aptitude from the Differential Aptitude Test still seems inadequate, her teacher can then go to a special aptitude test that concentrates only on arithmetic ability.

This test will provide specific information about her ability to solve abstract problems, to perform simple arithmetic functions, or to think in terms of mathematical relationships. In this case, the factor of intelligence relating to mathematical reasoning as suggested by Thurstone (number, or numerical ability) is further broken down into factors within factors.

The growth of tests of special aptitude has been quite dramatic for two reasons. First, early general intelligence tests were heavily loaded with language since vocabulary and the effective use of language were considered to be essential to intelligent functioning. Because of this, such factors as mechanical and other nonverbal skills and abilities could not be assessed. Researchers soon discovered that success in life need not be dependent on verbal ability and that manual and vocational skills could be the means to success nonverbally. In addition, the increased emphasis on guidance activities in the schools led to the search for more adequate ways to measure vocational and occupational skills. This resulted in the development of tests to assess every conceivable special aptitude including mechanical speed, clerical ability, visual-motor coordination, manual dexterity, and visual and auditory perception.

In addition to the aptitudes involving sensori-motor activity, many others were identified, and tests were invented to assess them as well. We have already mentioned the Seashore Measure of Musical Talent. There are others to test artistic talent and creative ability. The list of special aptitude tests is formidable, and like the multiple aptitude batteries, they arose from the theory that intelligence consists of multiple factors rather than a single factor. Some are excellent tools that help teachers identify children's specific abilities and plan ways to enrich their lives and assure them a measure of success. Conversely, these tests also indicate that music or art, for example, may not be the route for a given child to travel.

The variety and diversity of available measuring instruments attests to the persistence of some 70 years' research into the nature and function of intelligence. It also serves as a reminder that intelligence is perhaps the single most important trait of concern to teachers, regardless of whether they view it as a *single* underlying inherited factor that transcends and permeates all cognitive behavior or as a *group* of factors, each performing a special function but related closely to all the others. Although the actual stuff of intelligence may never be known, it is clear, from first hand observation, what it *does*. It is the basis for cognitive activities such as reasoning, using judgment, solving problems in light of experience, seeing relationships, doing abstract thinking, perceiving accurately, structuring information, dealing effectively with the environment, exhibiting motor skill and sensory acuity, demonstrating motivation and drive, and so on. The language describing the *function* of intelligence has grown with the research, providing teachers with increasingly accurate ways to describe children's potential.

Individual Intelligence Tests

From time to time, the assessment of certain children's potential requires more refined procedures than group tests provide. In the case of Alice, for instance, an initial test of general intelligence erroneously indicated that she was retarded. An individual intelligence test, on the other hand, afforded the examiner an opportunity to observe her performance more closely. Tests of this kind are administered by specially trained examiners who know how to evaluate not only the rightness or wrongness of a child's answers, but also the *quality* of the answers. In the hands of a qualified professional, the *way* in which Alice answered the various questions yielded important clues about the reasons her intellectual potential appeared to be lower than normal. Even though her I.Q. score on the individual test was still quite low, the quality and nature of her responses clearly indicated the presence of serious emotional problems that had developed over several years. The examiner was able to determine that experience was a handicap to Alice's learning potential rather than a help.

The individual intelligence test, then, is considered not only as a powerful test of intellectual potential but also as a clinical instrument for uncovering emotional and other personality characteristics. As a standardized test of intelligence, it provides an objective measure of intelligence that is stated as an I.Q. As a clinical tool, it affords opportunities for interactions between psychologist and child not possible on group tests. These interactions provide more subjective information about the *qualitative* behavior of the child—information with which the examiner makes qualitative judgments about the child's personality structure.

We will mention these tests again in our chapter on personality assessment, but for now we would like to make the important point that personality characteristics often play a significant role in the way people learn and in the degree to which their innate potential is realized. As in Alice's case, the quality of personal growth and development can dramatically affect the measurement of intelligence and sometimes lead to I.Q. scores that do not represent the child's true intellectual capacity. Thus, Alice's measured performance on the tests combined with the examiner's assessment of the quality of her performance to provide an accurate assessment of her intellectual capacity.

The Binet and the Wechsler intelligence tests Like the general tests of intelligence, the two current and most widely used individual intelligence tests were also designed by Binet and Wechsler. The Stanford-Binet Intelligence Scale[11] is the direct descendent of the original Binet Scale of 1905. Refined and revised several times over the years, it still holds a place of great significance in the field of psychological testing. An analysis of its items shows that the test still reflects Binet's original belief that intelligent behavior is largely dependent upon good language acquisition and usage. Also evident is the deliberate exclusion of items that might test group or special factors of intelligence. Instead the scale shows that a single general factor of intelligence is assessed.

David Wechsler's original Wechsler-Bellevue Intelligence Scale,[12] published in 1939, has also been revised several times. Originally an instrument to measure adult intelligence, a version was later developed to measure the intelligence of children. Perhaps the major difference between the Wechsler and Binet is that the Wechsler recognizes, through a separate section of the test, the importance of a nonverbal or performance factor of intelligence.

Both the Wechsler and the Binet are widely used to obtain objective measures of intelligence as well as to assess the *quality* of intellectual performance. In addition, both are used to gain knowledge of personal growth and development. For this reason, both tests are used extensively as clinical instruments to diagnose strengths and weaknesses in both cognition and emotion. The tests maintain Binet's and Wechsler's long-standing belief that intelligence must be assessed as a global construct, intellect being only one of several dynamically interacting characteristics. Thus the tests require the examiner to delay judgment about a child's potential until intellectual behavior can be related to physical and emotional growth in the context of the individual's life experiences. In this respect, individual intelligence tests are invaluable diagnostic tools when teachers do not feel satisfied with the I.Q. score yielded by a group intelligence test.

REVIEWING THE USES OF INTELLIGENCE TESTS

With this background on the current meaning of intelligence and the major types of intelligence tests in use, we will briefly review the uses of these tests. The discussion must be prefaced with the reminder that I.Q. scores and mental ages are only objective expressions for the tenuous construct of intelligence. Each time teachers use such scores, they should recognize that such tests are not wholly adequate for describing cognitive ability.

Screening

The initial screening of individuals on the basis of a group general intelligence test can serve a variety of purposes. From the wide variations in scores, a teacher may wish to identify students clustered at either the lower or upper levels of the distribution. Since most children's scores will tend to cluster around an average score, those at the outer limits can be easily identified for further study.

Although the usual purpose of this kind of initial screening is to place students in particular curriculum tracks, the more important reason is to identify those who seem to deviate significantly from the average. An extremely low score, for instance, should send a teacher immediately to a more specific evaluation procedure, one that will verify or reject the initial assessment or shed further light on the reasons for the low score. An unusually high score should also be a signal to look more deeply into the child's potential. Such wide variations among children are most common at the lower grades. Later, when the measurement of intelligence seems to stabilize, such extreme scores should be cause for more concern.

Most group intelligence tests have sections devoted to both verbal and nonverbal functions. Each will yield a separate I.Q. score, sometimes with extreme differences between the two. This also is a signal to examine the nature of the discrepancy. Perhaps the child's experiences have been heavily loaded with language and few opportunities for motor development or the development of mechanical skills. Or, as is sometimes the case, the discrepancy may be an important clue to deeper problems, perhaps of an emotional nature.

We should emphasize that the *major* use of general intelligence tests for classroom teachers is to provide a first impression of children's cognitive potential, an impression that actually tells very little about the total child but that should be used as one input among several for evaluating behavior. Remember, a single score is not a definitive classification of intelligence.

Interpreting Academic Achievement

In the primary grades, the I.Q. is relatively unstable and may seem to change dramatically from one testing to the next. This is due to the wide variation in experiences young children bring with them to the testing situation. For this reason, comparing intelligence test results with the results on achievement tests is somewhat unreliable. Later on in the upper elementary grades and beyond, the experiences necessary to success on achievement tests are more similar to those for intelligence tests. Both require heavy portions of reading and language ability, and both are constructed of items consisting of material learned in school. Thus, a child who achieves high scores on an achievement test ought to do the same on the I.Q. test. Generally speaking, the two types of tests correlate quite well; that is, high achievement scores normally go along with high I.Q. scores.

Accordingly, when teachers assess their children's academic achievement, they need to know how closely the two measures correspond. For example, if Suzy's I.Q. score in grade five is 120, and her achievement test score is equal to that of a normal fourth grader, the scores suggest that she may not be learning as much or as well as she should. Such comparisons of intelligence and achievement scores provide teachers with diagnostic tools, to improve their instructional activities. Without the comparison, a teacher might well conclude that Suzy is achieving adequately and that special attention is unnecessary. The intelligence test score, then, helps teachers relate children's *actual* achievement to their *potential* for achievement, thus providing an important bit of information with which to individualize and strengthen instructional strategies.

Setting Expectations

With the general idea of each child's potential provided by the initial screening, teachers can begin the process of diagnostic teaching. By determining that Andrew, for instance, seems to function better on items requiring good vocabulary and language skills than on the nonlanguage section, a teacher might consider two long-range goals for him.

First, since the reading and other language activities in the regular curriculum will probably come relatively easy for him, his teacher should call for more advanced work from him than from some of the other children. He should be expected to read more books and more demanding books; he should be given writing and research projects to increase his vocabulary and build his skill in using language in more creative and meaningful ways. In short, since he is more capable than others in this area, his teacher should expect cognitive behavior of a higher order and quality. He should work harder and learn more, simply because he has the ability to do so.

Second, since he seems less able in the nonlanguage, or performance area, his teacher should be more cautious in assigning work in mathematics and other related subjects. His relatively low performance score will help determine the teacher's expectations of him *at least for the time being*. However, the teacher should watch his behavior closely to determine whether his performance ability is really lower than it might be or whether other factors such as motivation or experience are causing the lower score. As his behavior provides more and more clues to his probable performance ability, the teacher's expectations can become more definite. Simply by getting him involved in projects that require manual dexterity and physical coordination as well as the use of arithmetic to solve problems, the teacher might increase his interest, and he may become enthusiastic over a new area of activity.

Using group intelligence tests to set expectations and determine how children can best profit from school is only one source of evaluation. Along with daily observation, achievement test scores are particularly important since they help teachers compare real performance with the potential indicated on the intelligence test.

Identifying Special Aptitudes

Tests of special aptitude such as the Differential Aptitude Test help teachers follow up on the clues to special abilities indicated either by general intelligence tests or classroom behavior. With dozens of special aptitude tests available, teachers can assess a multitude of special abilities. Such tests are useful not simply to identify special aptitudes, but to help teachers set realistic and challenging expectations. One of the most important things such tests can do is provide the diagnostic information needed to make a student's learning experiences as productive and fulfilling as possible. By providing special curriculum and learning activities, teachers will keep students interested in learning and excited by it. Finally, they will be helping assure students a full measure of success later in life by recognizing and nurturing special talents as early as possible.

Identifying Problem Cases

Unfortunately, learning does not come easily for all children; for some it is downright discouraging. Limited intelligence, a wide array of emotional problems, and a variety of learning disabilities are some of the special problems that teachers must identify. By following up a particularly low score on the general intelligence test, teachers can prevent serious mistakes in judgment about a child's potential and help to identify the sources of the problem. For example, otherwise intelligent children have been mistakenly considered lacking in intelligence because other factors seriously inhibit the learning process. Such factors as emotional or personality problems as well as learning disabilities often make it difficult or impossible for a child to use certain cognitive modalities to their fullest. The learning disabilities include visual or hearing impairment, central nervous system dysfunction, and poor sensori-motor ability. All of these add physiological factors to the emotional factors that tend to limit the potential of the learning process. Both kinds of problems can be identified and diagnosed quite adequately with individualized intelligence tests such as the Binet and the Wechsler. Chapter 11 includes a fuller discussion of evaluation procedures for such "special" children.

Educational Guidance

The term guidance has acquired an extremely broad meaning in recent years. Formerly, it meant the process by which a high school guidance counselor helped students select a college appropriate to their needs and income. While some testing was done, generally the counselor examined the records of the students and met with them to discuss plans for college. They would look together at various college catalogs and make a decision based on something short of full information.

Until relatively recent years, guidance positions were filled by former teachers who did not necessarily have a background in psychological and educational assessment. Now, guidance counselors are more likely to have both teaching experience and additional academic and practical experience in learning and human behavior. Often they are skilled psychological examiners, capable of administering and interpreting both general and individual tests of intelligence. Their assessment of young people's strengths and weaknesses often gets them off to a good start in college. For counselors, the results of intelligence tests provide important information about the general as well as the special aptitude of secondary students and are helpful in guiding them toward intelligent college choices.

In addition to the role played by guidance counselors in college placement, commercial aptitude tests such the Scholastic Aptitude Test have also become commonplace predictors of academic success. In college, intelligence testing continues with graduate school admission policies nearly always requiring evidence of ability to do advanced academic work. The Medical School Aptitude Test (MSAT) or some other of a large variety of such instruments replaces the SAT at this level.

Guidance has also found its way into the school learning environment where intelligence test results are used as diagnostic and placement tools. Guidance counselors and school psychologists are available to children and teachers throughout the elementary and secondary grades. They play an important role in determining appropriate curricula and grade placements at all levels, and their interpretation of intelligence test scores helps the teacher in diagnosing intellectual strengths and weaknesses.

Vocational Guidance

In addition to guiding students toward college, counselors have become important resource persons for those who choose vocational or occupational careers. They are able to help young people make intelligent choices partly on the basis of vocational test results. There are dozens of these available, and they are examples of the special aptitude tests we have spoken about. Tests of mechanical ability, tests of clerical speed, tests of manual dexterity, tests of commercial and business aptitude—all are designed to identify those aspects of intelligence that might serve the student well in years to come.

Beyond the schools and into the world of work, business and industry use a bewildering array of aptitude tests in the selection and placement of job candidates and in consideration for promotion to more advanced jobs. Selecting, classifying, placing, diagnosing, and evaluating people to find out how intelligent they are or what specific kinds of intelligence or aptitude they have has become an inherent feature in work as well as school. In all these areas, professional and responsible use of tests is essential.

Research

The value of intelligence testing for research cannot be underestimated. Research into the nature of intelligence led directly to the development of the tests themselves. The results of those first Binet-Simon scales in turn provided the important data that led to the theory that more than a unitary or general factor of intelligence was responsible for learning. Thus emerged the tests of multiple aptitude and then the myriad of special aptitude tests of which we have spoken. These in turn have generated even more data about how intelligence seems to function, and they have provided more information for those who continually probe the complexities of human behavior for clues about the intellect.

In addition to studies into the nature of intelligence itself, extremely important research is now being done that has already had enormous impact in the field of social science. Intelligence test results are helping psychologists probe the effects on intelligence of such factors as the individual's environment and physiology. Of particular importance are studies currently under way that are attempting to determine the degree to which inheritance affects intelligence. One researcher, for instance, has suggested that Blacks generally score lower on I.Q. tests because they are genetically less intelligent to begin with; that is, they have inherited less general cognitive ability than members of other racial groups. We will discuss this theory and the controversy it aroused in a later chapter.

In these and other current studies, intelligence scores are believed to be the concrete evidence of intelligence at work, and the behavior of those who take the tests is observed even more carefully than the scores themselves. Observing the function of intelligence through behavior of individuals is the only way in which researchers can theorize about its nature. The more they learn, of course, the more information becomes available to classroom teachers.

All of the above, as well as other uses of I.Q. scores, are examples of the ways in which the measurement of intelligence assists in understanding the nature and function of intelligence. Whether a standardized group test of intelligence is administered to a fourth grade class, a test of clerical accuracy to a high school senior, or a test of manual dexterity to a factory worker, the result is generally the same. Intelligence tests are used to provide information about individuals' ability to perform cognitive functions. This information is but a single input among many in the task of evaluation. As Binet and Wechsler both have stated, intelligence is a global construct, its measurement requiring a variety of inputs including intelligence tests but also including such other inputs as physical and psychological examination. Thus to gain an adequate understanding of the global process of intelligence, teachers must maintain an emphasis on assessment and evaluation rather than testing. Testing alone simply yields arbitrary scores that have no meaning by themselves. When interpreted in the context of the personal, physical, and intellectual components of the individual, they become meaningful for assessing potential and making intelligent evaluations.

In spite of the many criticisms of the intelligence testing movement, then, we have gained much from the research of those who continue to search for better ways to understand and foster cognitive development. As we have said before, the fault of poor testing, measuring, and evaluating is not inherent in the instruments themselves but in the people who use them. Educators who understand how these instruments work and what the scores mean will assure children of the most effective program of tests, measurement, and evaluation.

IMPORTANT POINTS TO THINK ABOUT

1. As you examine the scores of fourth grade children on a general intelligence test, what clues might you discover that tell you of their individual potential strengths? If the test has both verbal and nonverbal sections, what results might suggest potential problems?

2. If you discover that Ted's nonverbal I.Q. score is 114 and you know he is succeeding in arithmetic at the third grade level, what further testing steps will you consider?

3. If Suzy's scores on a multiple-factor intelligence test indicate good arithmetic reasoning ability but poor verbal ability, how will you set realistic expectations for her?

4. If Jimmy's scores indicate good verbal as well as nonverbal intelligence but his academic performance is consistently low, how might an individual intelligence test help you find ways to encourage him to work up to his potential?

5. Can you make a statement in which you clearly describe the global nature of intelligence as set forth by both Binet and Wechsler?

NOTES

1. A. Binet, as quoted in J. D. Matarazzo, *Wechsler's Measurement and Appraisal of Adult Intelligence* (Baltimore: Williams and Wilkins, 1972), p. 66.

2. D. Wechsler, as quoted in J. D. Matarazzo, p. 74.

3. A. Binet, as quoted in J. D. Matarazzo, p. 66.

4. D. Wechsler, as quoted in J. D. Matarazzo, p. 79.

5. A. Binet and T. Simon, *The Development of Intelligence in Children* (The Binet-Simon Scale), translated by E.S. Kite (Baltimore: Williams and Wilkins, 1916).

6. C. Spearman, *The Abilities of Man: Their Nature and Measurement* (New York: Macmillan, 1927).

7. L. L. Thurstone, *Primary Mental Abilities*, Psychometric Monographs, No. 1 (Chicago: University of Chicago Press, 1938).

8. R. B. Cattell, "Theory of Fluid and Crystallized Intelligence: A Critical Experiment," *Journal of Educational Psychology* (1963).

9. Mary N. Meeker, *The Structure of Intellect: Its Interpretation and Uses* (Columbus, OH: Merrill, 1969).

10. D. Wechsler, as quoted in J. D. Matarazzo, p. 77.

11. A. Binet and T. Simon.

12. D. Wechsler, *Manual for the Wechsler Adult Intelligence Scale* (New York: The Psychological Corporation, 1955).

CHAPTER NINE

ASSESSING ACHIEVEMENT TO IMPROVE INSTRUCTION

IMPORTANT POINTS TO WATCH FOR

Achievement tests and intelligence tests both require experience for successful answers.

Achievement tests verify teachers' assessments of youngsters' intelligence or cognitive potential.

Most standardized achievement tests are norm-referenced. Children's scores on norm-referenced tests can be compared with those of a large standardizing group from which norms were developed.

Critics of standardized achievement tests point to several shortcomings of such evaluation instruments:

- They create a tendency to teach to pass the test.
- The subject matter on the tests is inadequately sampled.
- Factual matter is overemphasized.
- They provide limited diagnostic information.

Informal and teacher-made achievement tests are usually criterion-referenced. The scores on criterion-referenced tests can be used to evaluate and diagnose individual progress.

Carefully stated instructional objectives are vital to the construction of good criterion-referenced tests.

Item analysis is the process by which the usefulness of items on norm-referenced and criterion-referenced achievement tests is determined.

Norm-referenced and criterion-referenced achievement tests are not different kinds of tests. The difference lies in the way children's responses are interpreted.

Norm-referenced achievement tests are useful:

- To compare one group of children with others.
- To compare achievement with intelligence.
- To determine individual progress to a limited degree.
- To assess curricula and teaching strategy.

Criterion-referenced tests are useful:

- To diagnose learning.
- To diagnose and improve instruction.
- To determine individual progress.

ACHIEVEMENT AND INTELLIGENCE TESTS ARE OFTEN SIMILAR

In Chapter 6, we pointed out that achievement tests and certain intelligence tests seem very much alike. The questions on one often seem much like those on the other. Both are concerned with subject matter and experiences, and both require this information for successful answers. One well-known standardized achievement battery, for example, includes a test of mathematical computation. One of the items asks the children to solve the following:[1]

$$
\begin{array}{r}
532 \\
\times\ 32 \\
\hline
\end{array}
$$

f. 16,924
g. 2,660
h. 17,024
i. 17,004
k. NH

An equally well-known aptitude battery asks the children to solve this example:[2]

$$
\begin{array}{r}
484 \\
\times\ 25 \\
\hline
\end{array}
$$

A 2485
B 2486
C 2496
D 3486
E none of these

While these two items are so much alike that it would be impossible to determine which came from the intelligence test and which from the achievement test, others are more easily identified. For instance, the language section of the same achievement test includes this item:

Part of the folklore of the _____ is the story of Johnny Appleseed, an early settler.

5. United States
6. United states
7. united States
8. united states

Here is an item from the Verbal Reasoning section of the same aptitude battery:

19. .... is to potato as beater is to ....

   A. mashed — egg
   B. skin — steak
   C. skin — egg
   D. masher — winner
   E. masher — eggs

The achievement test item clearly calls for a bit of information taught in the language curriculum of all schools. To answer the item successfully, the child must remember one of the rules of capitalization and have achieved the reading skill and vocabulary necessary to understand the question.

The aptitude item also calls for the skill of reading and the acquisition of sufficient vocabulary, but it goes one step further. It asks the child to *apply* those common curriculum experiences to a relatively uncommon activity, that of making analogies. To decide that masher is to potato as beater is to egg requires the ability to see relationships among things and to apply information to solve a rather unique problem. Making analogies, seeing relationships, and solving new problems in the light of experience are functions of intelligence and considered fundamental to the learning process.

Further comparison of items from both kinds of tests would reveal that achievement tests usually ask students to remember previously acquired skills and information. While intelligence tests also ask for such memories, they ask additionally that certain kinds of cognitive functions be applied to the memories. As intelligence tests become more advanced, they will make more and more demands upon the higher cognitive processes of reasoning, judging, generalizing, and evaluating. Ability to perform these functions indicates the ability to perform even more complex and abstract functions in the future, thus enabling teachers to make statements about the child's *potential* to learn.

Achievement tests, then, differ from intelligence tests in that intelligence tests use information and skills gathered in the past to assess *future* potential, while achievement tests ask those being tested to show their accumulated knowledge and skills.

WE MEASURE ACHIEVEMENT BY MEASURING BEHAVIOR

Even though classroom teachers administer intelligence and aptitude tests they do so relatively infrequently, perhaps as seldom as once a year for group intelligence tests. Depending upon the results, a teacher might follow this test with a specific or a group aptitude test or decide that a child or two needs individualized assessment.

This in no way means that intelligence testing is less important than other evaluation techniques. On the contrary, it sets the stage and provides the guidelines for all other testing and measuring. As we indicated in the previous chapter, the measurement of intelligence helps teachers determine goals and plan learning activities for their children, goals stated in terms of expected behavior and learning activities planned to elicit it. The effectiveness of both the goals and the learning activities is, in turn, measured by the children's actual behavior.

STANDARDIZED ACHIEVEMENT TESTS

The Stanford Achievement Test described in Chapter 7 is one of a great many general achievement tests that have been developed and standardized for classroom use. The Stanford and others are really *batteries* of separate tests, each of which measures achievement in a specific area of the curricula. Eleven tests make up the Stanford; a listing of their titles will indicate the broad curricula coverage included in the total battery:

Test 1. Vocabulary
Test 2. Reading Comprehension
Test 3. Word Study Skills
Test 4. Math Concepts
Test 5. Math Computation
Test 6. Math Application
Test 7. Spelling
Test 8. Language
Test 9. Social Science
Test 10. Science
Test 11. Listening Comprehension

STANDARDIZED ACHIEVEMENT TESTS ARE NORM-REFERENCED TESTS

Nearly all standardized achievement batteries are norm-referenced tests. Standardization indicates that the test items have been carefully selected from the curricula of schools throughout the country and that children's scores can be compared to thousands of others from school systems in all major geographic regions of the country. For instance, third grade children who take the achievement test will be compared, on the basis of an average or norm established during the standardization process, with all third grade children in the standardizing group. Thus, if a child's score compares closely with the scores of children in the standardizing group at the 50th percentile, the child has achieved more than 50% of what the standardizing population did. The inference, since the standardizing group is supposedly a random sampling of all third grade children in the country, is that this child's achievement in school is better than that of 50% of all the third graders in the nation. The scores of the standardizing group, then, are the norms against which teachers compare their children.

Percentile rank is one way to represent norms. Grade equivalent is another; stanine scores yet another. Whenever norms such as these are used to describe children's behavior on standardized tests of achievement, the tests are called *norm-referenced* tests. They are valuable in helping teachers measure children's achievement as it compares with that of children throughout the nation.

As yardsticks against which to compare children's achievement, standardized achievement tests, when administered and interpreted in strict accordance with the instructions, provide useful information about how youngsters "stack up" against national norms.

STANDARDIZED TESTS IN SPECIAL AREAS

The Stanford Achievement Battery is essentially a survey or general achievement test. Its major purpose is to provide information about children's achievement from a cross section of the nation. The number of items written for any one subject is quite small. In the arithmetic tests given at the end of grade five and the beginning of grade six, the combined items in Math Concepts, Math Computation, and Math Application total 112. Given the enormous amount of math information children have achieved by the end of grade five, 112 items seems a very small sampling indeed. However, the sampling procedure that determines the number and nature of the items to be included is carried out just as carefully as is the sampling of the test population. The fact that math is only one of several subjects to be tested determines, in part, the shortness of each test in the total battery. For this reason, the achievement battery, like the general intelligence test, is often used as a screening device to identify apparent weak areas. When, for instance, a teacher discovers that a student's grade level scores on the math tests are somewhat lower than those of the national norms, the teacher might consider a more complete achievement test, this time only in math. Special achievement tests at all grade levels have been published in abundance for most subjects and for most skills, particularly tests of reading readiness.

LIMITATIONS OF STANDARDIZED ACHIEVEMENT TESTS

Standardized achievement tests, whether general batteries or tests of specific achievement, must be used in conjunction with other evaluation procedures. To use and interpret them in isolation will be much like using a single group intelligence test to assess cognitive ability.

The Tendency to Teach to Pass the Test

When teachers become too dependent upon standardized achievement tests, the tendency is to tailor instruction to the material on the tests.

Although teachers try not to, they come to be influenced by the subject matter they know is included. Thus arises the familiar criticism that schools tend to teach to pass tests. Considering the millions upon millions of standardized tests given each year, it is easy to imagine that schools sometimed *do* teach partly to pass tests. Perhaps this is understandable, given the importance of comparisons among children in various areas. Teachers always want to know that their children are doing as well as everyone else's. Too much dependence upon the results of standardized tests, then, tends to standardize teaching strategies and limit them to the skills and subjects sampled by the standardized tests.

Inadequate Sampling of Areas to be Tested

A second limitation is the small number of items for each skill or subject area. There is simply too much knowledge in the heads of a tenth grade class to be adequately sampled by 40 or 50 questions. There almost certainly will be many skills and areas of content that the sampling procedure misses.

Overemphasis on Factual Material

A third limitation is the heavy emphasis on factual material and the necessity of memorizing large amounts of material to be given back by rote. When too much emphasis is placed on rote memory, difficulties in relating these memories to new learning occur and development of the higher cognitive functions may suffer.

Limited Use for Diagnostic Purposes

Finally, the use of general achievement batteries for diagnostic purposes is very limited indeed. Often such batteries are administered at the beginning of the school year with a different form of the same battery given at the end of the year. The results of the first test are often used to "diagnose" children's achievement weaknesses, and the results of the second are used to measure the growth that has occurred during the year. If other, more specific tests are not used to further diagnose the weaknesses suggested by the general battery, diagnostic testing will be severely limited.

INFORMAL ACHIEVEMENT TESTING

In the chapter on teacher-made tests, we emphasized that the major testing, measuring, and evaluating procedures are carried on day after day by the teachers themselves. As important as standardized tests might be in the overall evaluation process, face-to-face relationships with children yield far more information about their growth and development than do standardized tests. Even though teachers' measurements are not "standardized" and as rigidly administered, they do what no other measurement technique can. They demonstrate how much and how well children are achieving, *not* in comparison with nameless and faceless children from other places, but in terms of their own unique and individual capacities and styles.

To understand just how important is the process of informal evaluation of achievement, teachers need only remind themselves that standardized tests are built upon just such teaching and learning behavior, since the items on these tests are taken from classroom material. In short, the behavior teachers observe daily is the behavior sampled by the test makers and then sent back to the schools as items on standardized tests.

INFORMAL AND TEACHER-MADE ACHIEVEMENT TESTS ARE USUALLY CRITERION-REFERENCED TESTS

We have said that standardized achievement tests are norm-referenced so that the scores obtained on the tests are examined with reference to national norms established by the test publishers. They are never examined with reference to the specific behavior of the child taking the test. When Suzy scores 87 on the spelling subtest of an achievement battery, the score is related to other 10 year olds who took the same test. If 87 translates to a grade equivalent of 4.6 or to a percentile rank of 58 or to a stanine score of 5, her achievement must be considered with reference to those norms and how they relate to her individual progress.

This limitation of standardized tests has given impetus to a relatively new approach to test construction. Most teachers want to know how each child is doing with reference to instructional objectives prepared for children in a particular classroom. Testing to discover how much and how well a child has achieved with reference to a given learning objective is called *criterion-referenced* testing.

CRITERION-REFERENCED TESTS AND INSTRUCTIONAL OBJECTIVES

In Chapter 3 we pointed out the need to set goals for effective teaching and evaluation. Carefully stated, long-range educational goals set the stage for the more specific instructional objectives of teaching units and of single lessons. These specific instructional objectives are one of the vital ingredients of the new and fast-growing evaluation technique of criterion-referenced testing.

Simply stated, a criterion-referenced test is one that measures a child's achievement in terms of a stated instructional objective. A teacher might decide, for instance, that one instructional objective for an arithmetic lesson is to teach the children to use lines of latitude and longitude to locate points on a globe. Stated in behavioral terms the objective might read:

> Using their understanding of latitude and longitude, the children will be able to locate on the globe 20 major cities of the world.

If it is desirable for children to have a success rate of 100%, this accuracy becomes the *standard*, or *criterion*, against which their behavior is measured. Any child who "measures up" to this criterion by locating all 20 cities is said to "meet the criterion." A child who locates only 17 of the cities falls short of the criterion.

Usually, teachers hope for 100% success but more realistically set the standard a little lower and reword the objective accordingly:

> Using their understanding of latitude and longitude, the children will be able to locate 16 out of 20 major cities in the world.

Stated in this way, the objective establishes a criterion or, standard of behavior, that not only can be met but that also can be exceeded. The degree to which youngsters meet or exceed the stated objective determines their success. Their behavior is described *with reference to the criterion that is established in the objective*.

In a very real way, teachers have been using a form of criterion-referenced evaluation for generations. Whenever they say that they expect children to learn the multiplication facts or be able to describe the duties of the Vice President of the United States, they establish criteria. They probably already have an idea which children will or will not meet the criteria, but they must constantly set standards for them.

However, in the strict sense of the term, the casual hope or expectation that the children will be able to learn certain things does not constitute the setting of a criterion. The criterion must be established clearly and precisely in the instructional objective. The instructional objective, in turn, must be stated *prior* to the actual instructional process. Teachers then observe children's learning behavior to determine the degree to which each has met the criterion.

THREE INGREDIENTS OF CRITERION-REFERENCED TESTING

Criterion-referenced testing, then, as currently defined involves three definite ingredients.

1. Learning behaviors to be demonstrated by children must be stated clearly and explicitly *prior to* the learning experiences themselves. (Example: The child will be able to punctuate a four-sentence paragraph.)

2. The acceptable levels of success must be stated explicitly. (Example: Punctuation must be done with 80% accuracy.)

3. Situations and conditions must be made available in which children can demonstrate how well they have met the criterion. In other words, teachers must either observe children's behavior carefully in the actual learning situation or they must construct a test by which to measure their success.

Before we describe criterion-referenced instruments that are more formal and produced commercially for class use, we need to make a few important points about norm referencing and criterion referencing.

NORM-REFERENCED AND CRITERION-REFERENCED TESTS ARE NOT DIFFERENT KINDS OF TESTS

So much controversy has been aroused about the shortcomings of norm-referenced tests and the usefulness of criterion-referenced tests that one might think the tests themselves are dramatically different from each other. This is not so. Many items on standardized achievement tests are nearly word for word the same as those on criterion-referenced tests designed by teachers. The important difference lies not in the items on the tests but in the interpretations of their answers. Since teachers test children to learn more about them, their interpretation of the answers on the tests is important in setting new objectives. In short, teachers make important judgments from children's test behavior.

JUDGMENTS FROM NORM-REFERENCED TEST RESULTS

Since norm-referenced or standardized achievement tests are constructed with items sampled from school curricula throughout a wide area, teachers must remember that judgments about individual children must be made with reference to the scores of the sample population. Judgments about spelling ability or Timothy's map reading skills with reference to their individual progress are limited with norm-referenced tests. Teachers can compare their responses only with those of the normative or sampling group; their judgments are then comparative in nature. Kim has achieved more than 70% of the population in spelling. Timothy knows more map skills than 80% of the children who took the test. However, this does not mean that Kim or Timothy should become complacent in these academic areas and relax their efforts. A teacher's judgment on the basis of their standardized achievement test answers is based on a sampling of test items that is very small compared with the enormous number that could be included if there were time to answer them all. The small number of items and the norm-referenced nature of the standardized achievement test signal the need for cautious judgment. The limitations do not destroy the usefulness of the standardized tests, but they restrict the usefulness to information of a comparative rather than a specific nature.

JUDGMENTS FROM CRITERION-REFERENCED TEST RESULTS

If teachers wish to know more specifically Kim's spelling ability or Timothy's map skills, they must use standards other than those of the national sample. Given the developmental nature of growth and learning and the fact that each child holds an ever-shifting position along this continuum of development, teachers' standards must be set with reference to *individual needs and abilities*. Although Kim may well be a better speller than 70% of the fourth graders in the country she may, in fact, be even better than that according to her personal continuum.

Robert Glazer[3] has described this learning continuum in a clear-cut and helpful way. He says that the achievement position of any given child can be related to a continuum of achievement that begins at the point of zero achievement and continues through the point of perfect achievement. In Timothy's case, for instance, the continuum of map reading skills begins at zero and proceeds through a series of developmental stages to the point of perfect map reading ability.

The various stages along the continuum might be labeled as percentages of perfection as in Fig. 9.1, or in terms of numbers of skills to be mastered at each point. The important thing is that the continuum of achievement is constructed directly from a teacher's instructional objectives. Perfect map skills does not mean the mastery of all map skills known to man. It means that a teacher has identified 20 specific map skills to teach during a unit on geography. As the unit begins, some children will stand at zero on the continuum while others will be found at various points depending on their experience with maps.

Judgments about any child's map reading ability are then made with reference to clearly stated objectives or levels of achievement. Each objective and each level becomes a criterion against which the teacher can compare the youngsters' responses. If the 40% point of the continuum includes 8 of the 20 map skills, it becomes a very simple matter to decide whether Timothy is exceeding the objectives. With reference to the criterion, in other words, Timothy's progress can easily be established and described. As the unit began, Timothy was found to know already 60% of the map skills to be taught throughout the unit (see Fig. 9.2).

The criteria set along a continuum, then, are based on an instructional objective so that the achievement of any child can be *referenced* to those criteria at any time. Thus teachers have the advantage of making judgments in terms of individual progress according to an essentially indi-

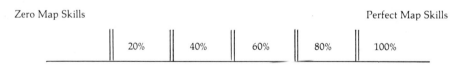

Zero Map Skills   Perfect Map Skills

20%   40%   60%   80%   100%

Figure 9.1

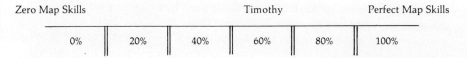

Figure 9.2

vidualized learning continuum for each child. Judgments from test items using this concept can be extremely helpful in evaluating individual progress and diagnosing individual behavior. The diagnosis, in turn, is vital in helping teachers set realistic objectives for each child.

HOW DO TEACHERS KNOW TEST ITEMS ARE APPROPRIATE AND USEFUL?

Item Analysis of Norm-referenced Tests

In Chapter 7, we showed how test publishers analyze the individual items on tests to determine their appropriateness and usability. Through a process called item analysis, each test question undergoes rigorous examination that will decide whether it will be included in the final test package. Although classroom teachers are not directly involved in item analysis of norm-referenced tests, those who understand the process are more knowledgeable in selecting and using standardized tests. An understanding of the principle of item analysis for norm-referenced tests also helps teachers recognize the essential differences between norm-referenced and criterion-referenced evaluation instruments.

To determine a test item's usefulness or strength, test makers first judge the abilities of children who will take the achievement test they are attempting to standardize. On the basis of similar tests, they identify a group of children who seem to be the most capable. Test publishers believe that this figure should include approximately 30% of the group. They also identify the 30% that seems to be the least capable. Both groups are identified because they help determine whether a given test item is useful. The bright youngsters should get a good question right and the slowest youngsters should get it wrong. The bright children, by virtue of their native intelligence and their experiences will know more than the lowest group about virtually any subject.

Having identified these two groups of children, test makers test the entire sample group and analyze the children's responses to each test item. If most of the top children get the item right and most of the lower group get it wrong, the test item is said to *discriminate* and is usable. If a large number from the top group gets the item wrong and a correspondingly large number of the lower group gets it right, the question does not discriminate and it is rejected or rewritten.

Norm-referenced test makers finally include only those items that discriminate and are therefore useful. Their tests are valid and reliable measurement instruments to the degree that a significantly larger proportion of bright students answer each item correctly than will the same proportion of slower students.

The "Show of Hands" Item Analysis

There is a relatively simple way to analyze items on teacher made tests, the "show of hands" item analysis. Although teachers usually do not do an item analysis on every test they compose, this technique helps teachers get into the habit of identifying poor items and taking more care in constructing useful ones. Terry Tenbrink[4] describes this method as one that can be done very simply right in the classroom. After arithmetic tests are completed and graded, they are divided into two equal piles. The first contains the upper 50% of the tests; the second of course includes those with scores below the 50th percentile. This divides the class into the brighter and slower children.

After passing the papers out to the class with the top 50% going to one side of the room and the lower 50 to the other, the teacher simply calls for a show of hands in response to items: "Raise your hand if item number one is correct on the paper you have." A glance will indicate that twelve of the top students answered the item correctly while only six of the lower group did so. The show of hands gives a quick indication that this item probably discriminates.

As the teacher continues through the list, bad items will quickly be identified when a large number of hands are raised in the lower group. By noting the number of hands raised from each group in response to each item, the teacher obtains a crude but effective item analysis like that used for norm-referenced tests. Questions that obviously discriminate can perhaps be used another time. Those that do not should be analyzed for ambiguity or other faults and either rewritten or rejected. The norms in this case are, of course, *local* or classroom norms rather than *broad* or national. The class is the sample group; their behavior on tests determines what the norms will be. If the teacher decides, from the responses of the class, that an average score on this arithmetic test is 70, the test has a norm against which to reference each child's performance.

Item Analysis of Criterion-referenced Tests

Analysis of items on norm-referenced tests depends upon a wide variance in children's responses. If all the children got all the items right or all of them wrong, there would be no variance and the items would not discriminate. This is not the case with criterion-referenced tests since they do not involve norms against which to compare individual children.

Instead, criterion-referenced tests measure the degree to which each child achieves the objectives established for an instructional unit. If instructional objectives call for the correct naming of all 13 original colonies, for instance, that information will be called for in the test items. There is no reason for this item to discriminate. All the children should get it right because this is one of the things the teacher set out to teach them.

Analyzing the items on a criterion-referenced achievement test, then, is a relatively easy matter. Teachers simply prepare a chart listing the behaviors they hope to see in the children after the teaching and learning have been done. Test questions are based precisely on instructional objectives. Suppose, for instance, a teacher wishes to test tenth graders on English composition skills. The objectives have stated that the youngsters will be able to demonstrate their composition skills by answering questions about a poorly written selection. Skills to be demonstrated include capitalization, punctuation marks, good sentence structure, and proper sentence placement. The chart will look something like Fig. 9.3.

The chart in Fig. 9.3 lists all the children and all the items on the test. After correcting the test, the teacher places a plus sign after the names of the children who got an item right and a minus sign after those who got it wrong. The predominance of plus signs below item four indicates that the youngsters have learned the capitalization skill called for in the instruc-

Item	Capitalization 1 2 3 4	Punctuation 5 6 7 8	Sentence Structure 9 10 11 12	Sentence Placement 13 14 15 16
Name				
Timothy	+			−
Kim	+			−
Ted	+			−
Mike	+			−
Jimmy	+			−
Tomilee	+			−
Chad	+			−
Andrew	+			+
Darra	+			−
Jonas	+			−
Richard	−			−
JoAnne	+			+
Cheryl	+			−
Bill	−			−
Brian	+			−
Joe	+			−
Art	+			+
Alice	+			−
Suzy	−			−

Figure 9.3

tional objectives. Item 13 tells just as quickly one of two things: either the question or the teaching is poor. If the question were rewritten in more precise terms and most of the children then got it right, it would be safe to say that the test item and not the teaching was poor. The tabulations for the other 14 items enable the teacher to identify possible problems. In general, the majority of students answer an item correctly, it is most likely a good one, and most of the children have learned the behavior called for.

Gronlund[5] suggests that teachers can get a clearer picture of whether their test items indicate good learning and whether their instructional objectives have been met by including both pretest and posttest behavior in the chart. In this way, teachers can readily evaluate the appropriateness of each test item. For instance, if a science objective states that the children will be able to name the parts of an electric cell (flashlight battery), teachers will ask that question before they begin teaching the unit on electricity. If Suzy can name none of the parts on the pretest and all of the parts on the posttest, it is safe to assume that the teacher has achieved the objective. According to this suggestion, the chart might be modified to include both pretest and posttest responses as shown in Fig. 9.4.

A tabulation such as Fig. 9.4 provides an instant assessment of the test and the strength of its individual items. It also gives important insight into the individual growth and needs of each child.

| Name | Knowledge | |
| | 4 parts of electric cell | |
	Pre	Post
Timothy	0	3
Kim	0	4
Ted	2	4
Mike	0	3
Jimmy	0	4
Tomilee	1	3
Chad	0	4
Andrew	0	4
Darra	0	3
Jonas	1	2
Richard	2	4
JoAnne	0	4
Cheryl	0	4
Bill	1	3
Brian	1	3
Joe	0	2
Art	1	3
Alice	0	4
Suzy	0	4

Figure 9.4

FORMAL CRITERION-REFERENCED TESTS

With the growing interest in instructional objectives, educators will begin to see a rapid growth in the number of commercially produced tests based on the principle of criterion referencing. Several are already available in mathematics and reading, and they are constructed in the same way that a teacher would construct a classroom criterion-referenced test. Instructional objectives are clearly stated for the behaviors to be learned, and then test items are constructed to determine whether or not the children achieved the objectives.

In the case of commercially published tests, teachers do not need to write out instructional objectives since this is already done by the publishers. For instance, the *Individual Pupil Monitoring System, Mathematics*[6] lists children's specific behaviors in mathematics. Each objective is numbered and keyed to a test section containing the items constructed to measure that specific behavior. Objective number 211 states that each student should be able to solve addition problems with sums of 7 through 10, using the vertical form. The test items for objective number 211 include examples calling for this behavior. If the children get them right, they demonstrate their competence to add with reference to a specific predetermined criterion. This is a criterion-referenced test item.

CRITERION-REFERENCED TESTS TO MEET INDIVIDUAL NEEDS

The title of the particular evaluation system just mentioned, *Individual Pupil Monitoring System* (or IPMS) suggests the major reason for the growing popularity of criterion-referenced evaluation. Unlike norm-referenced tests, which limit evaluations to a comparison with some broader norm or standard of behavior, criterion-referenced tests allow teachers a closer look at individual progress. Teachers are more interested in how much their children grow with reference to their own needs than with reference to the achievement of children around the country. For this reason, they seek ways to measure growth by standards set at the local level, standards that are more realistic measures of actual progress. Testing, measuring, and evaluating in this way also affords a more reliable method of diagnosing learning. Teachers know in advance the behavior they wish to observe and call for it on a test. If Sally seems to have trouble adding, test item 211 gives immediate evidence of this and the teacher knows exactly which mathematics behaviors need to be improved.

A CRITERION-REFERENCED READING TEST

Some criterion-referenced tests have evolved as a vital component of a unique instructional system. One of these is the *Wisconsin Test of Reading Skill Development.*[7] A brief look at the individualized reading skills tests in this evaluation system will show how criterion-referenced tests are linked closely to the specific instructional objectives of the program.

The total program is called *The Wisconsin Design for Reading Skill Development.*[8] Like the IPMS mentioned above, the Wisconsin Design was developed with the principle of individually guided instruction in mind. The intent of its authors, to address themselves directly to children's individual needs and progress, is evident in their statement of the design's four fundamental purposes:*

1. To identify and describe behaviorally the skills which appear to be essential for competence in reading.

2. To assess individual pupils' skill development status.

3. To manage instruction of children with different skill development needs.

4. To monitor each pupil's progress.

Developed as a supplement to *any* reading program, the design is an attempt to identify the specific reading skills normally taught in the elementary grades and to describe them in *behavioral* terms as *instructional objectives*. For instance, an early reading skill is recognizing initial consonant sounds. The authors identify this skill by stating it as an instructional or behavioral, objective.†

Given a familiar word pronounced by the teacher, the child indicates which of three other words begins with the same consonant sound.

Using this objective, the teachers develop whatever teaching strategies they wish to help children learn how to recognize initial consonant sounds. Later, when children are tested, an item from the Wisconsin Test of Reading Skill Development reads like this.‡

Put your finger on the top. Next to the top is a **saw**. Which picture in this row starts with the same sound as **saw**? Listen. **Tie . . . boot . . . sun**? Fill in the circle under the picture that starts with the same sound as **saw**.

This and fourteen similar test items verify that the children know how to recognize initial consonant sounds. Later the somewhat higher level skills of reading comprehension are taught. One of

*Reprinted with permission of National Computer Systems, Inc. (Minneapolis, Minn.) from Wisconsin Design for Reading Skill Development, Rationale and Guidelines, p. 1.

†Reprinted with permission of National Computer Systems, Inc. (Minneapolis, Minn.) from Wisconsin Design for Reading Skill Development, Rationale and Guidelines, p. 123.

‡Reprinted with permission of National Computer Systems, Inc. (Minneapolis, Minn.) from Wisconsin Design for Reading Skill Development, Test Administrator's Manual: Word Attack Level A, p. 20.

the objectives from this section refers to the ability to identify the central thought of a passage.*

The child identifies a central thought of a passage that contains no organizer (topic sentence) and has both relevant and irrelevant information.

Another comprehension objective this time relating to the ability to determine obscure meanings of words in a reading selection, is stated in this way:†

The child uses direct and indirect clues to determine the obscure meaning of a familiar word in context.

In this way, an entire sequence of behavioral, or instructional, objectives has been developed for use by any teacher using any system of teaching reading. The list of objectives was derived from the teaching-learning environments or actual classrooms and carefully stated and restated until experienced teachers and reading experts agreed about their accuracy and appropriateness. The testing items were then constructed directly from the objectives, providing an excellent example of formal criterion-referenced test construction.

In a very real sense, such formally constructed tests can be said to be standardized. Although the standardizing or pilot testing procedures do not yield the typical norms found on norm-referenced tests, they do identify a standard of performance and achievement against which to measure children's progress. In identifying and listing the reading skills thought to be essential to successful reading through the elementary grades, test makers establish standards of sorts. To use such formally constructed tests, teachers must accept these standards as compatible with their own and develop their teaching strategies accordingly. In a way, this might tend to diminish the value of the test for diagnostic purposes.

One danger in the growing availability of criterion-referenced tests developed by those not close to individual school systems is that teachers might find in them an easier, but not necessarily more appropriate, way to identify and state their instructional objectives. While reading and mathematics seem to lend themselves rather well to a generally acceptable set of objectives and associated test items, other subjects such as literature or history do not. In the final analysis, classroom teachers must assume full responsibility both for determining the objectives for their children and the testing, measuring, and evaluating procedures that will help them decide how well they have achieved the criteria stated in the objectives.

---

*Reprinted with permission of National Computer Systems, Inc. (Minneapolis, Minn.) from Wisconsin Design for Reading Skill Development, Rationale and Guidelines, Addendum, p. 6.

†Ibid., p. 7.

BANKS OF OBJECTIVES FOR CRITERION-REFERENCED EVALUATIONS

Some publishers and state departments of education have recognized the growing interest in setting clear objectives and then building instructional programs around them. They have examined typical curricula in all subject and skill areas and have constructed long lists or banks of instructional and behavioral objectives. Teachers and local school systems may select from such materials those objectives that seem to meet their particular needs. One advantage of such lists is that the objectives are usually constructed with a high degree of precision and teachers can usually find some that are appropriate for their children. A disadvantage is that teachers come to depend upon someone else to state their instructional objectives. When this happens, there is always the possibility that teachers will adjust their teaching strategies and their children's behavior to the objectives rather than build the objectives around the youngsters' specific and unique needs.

In addition to the establishment of banks of objectives, criterion-referenced test items will undoubtedly become established as well. Not only will lists of instructional or behavioral objectives be available from which to select, teachers will also be able to select test items to assess the degree to which each objective has been met. Somewhere between the selection of objectives and the administration of the test items, teachers will have to arrange the necessary learning experiences. When this happens, of course, teachers increase the probability that their teaching and evaluating strategies are determined, in large part, by someone else.

WHEN DO TEACHERS USE NORM-REFERENCED TESTS?

To Compare Their Children with Others

The standardization process of norm-referenced tests suggests one of their uses. Through the norms derived from the performance of the test's sample population, teachers compare their children's achievement with that of the norm group. Grade-level norms in addition to age levels, standard scores, percentile scores, and stanine scores allow various kinds of comparisons.

In a later chapter, we will discuss some of the criticisms that have arisen about this aspect of both achievement and intelligence testing.

To Compare Achievement with Intelligence

We discussed the use of norm-referenced tests for comparing achievement with intelligence in Chapter 7, but it bears repeating. Much of the activity required in taking an achievement test, such as memory, judgment, and reasoning, is cognitive in nature. Intelligence tests, which require many of the same cognitive activities, allow teachers to predict students' probable success in subsequent academic work. Achievement tests are thus used to indicate whether students are living up to their cognitive potential.

Teachers must take great care when they use achievement tests in this way. They should be sure to use intelligence tests and achievement tests that have been standardized against essentially the same populations of children. If they do not, they will not be able to determine whether poor performance indicates failure to live up to cognitive potential or whether the differences in scores are caused by the differences in the two standardizing groups.

To Determine Individual Progress

Using norm-referenced tests to determine individual progress is not particularly helpful. Since most achievement tests sample the curriculum content with small numbers of items, any child in a class may know a great deal more about geography than is covered by the few test items relating to it. Individual progress must be measured more intensively by providing each student with as many chances as possible to show how much he or she knows about a subject. Evaluating to keep track of individual progress implies diagnostic testing for the improvement of learning. This can be done effectively only with adequate numbers of test items that provide more information about individual strengths and weaknesses than do most standardized achievement tests.

To Assess Strengths and Weaknesses of Curricula

The results of achievement tests often vary significantly from city to city, from school to school, and even from grade to grade within a school. When such differences occur, they indicate a need for curriculum revision. The backgrounds of large groups of children in one school for instance, may not be adequate for good performance on a particular achievement test while children in a school across town do well on the same test. When this occurs, educators may wish to modify the curriculum of the first group by providing more enriched content or by developing different teaching strategies.

WHEN DO TEACHERS USE CRITERION-REFERENCED TESTS?

To Diagnose Learning

The limitation of norm-referenced tests for diagnosis of individual strengths and weaknesses is the major reason for the remarkable growth in the use of criterion-referenced tests. The process of writing a test item for criterion-referenced tests based on clearly stated instructional objectives is simple. Moreover, criterion-referenced tests measure individual performance at a given point in time rather than performance as it generally compares with national norms. Actual performance, directly related to teachers' daily teaching-learning strategies, clearly indicates children's specific needs and can suggest reasonable instructional objectives for them. Carefully constructed criterion-referenced tests indicate how much extra help in arithmetic Suzy will need and exactly what kinds of arithmetic problems on which she needs help. This degree of diagnostic precision is not available through the use of norm-referenced tests.

To Diagnose and Improve Instruction

Increasingly, teachers are being held accountable for their children's academic performance. In a later chapter we will discuss how severely both teachers and their schools are chastised when the results of their standardized testing programs fall below the national norms. Criterion-referenced tests are an excellent device by which teachers can monitor and improve their teaching effectiveness. Skillful writing of instructional objectives is not particularly difficult, but it requires attention to detail and to the components of good objectives discussed in Chapter 3. Good objectives make it more likely that teachers will employ good teaching strategies to achieve them. When teachers aim toward clearly stated and understood objectives, they tend to be more thorough and to stay on the track.

Objectives also provide the framework for testing procedures. Stating the criterion of success is not difficult when teachers know in advance what they wish that success to be. When children answer questions correctly on a test, they show, in effect, how well the teacher has taught them. Their performance provides valuable clues to the ways in which teachers can vary their teaching strategies and sometimes even their personalities in order to do a better job.

BOTH NORM-REFERENCED AND CRITERION-REFERENCED TESTS ARE IMPORTANT

In spite of the rapid growth of criterion-referenced tests, they do not foreshadow the demise of norm-referenced tests. Despite the shortcomings, comparisons of children with national norms is an important educational activity. Educators may become less dependent upon norm-referenced tests for setting curricula or for determining grade placement, but national norms will remain as a kind of assessment of the country's educational status. They offer a reminder of how much and how well educators are doing as a national group, and they serve as benchmarks and broad guidelines within which to develop teaching-learning strategies at local levels. When children vary significantly from the norms, teachers should be concerned and should seek the reasons.

At the very least, norm-referenced tests serve as screening devices by which to identify possible areas of strength or weakness. Used intelligently, some norm-referenced tests, particularly those that measure achievement in specific areas such as mathematics or reading provide one input to teachers' efforts to improve learning.

Finally, as research tools norm-referenced tests provide an ever-growing body of data for the study of human behavior. Without such data, researchers would not have the information necessary to continue building their understanding of how people think and learn.

Criterion-referenced tests, on the other hand, serve as on-site evaluation tools for the diagnosis and improvement of learning and teaching alike. They provide a degree of precision and objective assessment not possible in traditional teacher-made test procedures. They force teachers to be more exact and more professional in how they accommodate individual differences. And they offer a powerful technique for paying more than lip service to individualized instruction.

SUMMARY

The uses of achievement testing are both broad and specific. Standardized tests help teachers assess where children stand with reference to national norms. Teacher-made and other locally constructed achievement tests indicate children's exact strengths and weaknesses. Standardized tests are limited in this respect, and these limitations have led to severe criticism of the testing movement in general and to the production of criterion-referenced test procedures. Although nothing new in principle, particularly for effective teachers, criterion-referenced testing materials reflect the trend toward more precision in teaching through the writing of instructional and behavioral objectives.

Whatever form of achievement evaluation tools teachers come to use most frequently, they must remember that the most important will be those they administer daily. Not all will be criterion-referenced; most will be observations and descriptions of children's behavior, which are important in helping teachers find ways to improve children's achievement. Standardized tests, criterion-referenced tests, and good observation techniques are the tools by which teachers evaluate how much and how well their children have learned. All can be enormously helpful, and all are important to the overall program of achievement testing.

IMPORTANT POINTS TO THINK ABOUT

1. Imagine that the children on page 200 are your tenth graders. How would you use the results of a standardized achievement test to determine how well each is living up to his or her intellectual potential?

2. How would you use the results of a criterion-referenced test to gain the same information?

3. Can you draw a tentative plan for the appropriate use of both norm-referenced and criterion-referenced tests for the entire school year?

4. How would you explain to a concerned parent the major differences between norm-referenced and criterion-referenced achievement tests?

5. Plan a lesson about cloud formations. State your instructional objectives very clearly and then construct a five-item criterion-referenced test on the subject of cloud formation.

NOTES

1. Stanford Achievement Test, Intermediate Level I (New York: Harcourt Brace Jovanovich, 1972).

2. Differential Aptitude Tests, Form L (New York: The Psychological Corporation, 1961).

3. R. Glazer, "Instructional Technology and the Measurement of Learning Outcomes," *American Psychologist* 18 (1963).

4. T. Tenbrink, *Evaluation, A Practical Guide for Teachers* (New York: Macmillan, 1973).

5. N.E. Gronlund, Preparing Criterion Referenced Tests for Classroom Teachers (New York: Macmillan, 1973).

6. Individual Pupil Monitoring System, Mathematics (Boston: Houghton Mifflin, 1973).

7. W. Otto and E. Askow, Wisconsin Test of Reading Skill Development (Madison, WI: University of Wisconsin Press, 1972).

8. W. Otto and E. Askow, *Wisconsin Design for Reading Skill Development* (Madison, WI: University of Wisconsin Press, 1972).

CHAPTER TEN

ASSESSING PERSONAL GROWTH TO IMPROVE INSTRUCTION

IMPORTANT POINTS TO WATCH FOR

The development of a healthy personality is essential to success in school.

Personal growth is developmental in its formation.

Teachers need to know how to evaluate personal development as it relates to the stresses and demands of cognitive learning at any age or grade level.

Good personal growth is *learned* just as subject matter. It does not happen as a natural consequence of maturation.

As teachers evaluate children's personal growth in the primary grades, they should watch for evidence of security and trust.

In the middle grades, they should watch for evidence that children have begun to achieve a degree of mastery over their environment and a growing sense of independence.

In junior and senior high school, teachers should watch for evidence of increased identity formation and relatively healthy responses to the stresses and strains of adolescence.

GOOD PERSONAL GROWTH IS ESSENTIAL TO LEARNING

In Chapter 2 we discussed the importance of personal and emotional development to successful learning. We spoke of the need for children to "feel good about themselves" in order to be comfortable and successful in the learning environment and, drawing on Alice's story as an example, we showed how deficits in emotional development can potentially destroy a child's chances for a normal life.

Alice's story points up two extremely important facts. First, even in today's school systems, there are still individuals whose lack of understanding of child growth and development can lead to tragic consequences for children. Second, the number of such individuals is diminishing as more professionals knowledgeable about human growth and development enter the teaching field. These professionals bring a sophisticated understanding of testing, measuring, and evaluating that includes knowledge of the techniques and materials of testing, the nature of child development, and the dramatic relationship between personality development and cognitive growth.

Good personal growth is essential to learning. Children who are happy and well adjusted feel good about themselves and seem to respond to the learning task with spirit and enthusiasm. Even children who are not as intellectually strong as others often seem to accept their cognitive shortcomings without undue stress. When their personal and emotional lives are in order, they are able to "roll with the punches" that are part of every school day. Such children have benefitted from a combination of gifts, all contributing to that quality of the human condition known as "well adjusted." For each child the combination of gifts is unique—a particularly loving set of parents, for instance, or a background of especially enriching experiences, or an environment in which brothers and sisters reinforce and encourage each other. Whatever the combination of circumstances, such children are usually wholesome and outgoing in class and a delight to teach. They have attained a level of personal and emotional growth that allows them to thrive in a school's demanding and often difficult learning environment.

Teachers are responsible for fostering such personal growth. To foster it they need to know how to recognize it. Recognizing it is what testing, measuring, and evaluating is all about. Teachers observe and test youngsters not only to determine their intelligence or their degree of achievement, but also to determine where each stands on the developmental continuum of personal growth. Through these evaluations teachers can determine why Timothy has difficulty learning geography or why Suzy is unable to keep up in science. Deficits in personal functioning may well inhibit what should be successful cognitive experiences. If the evaluations are accurate, they will provide the diagnostic information needed to help children overcome their deficits or learn how to work around them. In short, teachers constantly test, measure, and evaluate youngsters' personal growth in order to identify emotional trouble and to assess the degree to which inadequate personal growth affects learning. Whether deficits in personal growth are long- or short-term, teachers must know how to recognize and evaluate them.

The purpose of this chapter is to help you become sensitive to the ways in which personal and emotional development dynamically affect development of the intellect. While we have no intention of presenting a course in abnormal psychology, we wish to prepare future teachers for some of the personal behavior dynamics of the classroom. Such behavior, if it is serious enough, can adversely affect how much and how well children learn.

THE DEVELOPMENTAL NATURE OF PERSONAL AND EMOTIONAL GROWTH

The field of personal and emotional development has been exhaustively researched. Freud, perhaps, should be considered the pioneer, owing to his recognition that small children had personalities of their own and were not to be considered as "midget adults." Although the psychosexual aspects of his theory have been criticized, his recognition that early childhood was the most significant growth period for personality development has been accepted completely. Subsequent researchers such as Benjamin Bloom, James McVee Hunt, Burton White, and Erik Erikson have verified and reinforced Freud's statements about early childhood. Whatever their specific and unique contributions to the current understanding of personal growth, all would agree on two points at least. First, the quality of life during the first six or so years has enormous significance for later stability and emotional strength. It is currently recognized, for instance, that stimulus variety during early childhood plays a major role in successful cognitive development, that human warmth and affection are essential to a secure emotional state, and that a nutritionally balanced diet establishes the foundation for good physical development.

Second, all agree that these early years constitute a time of rapid growth and development, physically, cognitively, and personally. This period of rapid growth is followed by a plateau of several years of quieter and more subdued activity during which children seem to be integrating and practicing the skills and responses learned during the early years. Although new skills and behaviors are learned during this period, they are acquired at a more leisurely rate and without the extreme growth spurts of early childhood.

The onset of adolescence introduces youngsters to an entirely new world to assimilate and integrate into their personality structure. Once again, a period of rapid growth and change in physical, intellectual, and emotional development gets under way. Teachers of preadolescents and adolescents are often amazed at the variety and intensity of responses to this period in life. The onset of physical maturity, the emerging recognition of mature sex roles, and the growing awareness that childhood is becoming history while the responsibilities of adulthood loom ahead occasion a multitude of questions and anxieties. Such behavior provides dramatic evidence of the developmental nature of growth. Teachers must not only recognize and understand such behavior in general but, more importantly, identify specific behaviors that seem to inhibit an adolescent's full development. To respond accurately, teachers must be sensitive in their observations to individual differences in personal growth. Only in this way can teachers effectively help each youngster through the difficulties of adolescence.

The development of personality, then, is a process in which each important event becomes the emotional foundation for the next. Children who have experienced an emotionally rewarding early childhood will tend to be more secure in responding to the excitement and challenges of school. If elementary school experiences are rewarding, both academically and personally, and if their out-of-school experiences continue to be supportive and secure, they will move into adolescence without the extreme anxiety this experience generates in some young people.

Although teaching would be simplified if the thousands of children one encounters during a teaching career were emotionally secure and stable, this is not the case. An understanding of what constitutes good personal and emotional development is therefore vital to helping children who experience sudden departures from normality or who have longer-term and more deeply rooted personal deficits. Knowing the developmental nature of personal growth will not make teachers clinical psychologists but will provide a framework of the normal and healthy personality that can serve as a guide in observing and evaluating children.

THE IMPORTANCE OF SOCIAL RELATIONSHIPS TO PERSONAL GROWTH

Personal growth is largely a product of the social and interpersonal relationships children experience throughout their lives. Not only are their basic personal and emotional traits heavily conditioned and shaped by their interactions with others, but these interactions are often the underpinnings of abnormal behavior. The development of good social relationships is essential to productive learning in one of the most intensely "social" environments—the classroom. Nearly all the personal and emotional behavior teachers observe takes place in the context of this social scene. Very often the quality and nature of social relationships give teachers important clues to the quality and nature of personal development. Do children share with each other or exhibit selfish behavior? accept or reject the friendship of others? react with aggression or submit to the taunts of others? The daily social events of the classroom provide the information from which teachers can construct strategies for building a healthy social environment, one that will foster the personal strengths necessary for successful learning. The classroom social scene includes not only the children's interactions but also the teacher's, whose personality is very important to the social structure of the class. The quality of the teacher's personal and emotional growth exerts a powerful influence on the personal and emotional growth of the youngsters.

From kindergarten through senior high, the total classroom scene of children interacting with each other and with the teacher provides the environment in which social relationships are forged and personal and emotional strengths are developed. If personal growth is healthy during the crucial first six or so years of early childhood, children come to school well prepared to tackle the second period of development. Those whose early years were not so productive of personal strength find in the classroom environment many threats to an already fragile ego.

KNOWING ABOUT NORMAL PERSONAL GROWTH WILL HELP TEACHERS RECOGNIZE ABNORMAL GROWTH

Teachers have a responsibility, then, to understand what constitutes healthy personal growth and recognize behaviors that signal a departure from it. Using appropriate evaluation activities, teachers are more likely to spot inadequate personality development and are better able to restructure the learning environment to create conditions that can complement a child's personal growth. However, let us stress that most children's behavior, in spite of its often erratic nature, is normal and natural. Change and crisis are very much in evidence in all children. While some children respond to a crisis with an ego strength that allows them to grow, others respond with anxiety that can inhibit healthy personal development. Teachers need not be as concerned with erratic and uneven growth patterns as they are with growth that seems to stop. When growth stops, teachers witness children's inability to change and adjust successfully to the stresses and strains of the environment. By knowing about normal and healthy personal growth, teachers are able to recognize behavior that signals that normal development has been stopped or seriously inhibited.

ASSESSING THE PERSONAL STRENGTHS OF CHILDREN IN THE PRIMARY GRADES

The kindergarten teacher receives the child into his or her first experience away from the relative security of home. In this situation, behavior differs dramatically from one child to another.

Charlie is outgoing and self-assured. He saunters in on the first day as though the kindergarten were simply an extension of the world he just left. This new environment holds no threat for him, and he explores each nook and cranny with great confidence. He tucks into his mind those areas that have particular interest for him, making a mental note to come back and explore them in depth. If he doesn't know what something is or what lies behind a closed door, he simply asks. If he wants to know more about a child who looks particularly interesting, he goes to the child and finds out. When instructions are given to sit quietly, or to listen carefully, or to fold papers for art work, Charlie goes about the job with good humor and with a healthy curiosity about what will happen next. When he fails, there is no tantrum and no tears; he simply looks around to ask for help. He seems to sense that the classroom, with its teacher and all of its equipment and materials, exists for one purpose only—to fulfill Charlie's needs and to answer his questions.

Kindergarten teachers watch for behavior like this and hope for many more Charlies. His behavior signals a child whose personal growth, during the first years, has been relatively healthy. He has come through his earliest year or two with good feelings about the people around him who gave him affection, warmth, and a full share of physical attention—cuddling him often and showing him in many ways that he is loved and wanted. Having gained his first important personal milestone during this time, he has learned to trust the people in his world and, through them, the world itself.

Charlie's behavior in kindergarten paints a further picture of his early years. During Charlie's next two or three years, his trust in others led to greater mobility and explorations of a wider world, including the world of himself. His natural curiosity about his body has been satisfied through natural exploration and questioning—exploration and questioning accepted with the same patience and affection that marked his earlier experiences. His increased mobility during these few years, along with his increasing size, also brought the need for restraints and for learning such important social behaviors as toilet training. His behavior on the first day of school reveals that his growing need for autonomy was not inhibited by harsh controls or by feelings of shame over normal and natural behavior. His personality, at the age of three or so, was probably marked by good feelings about himself—feelings of relative autonomy to explore and learn without shame.

In his relations with other children, Charlie is quite uninhibited. Although very much aware of his maleness through the toys and objects he selects and rejects, Charlie is able to balance his sex role with a willingness and ability to relate unself-consciously to boys and girls alike. This behavior, along with his unabashed attempts to get close to his teacher indicate that his personal development during the past three or so years has resulted in strong feelings of autonomy. His questions about his maleness and his growing awareness of male and female roles were most likely accepted by his parents as natural and important to good personality development. They very likely responded to his growing need for autonomy with patience and understood his attempts to compete with his father for his mother's love. Not needing to feel guilty about his behavior during these years, Charlie has become a child with an ego ready to withstand the pressures of school and to move, with security and self-assurance, into the next important stage of personal development.

A student like Charlie is a delight to teach. His independence and good feelings about himself help him acquire more easily the skills and information that are the stuff of formal learning. His emotional readiness to learn is clearly identifiable by his classroom behavior.

However, all children are not equally ready for school. Sally is having a problem getting her coat unbuttoned and seems embarrassed to ask another child for help. Bill has a look of sheer terror on his face that tells of a personality still insecure in new situations and needing lots of help and reassurance that this place is safe. Tony looks but is afraid to touch. His curiosity is great but the rules he has learned have taught him not to explore things that belong to others. It will take time to help him understand that the world *must* be explored and that touching and finding out about things is not something to feel guilty about.

Paul is belligerent and seems to think that everything must be gained through brute force. He pushes other children aside and demands to have what they are enjoying. Resistance to his demands leads instantly to a fight. His behavior is not necessarily a sign of personal strength but perhaps of serious weakness. His teacher, knowing that he will be a problem, will observe him carefully to discover what motivates his behavior. Is his belligerence a sign of self-assurance that he can get what he wants by force? Or does it reveal that he is emotionally, or perhaps intellectually, incapable of getting it by more reasonable and acceptable means?

The remarkable variety in children's behavior is nowhere more apparent than during the beginning days of school. Perhaps it is a good reminder that stages of development must never be interpreted to mean that all children can or should be expected to fit the developmental theories. Knowing the ideal behavior as children enter the juvenile stage of personal development provides a benchmark against which to measure variations and toward which to strive in helping children gain personal strength. However, it may be impossible to completely change Paul's behavior from constant belligerence to courteous interaction. Although his behavior indicates that he has not yet reached a level of personal growth that will foster success and happiness in school, his teacher can at best work with him patiently to initiate changes. Observing his behavior constantly and carefully is the teacher's best way of measuring and evaluating his personal growth and, as a result, of being able to find the strategies to begin the change.

As teachers observe and evaluate children's personal behavior in the primary grades, what do they look for? First, for a sense of security that shows that children are comfortable both with what they are and where they are. Do they move about the room with obvious self-assurance? Do they accept suggestions and assignments without expressions of anxiety and insecurity? Do they relate to other children openly with neither undue aggression nor reticence? Do they respond to failures without excessive frustration and with the understanding that failure is often a part of learning? In short, have they brought from early childhood a degree of trust in people and in the world? Have they developed the courage to take initiative to explore and question without fear of humiliation? If not, their personal strength may vary from near optimal adjustment to being nearly incapacitated emotionally.

It is no accident that the formal atmosphere of the school begins when children reach the age of 5 or 6. For centuries, those concerned with education and religion have agreed that this is the age at which significant changes seem to take place. The Catholic Church long believed that age 7 was the beginning of the ability to reason, and thus important religious activities such as baptism began at this age. Societies throughout the world have sensed that this was the age at which children are ready to begin formal learning.

Modern institutions have not departed substantially from this practice. In spite of occasional theories or curriculum innovations that attempt to begin schooling in the earlier childhood years, most societies still begin the educational process after five or six years of early childhood growth. Teachers in the primary grades have something more than the advantage of history to show them why this seems to be so. Piaget, Freud, Erikson, Bruner, and other researchers have investigated the importance of the early childhood years to successful learning. Piaget wrote of the need for well-developed cognitive structures at the sensori-motor and pre-operational stages of development, structures consisting of motor skills and memories necessary to concrete intellectual learning in kindergarten and first grade. Freud explained the need for children to feel secure and guilt free as they enter the world of school. Erikson said much the same thing and complemented Freud's findings with his carefully developed stages of personal development. Jerome Bruner speaks of the child's built in will to learn, a motivating force he believes to be at the heart of successful learning. His theory that intrinsic motivation is more powerful as a factor in successful learning than is the concept of external reinforcement helps explain what curiosity is all about. The curious child must have questions answered and must be allowed to ask the questions. Closely allied with curiosity, of course, is the need for children to acquire competence in the things they do. Without curiosity, there will be very little interest in learning and thus very little competence.

Children arrive on the first day of school, then, with the need to achieve and with a built in desire and curiosity to know. In addition to evidence of personal security, teachers watch carefully to note how well the children are able to fulfill their curiosity. Some have been stifled in this drive; others have not. Their behavior indicates that they have arrived at school with varying degrees of readiness to ask and learn—readiness that must include a fair measure of cognitive ability but that must also include an abundance of curiosity and emotional strength to learn.

Erikson would say that kindergarten children have entered the juvenile period, during which feelings of *mastery and inferiority* seem to be the major forces influencing their personal growth. At this time, the emotionally secure child begins to turn attention outward and away from the egocentric behavior of earlier years. The children must face a new environment, no matter how unready some may be to survive and master it. The teacher's responsibility for personal growth in the primary grades thus includes not only an evaluation of how each child comes to the new environment but a continuous assessment and evaluation of how each child relates to it. Knowing that Bill is terrified to start with indicates that his curiosity drive and his need to achieve competence will not flourish until his personal strengths allow it. On a continuum between inferiority and mastery, Bill has a long way to go. His teacher will look for gradual and continuous growth of mastery—whether he seems increasingly more comfortable; less shy, tearful, or withdrawn; more sure of himself around other children; more ready to volunteer; and most important, whether the classroom seems to become gradually safer for him. Once the classroom can provide the necessary shelter for his dependent moods while offering opportunities for the gradual emergence of independent behavior, the teacher has been successful in fostering Bill's personal growth.

During the kindergarten and primary grades, then, teachers watch carefully for behavior that indicates which children are emotionally ready to begin the difficult and challenging job of cognitive learning. Using Charlie's ideal behavior as a guide, teachers observe how other children deviate from this model. Since successful cognitive learning depends to a large degree on adequate feelings of independence and relative freedom from guilt and anxiety, teachers watch for behavior that invites encouragement and challenges and becomes increasingly independent. As each youngster shows evidence of increased or improved initiative and independence, teachers alter their teaching strategies slightly to keep the challenge of learning at the right level for each. Individualized assessment such as this leads to individualized instruction.

ASSESSING THE PERSONAL STRENGTHS OF CHILDREN IN THE MIDDLE GRADES

The elementary school experience, from kindergarten through grade six and including ages 6 through 12, is considered by Erikson as the time during which youngsters should achieve mastery over their environment. The first several years of this period are critical to children's well-being as they emerge from the security of home and family. Mastery seems easy for some, like Charlie, but not so easy for others.

After three or four years in the primary grades, teachers expect to observe a growing sense of independence. Most children will have gained some degree of mastery over their environment and over themselves. Even though Bill will still exhibit inferiority behavior, sensitive teaching and adequate challenge will have helped him to feel secure enough to enjoy school and want to be there.

Beginning at about the fourth grade, an important change in cognitive ability begins that calls for greater security and independence. The primary grades have provided the opportunity and challenge of learning the basic skills necessary to later success in learning. The ability to read, write, speak, and to do all of the concrete operations necessary for mastery of these important skills is gained, in varying degrees of success, before grade four. The skills of personal growth are achieved in varying degrees as well, and children must now be prepared for the suddenly increased subject matter demands of the upper elementary grades. The textbooks and the teachers now make the assumption that the basic skills are ready to be applied in the study of "subjects" like history, geography, and science. Less time is now spent on learning and practicing basic skills and more on the higher intellectual task of learning about the world and the people who make it work.

With students like Charlie in the classroom, teachers know what to expect. If his first years in school continued as his first day did, he has already mastered the basic skills and his personal sense of mastery is evident in his behavior. He gladly accepts the challenge and excitement of a unit on science or social studies, approaching his assignments with confidence and good nature, secure in the knowledge of his growing cognitive ability and in his feelings about himself. His personal independence has been enhanced by the skills he can bring to his work. His curiosity has not been diminished nor his drive to learn inhibited. By monitoring his cognitive and personal growth, his teacher can find ever more challenging things for him to do.

Children who are less well adjusted must also be observed and evaluated as consistently and as carefully as before. Bill is still unsure of himself and needs much encouragement to attack his assignment. As he reads, he still looks for approval and for help on harder words. He holds back when working in a group, waiting to see how other children will behave. More than likely, his behavior imitates someone else's, Charlie's perhaps, but not as accurately or as creatively. Still suffering from feelings of inferiority, Bill's mastery of his environment and of himself is still far from adequate for real success. He may not cry any longer, having come to accept his school and his friends as "safe" and nonthreatening, but he still defers to others in group activities. Yet he is beginning to speak up more often, and his responses in class discussions are more frequent. He is not nearly as devastated when he makes a mistake. He is gradually discovering that he is someone and that he belongs here. His teacher will observe that he is moving along the continuum of personal growth, not as rapidly or as successfully as Charlie, but he *is* moving and beginning to feel better about himself.

A teacher's evaluation of a child like Bill is extremely important. Less sensitivity to Bill's feelings, either because of impatience or lack of knowledge about child development, will lead to demands that threaten him. If he withdraws and makes excuses or refuses to do his work, a teacher's irritation and impatience will further diminish Bill's already fragile ego. The world of school, instead of exciting and delighting him, frightens him and fills him with anxiety. Whatever the reasons for his feelings of inferiority, they are compounded by the teacher's insensitivity, further inhibiting Bill's personal growth. Unfortunately, his diminished ego will not allow him to take the risks associated with learning, and his cognitive growth will also slow down. If teachers fail or refuse to recognize the behavior that paints the picture of a terrified child, they fail the child.

Similar problems can arise with a child like Paul, the belligerent child in the kindergarten class. Failing to understand that his actions are blatant signals of inadequate personal development, or responding to his belligerence with belligerence, reduces Paul's chances to improve his behavior. Knowing how to observe and what to observe will give Paul his best chance to enhance his personal development. Observing his actions carefully and noting them, as we described in Chapter 4, will accomplish several important things. First, it will provide an accurate and continuous assessment of his behavior. Such an assessment will paint a clear picture of his growth over a period of time and will suggest teaching strategies to help him change. Second, an ongoing assessment of this kind will help prevent emotional overreactions to his behavior, overreactions that are far too common in classrooms. Third, it will identify the incidents that seem to trigger his outbursts and the kinds of threats that seem to make him want to fight. Most important with individualized teaching strategies, Paul may come to know and like himself better when his aggressive responses give way to responses that other children perceive as friendly and likeable.

There is no way to effect truly successful changes in the behavior of a Bill or a Paul without knowing what to observe and how to observe. Understanding how children acquire mastery of their lives and how they shake off inferiority is essential to effective measurement and evaluation of personal growth. During the upper elementary school years, teachers' major concerns in the assessment of personal development are observing and recording behavior that provides clues to how well children are acquiring mastery. However, this is only a prelude to the development of teaching strategies that will help children fulfill their potential. In short, informed classroom observation will help teachers find the patience and the means of meeting every child's personal needs and of assuring each a maximum opportunity to move along his or her personal growth continuum.

ASSESSING THE PERSONAL STRENGTHS OF CHILDREN IN JUNIOR AND SENIOR HIGH SCHOOL

As children move through the elementary grades evaluations of personal development are based largely on the degree to which they have emerged successfully from the secure and egocentric world of home and into the challenging world of school. Here they have the security of knowing and spending the greater part of each day with a single group of classmates and usually one teacher. In addition, their physical growth has slowed from the dramatic rate of early childhood to the more measured and stable rate of the latency years. These physical and emotional conditions lend a degree of stability to the learning process. In addition, attendance in one classroom with one teacher during most of the day makes testing, measuring, and evaluating relatively easy. Thus teachers observe how well children master an environment that challenges them both intellectually and personally.

All this comes to an end as children enter junior high school. Instead of a single, usually sympathetic teacher to whom children can relate, they face a series of teachers, each with a different personality and each making different kinds of demands. The school day also makes different kinds of demands—demands on their ability to adhere to previously unknown rules and procedures. Complicating this new scene is the growing awareness that childhood is over, and the security of the elementary school gone forever. This awareness is dramatically sharpened by the physiological changes of adolescence, changes that bring heightened self-awareness and the need to acquire new behaviors appropriate to this age and place. The evaluation of personal growth during these years is made extremely difficult by the same learning conditions that the students face. Frequently, teachers complain that "there isn't time enough in the day for me to get to know my children," or "my job is to teach math, not to worry about emotional problems," or "if the parents and the elementary teachers had done their jobs, I wouldn't have to deal with this kind of behavior."

The behavior that occasions such complaints, adolescent behavior, often seems too difficult for both adolescent and teacher to understand, yet it marks a period in life crucial to future success. For the youngster who has begun physical adolescence in grade five or six, the transition to junior high will not be so traumatic. Chances are good that the reasons for the physical changes have been explained adequately or at least endured in an atmosphere of relative calm. For those who begin this important change during junior high, it is easy to see how complicated their lives can become. Adjusting to the cognitive demands of five or six different subjects and the same number of teachers, while running from class to class every hour, should be enough to ask of any child. To add to it the excitement and anxiety of physical maturation and emerging sexuality is to invite the possibility of personality problems. Moreover, when all of the child's energy is focused on trying to grapple with personal problems, there can be little left for subject matter. Adolescence, instead of being a time of healthy and open learning about oneself and of growing emotional security and awareness, often becomes a time of undue stress and strain because of the life and learning style our educational system imposes. Adolescence, like reading or arithmetic, requires a personal readiness that different children acquire at different times and in different degrees.

As teachers observe young people entering the seventh grade, they attempt to determine each youngster's readiness for adolescence, trying to determine what can be considered normal behavior for this age. Since adolescence is a time of great change, teachers watch for activities that indicate that changes are beginning. In addition to the obvious physical changes, cognitive changes also take place as intellectual functioning shifts from the concrete-operational to the formal-operational stage. Personal growth, therefore, is dynamically tied to these physical and cognitive changes and must be assessed accordingly.

The early adolescent will often exhibit excessively egocentric behavior, constantly combing hair, adjusting clothing, and looking furtively at his or her reflection. Emerging sexuality and stronger perceptions of sex roles are obvious as boys cast longing, self-conscious looks at girls and as girls giggle together in groups, discussing boys. While this growing awareness of each other along with their increased cognitive ability would seem to instill a growing sense of self-confidence, more often than not the opposite occurs. Even having attained a high level of self-assurance during the elementary grades and having mastered the personal skills necessary for success in that relatively safe environment, young adolescents often regress to experiencing strong feelings of inadequacy. As they did when they were younger, they become deeply and egocentrically concerned with their status in the world. This time the egocentricity is not so much a case of "everything should be mine" but "everyone should like me." Accordingly, many seventh graders seem obsessed with convincing themselves and others of their intelligence, sophistication, and especially their attractiveness.

Erikson calls this period of personal growth a time of identity formation. He sees children caught between the demands and anxieties produced by internal changes and those pressed upon them by the world outside. If identity formation is to proceed in a healthy manner, inside and outside demands must be met stimultaneously. Unfortunately, since the teenager's growing cognitive ability produces questions not so easily answered, the outside world often seems unwilling (or unable) to provide them.

Seventh graders' questions, then, are indicative of normal early adolescent behavior: "How come we have to obey all these rules when we see adults breaking them all the time?" "Why do you preach to us about the danger of smoking when you smoke?" "Why are we forbidden to use 'bad' language when books and movies are filled with it?" These and other questions chart the degree to which each teenager is coping successfully with the early adolescent years. The narcissistic primping and preening provides further clues, along with boy-girl flirtations and note passing.

Conversely, behaviors indicating less successful or less appropriate early adolescent growth are all too evident in some youngsters. The emerging adolescent is very much a comformist, so peer approval is enormously important—more so than that of adults. For the youngster who desperately needs to be liked and accepted, smoking, drugs, alcohol, skipping school, vandalism, and outright defiance of authority are frequent behaviors. By noting these behaviors, teachers build a systematic evaluation of each student, an evaluation essential to success in finding ways to change inappropriate behavior and to guide early adolescents safely through this often troublesome period.

Another look at the children we have followed since kindergarten will provide more specific portraits of adolescent behavior. Charlie was the star in kindergarten, his childhood environment having provided him with the personal security to thrive there. As he continued through the elementary grades, he gracefully acquired mastery of himself and his world. An intellectually capable and physically attractive youngster, he was also emotionally secure enough to withstand the normal stresses and strains of school. By the time he reaches seventh grade, he clearly has everything going for him.

Charlie is still an attractive boy but having grown very fast during the past few months, he is a little gawky. However, he seems to be handling his growth spurts without undue self-consciousness, wearing his jeans and a rugby shirt with more self-confidence than the other boys. His comb is not used quite as continuously either but he uses it often enough to allay his self-conscious fears. He also checks his reflection often enough to satisfy himself that he conforms both to his own perception of attractiveness and to that of the group. His awareness of girls and his conversations with them are typical of the early adolescent—self-conscious smiles, overly loud laughter, shuffling from one foot to the other—but, again, with a little more openness and less agitation. Charlie seems to understand this brief stage he is in and is patiently enduring it until he can go on to more mature relationships.

When Charlie questions his teachers about the mistakes adults make and about the inconsistencies in their demands, he does so honestly and with an obvious desire to understand the contradictions around him. When other children entice him with offers to skip school or sneak a smoke, he is mildly interested and may indulge. But he does so to satisfy his curiosity rather than to be one of the gang, and more often than not, he will politely decline the next offer. His sense of self-worth and identity are already stronger than that of most of his classmates.

His adolescence will be happy and fulfilling for him; his ego is strong enough to withstand its stresses and strains. His natural curiosity will lead him not only to question but to find answers to the problems in his life. Chances are good that he is already knowledgeable about the mechanics of sexuality and his understanding of his own emerging sexuality is based on its naturalness and individuality, rather than on misinformation and anxiety. In short, Charlie's behavior will be recorded as mildly self-conscious, open, and honest in his desire to know, relatively secure in his relationships with girls, desirous of being "one of the boys" but personally strong enough to resist the temptations proferred by troublemakers.

Bill, on the other hand, has temporarily lost the gains he made in the security of the elementary grades. He is almost a kindergarten child again, terrified of the world in which he is thrust. His lack of ego strength convinces him that no one sees anything very good or attractive in him. Bill betrays his anxiety over his unattractiveness by constantly tucking his shirt in, straightening his socks, smoothing his pants, combing his hair, squeezing real or imaginary blemishes, brushing lint from his sweater, finally making himself look unattractive by his nonstop activities. He glances constantly but furtively at the girls, as though he is desperately trying to satisfy his curiosity about them without being noticed, watching them to see if they are watching him. He hopes they are but he would be humiliated if they did.

Bill also fails to question the inconsistencies of the adult world. He lacks as much courage to question adults as he does security and self-confidence to join the group in which he so desperately seeks membership. Thus he is fair game for the offers Charlie so easily declined, eagerly accepting behavior he is not ready for and that will almost certainly be further destructive of his personal development. He will appear to be happier for a time as his membership in the smoking and class cutting groups fulfills his need to be "one of the boys," but his general behavior toward intellectual work and toward the other youngsters will remain inadequate. At times he will seem almost sure of himself as he challenges a teacher or insults one of the girls, but only when he is in the company and security of his friends.

Bill's behavior portrays his futile and inappropriate attempts to find himself in the world of the teenager. Emotionally, he has not yet grown successfully through the period of mastery and inferiority, yet he is expected now to survive in an environment often difficult even for a person like Charlie. It will be a long time before Bill achieves a sense of identity, and he needs every opportunity to catch up and feel comfortable with himself.

Suzy also requires special attention as she enters the seventh grade. She is feeling more than normal anxiety because she is still a preadolescent girl among girls and boys more physically mature than she. She too wants to be liked and invited to join the gang, but she is very quiet and the teenagers she is drawn to are not drawn to her. Consequently, she feels very much alone and wishes junior high could be more like grade six, where she was happy, where her friends were close to her, and where she felt secure and liked herself. Now her friends seem remote and different, having grown up without waiting for her. Although Suzy is also fair game for Bill's friends, she has been more fortunate than he throughout her early childhood and elementary school years. She has enough self-assurance to know that she doesn't need membership in the group that badly, and she resists the same invitations that Bill so eagerly accepts. Although she has more than normal anxiety about her status as a teenager, her anxiety about inappropriate behavior is even greater and she declines to participate. She is not as strong as Charlie though, whose refusals are accepted in recognition of his maturity. Suzy's refusals are met with derision, insults, and even roughhouse treatment. Her strength has become a liability, and she is rejected by both the good group and the bad.

Suzy's behavior is characterized by increasing withdrawal from class discussion and frequent absences from school. She will spend more and more time by herself as she comes to feel less and less a member of the class. Teachers who are willing to understand and help can increase her chances of surviving this and other adolescent episodes. Teachers who ignore these clues to the status of her personal growth miss the opportunities that might make all the difference to her.

Like Alice and the other children we have studied, Charlie and Bill and Suzy are also real. Each has entered adolescence bringing along a unique set of experiences composed of varying degrees and kinds of personal strength. Each occupies a place along the continuum of personal development—Charlie at the top, for instance, and Bill near the bottom. To understand these children, teachers must rely largely on their personal observations. There is no classroom test that will accurately record Bill's insecurity or Charlie's unusually strong self-assurance. Instead, teachers must know what constitutes early adolescent behavior in order to observe and record it faithfully. Only in this way can teachers express accurately the dynamic interrelationship of each child's physical, cognitive, and emotional growth. With these observations, teachers have the information they need to help each achieve successful personal identity and self-assurance.

SUMMARY

The personal behaviors teachers observe at any level, from kindergarten through senior high, are far too numerous to list with any degree of completeness. The types of behavior considered normal at various grade levels must be considered as being optimal expressions of personal development that can be used as yardsticks against which to compare and understand actual behavior.

Physical development plays a significant role in how children perceive themselves. Overweight children or those who tower over the other children will almost certainly experience feelings of personal inadequacy and express these feelings in their behavior.

Cognitive development also plays a significant role in how children perceive themselves. Intellectual failure or inadequacy diminishes the ego, and self-awareness suffers, convincing children that others feel about them as they do.

Physical, cognitive, and personal development interact dynamically, each affecting the other. To understand how dramatically different personal development can be among children of the same ages, teachers must observe and record how the personality develops and how it is affected by physical and cognitive development. In any grade, children's personal behavior occupies a continuum that includes maximum emotional development at one end and serious emotional deficits at the other.

Helping children to grow emotionally and personally is a teacher's responsibility just as much as helping them learn all of the skills and subjects they encounter throughout their school years. To do this effectively teachers need not be psychologists or psychiatrists. Rather, they need to know what constitutes adequate personal growth at each point along the continuum, and they need to take the time to observe the degree to which each child is achieving adequate growth. Finally, teachers need to evaluate their observations carefully in order to construct the kind of learning atmosphere in which each child's personal growth will have the best chance for optimal development.

IMPORTANT POINTS TO THINK ABOUT

1. Think about some of the small children you know who have recently started school. Can you describe some of their personality behaviors that might cause problems for them in school? Which behaviors give clues to feelings of mistrust and insecurity?

2. Imagine yourself teaching in grade four. Can you visualize and describe the personal behavior of a child who is self-confident and who has begun to master the world of learning?

3. Adolescence is a time of "storm and stress" for some children. Can you describe some of the personal behavior characteristics of young adolescents whose personal development has not yet reached a level of strong identity formation?

4. Personal growth, like cognitive growth, can be described as a continuum along which each child can be placed. Can you suggest specific behaviors to watch for at several points along the continuum, from early childhood to late adolescence?

5. How might academic progress be affected by strong feelings of insecurity? of mistrust? of low self-esteem? of inferiority?

ADDITIONAL READINGS

J. S. Bruner, *Toward a Theory of Instruction* (Cambridge, MA: Harvard University Press, 1966).

J. S. Coleman *et al., Youth: Transition to Adulthood* (Chicago: University of Chicago Press, 1974).

L. K. Frank, *On the Importance of Infancy* (New York: Random House, 1966).

D. Elkind, *Children and Adolescents* (New York: Oxford University Press, 1970).

E. H. Erikson, "Identity and the Life Cycle," *Psychological Issues* 1 (1959).

CHAPTER ELEVEN

ASSESSING CHILDREN WITH SPECIAL NEEDS

IMPORTANT POINTS TO WATCH FOR

New federal laws requiring maximum educational opportunities for all handicapped children will require that *all* classroom teachers understand the procedures for measuring and evaluating exceptionality.

One classification of children with special needs is *mental retardation.* Many thousands of these youngsters have profited from placement in the regular classroom.

Children are usually classified as *emotionally disturbed* when their fearful, hyperactive, destructive, or withdrawn behavior seriously affects their ability to succeed in school.

Many children with *sensory handicaps* are included in the regular classroom. Such handicaps include those associated with vision and hearing.

Speech-handicapped children must be evaluated with great care since speech is so fundamental to the vital process of communication.

Physical handicaps are generally medical problems, and assessment information comes from physicians. Two types of physical handicaps in regular classrooms are the crippling condition of *cerebral palsy* and the chronic health disorder of *epilepsy*.

Learning-disabled children are those who appear to have the capacity to succeed in school but who seem to break down in specific skills. The causes of learning disabilities are quite varied and may extend from mild temporary emotional upset to fairly severe neurological impairment.

This chapter was written especially for this volume by Professor Brian Cleary, Director of the Curtis Blake Child Development Center at American International College.

Gifted and creative children constitute another category of special need, one that poses special problems of assessment and teaching due to the voracious appetite such children have for knowledge.

Although many of the testing and measuring instruments for special children are highly specialized and generally are not administered by teachers in the regular classroom, teachers have to know how to interpret the results of most of these tests in order to provide the diagnostic teaching required by special children.

SPECIAL EDUCATION—A CHANGING SCENE

Less than 100 years ago society looked upon any handicap—physical, emotional, or mental—as some form of punishment or retribution from God. Children with such handicaps were hidden or institutionalized, doomed to live in a monotonous, unproductive, and stigmatized environment. Even the word "handicap" conveys a connotation of difference or deviance, and those so described are often regarded with a mixture of pity and suspicion.

There are over 8 million handicapped children in the United States, and according to the National Advisory Committee on the Handicapped, almost half of them are not receiving appropriate educational services. However, with teachers of special education receiving more intensive and better training and more funds being made available, the condition of the handicapped is improving.

NEW LAWS FOR THE HANDICAPPED

Perhaps the most important advance has been the changing perception of how handicapped young people fit into the educational picture. Until recently, children with special needs who received schooling did so almost on sufferance while most were excluded from regular schools and classrooms, their presence regarded as detrimental to other children. New laws and a changing national policy now recognize that the handicapped have a right to education. Under the law, that right may not be abridged because of lack of funds. Their education must be appropriate to their needs and potential, not just a token show of pious concern. By far the most important piece of legislation in this field is Public Law 94-142, enacted in 1975. Known as the Education for All Children Act, this law will have a great impact on education in the United States in the coming years. It will affect not only teachers in special education, but teachers in every school, at all levels. The law is designed to ensure that every handicapped child will receive a special education and the necessary related services.

The provisions of this law will have far-reaching effects on the teaching profession. First, the law calls for free public education for all handicapped children between the ages of 3 and 18. By 1980 this coverage will be extended to the age of 21. The law additionally provides for financial incentive grants for each child between the ages of 3 and 5 who is provided with special education. The grants encourage early identification and intervention.

A second provision is that an "individualized educational program" be developed for each child. In the form of written statement prepared jointly by a qualified school official, by the child's teacher and parents, and, if possible, by the child, the program must include an analysis of the child's present achievement level, short- and long range goals, and the identification of the specific services that will be provided to attain those goals. The statement must also indicate the extent to which the child is be able to take part in regular school programs, and it must make provisions for checking the progress of the child and adding any revisions that appear to be needed.

Third, handicapped and nonhandicapped children will be educated together to the maximally appropriate extent. This is a concept known as "mainstreaming." Handicapped children may be placed in special or separate classes only when the severity or nature of the handicap is such that education in a regular classroom cannot be achieved satisfactorily. This provision refers to something we will discuss in more detail later.

The fourth major provision is that tests and other evaluative instruments used for diagnosing and placing handicapped children must be prepared and administered in such a way as to eliminate any racial or cultural discrimination. Moreover, such testing should be conducted in the child's native language.

Teachers will feel the impact of the Education for All Children Act in a number of ways. Frequently, the responsibility of the teacher of children with special needs is greatly underestimated. However, in all but extreme cases, it is often the teacher who detects the handicap and makes the first referral. After the child has been evaluated, the teacher will be expected to implement the appropriate educational plan. Moreover, with the growing emphasis on mainstreaming, the teacher may find that there are many different types of exceptionality within one class. Consequently, teachers must have a working knowledge of identification, diagnostic, and remedial techniques for a wide range of conditions and learning needs. While teachers need not bear the brunt of the specialist's responsibility for diagnostic and evaluative work, they must be able to work effectively in interpreting and implementing prescribed techniques and, equally importantly, to report on progress or suggest modifications to the program if it is not producing the expected or desired results.

CATEGORIES OF SPECIAL EDUCATION

There are many categories of special education reflecting different physical, mental, and emotional conditions that exist among children. Many of these categories, such as the mentally retarded and emotionally disturbed, require highly specialized diagnostic and evaluative procedures that involve many disciplines including medicine, psychiatry, neurology, ophthalmology, optometry, and psychology. Teachers are seldom involved in initial referral and diagnosis in such cases but will often be called upon to provide educational programs and to evaluate educational progress. At the other end of the spectrum, there is a wide range of specific learning difficulties that an observant teacher should be able to recognize and make a referral before they develop into serious emotional and behavioral problems. The earlier such disabilities are recognized, the better the chances of successful remediation.

Looking at the various categories, we will consider the extent to which teachers might be involved in the identification, diagnosis, and remedial program. Often, it is not a matter of remediation but of adaptation. Many of these conditions pose the problem of helping a child adapt to a regular school program or at least to one that is as close to the regular program as possible. Adaptation, like mainstreaming, is a recurrent theme throughout much state and federal special education legislation; that is, children should be placed in the "least restrictive situation" commensurate with their educational needs.

The attempt to categorize children with special needs often reveals a tendency to construct mutually exclusive conditions. Many textbooks and authorities refer, for example, to such categories as mentally retarded, learning disabled, emotionally disturbed, physically handicapped, and so forth, often using only the initials M.R., L.D., E.D., or P.H.

Unfortunately, such divisions are frequently imposed at the administrative level where, for purposes of grant proposals, funding, staffing, purchasing, and so on, specific categories must be clearly defined. However, in actuality young people seldom fall into such neatly compartmentalized conditions. It is quite possible for a child to be learning disabled and emotionally disturbed, or mentally retarded and learning disabled. The important criteria for classification depend instead upon the priorities in the child's life. A dramatic example of this is the case of a microcephalic boy whose teacher spent many weeks teaching him to write his name. Although she was delighted at the child's achievement, which had been laborious and time-consuming, there was considerable doubt as to the value of this skill. Who was going to accept this child's signature as valid? Was writing ever going to be a valuable tool? The immediate priorities in the boy's life were to feed himself, dress himself, use the toilet himself, and master other life skills that would help him to become productive and self-sufficient. Obviously one must consider the priorities in such a child's life. Even though he may be capable of performing certain academic skills, the investment of time and effort may be out of proportion to the usefulness of the skills required.

The various categories of exceptionality are by no means as clearly defined as they may seem. The development of school programs must often be tempered with a careful consideration of the priorities of each child.

MENTAL RETARDATION

The first category we will consider is mental retardation. Despite many peoples' preconceived notions that the mentally retarded need to be institutionalized and cannot take part in educational programs, many thousands of mildly retarded persons have profited from regular schooling and are living useful, happy, and productive lives. The American Association of Mental Deficiency defines mental retardation as "sub-average intellectual functioning which originates during the developmental period and is associated with impairment in adaptive behavior." This definition sets forth three criteria to be considered. "Sub-average functioning" is usually based on an individual intelligence test with a score at least one standard deviation below the mean. The second criterion, "onset during the developmental period" means any time up to the midteens, when intellectual potential appears to be determined. Third, "impairment in adaptive behavior" refers to developmental milestones such as crawling, walking, and talking, in the early years, and later to academic and social adjustment.

Developmental, academic, and social adjustment are all important indicators of adaptive behavior. Thus there are two important aspects to be considered in mental retardation, intelligence and behavior. Children who perform lower than average on an individual test of intelligence may still manage to struggle along in the regular classroom and could hardly be considered retarded. Similarly, children who behaviorally cannot adapt to the regular classroom but whose measured intelligence is within the average range cannot be categorized as retarded. Such maladaptive behavior might well be the result of some emotional disorder. Clearly, cross-checking will serve to avoid the pernicious labeling of children as mentally retarded based entirely on a single criterion such as an intelligence test score. Cross-checking becomes even more important with very young children or children from deprived home environments. There are probably scores of children who because they rank in the low ranges on intelligence tests, and do poorly in academic work, are considered retarded but go into the world with some vocational skills to support themselves happily and independently.

Classifying Retarded Children

There are many methods of classifying retarded children, but most educators tend to use a method based on educational potential. Such measures, based on intelligence test scores, establish ranges that are rather arbitrary and are subject to a great deal of overlap from one school district to another. Generally, there are four divisions on the basis of I.Q. that are generally accepted in education. Children with an I.Q. between 75 and 80 (which range from minus 1.0 standard deviation to minus 1.7 standard deviations) are considered as slow learners or borderline retarded. Such children are capable of marginal success in the regular classroom but many tend to drop out, and very few graduate from high school. Yet most are able to become self-supporting, fairly well-adjusted adults.

Children with an I.Q. between 50 and 75 tend to have delayed academic skills; that is, they lag considerably in such areas as reading and mathematics, although they may eventually achieve at a fourth or fifth grade level. The majority of these children are placed in regular kindergarten or first grade classes, but due to poor achievement or maladaptive behavior, they are usually referred to special classes. Such children are generally categorized as educable mentally retarded. Upon leaving school they will be capable of unskilled or semiskilled work, but many will require further economic and social support.

At an I.Q. level of 25 to 50, children are generally considered as trainable retarded. Although I.Q. scores at this level are rather unstable, children within this range may be expected to have observable physical and sensory impairments that contribute to their intellectual shortcomings. Characteristically, unlike the educable mentally retarded, the trainable mentally retarded evidence developmental problems during the preschool years. Such children need training in self-care and often in language development. They are seldom able to master anything but the most basic skills at the first grade level. Most need constant care, although some may be capable of limited economic usefulness in a sheltered workshop.

The fourth and most severely afflicted group are the profoundly retarded with I.Q. levels below 25. Such individuals are seldom considered within the framework of special education, and most are institutionalized early in life and require constant care.

In 1967, the President's Council on Retardation identified about 3% of the population as retarded. Subsequently, the U.S. Office of Education modified this estimate, placing the incidence at 2.3%. These figures reflect definitions of mental retardation based on both I.Q. and adaptive behavior. If I.Q. were the only criterion, approximately 16% of the population would be considered retarded (minus one standard deviation is at the 16th percentile). By adding the criterion of adaptive behavior, the incidence drops to 3% or even lower.

A study of the various causes of mental retardation is beyond the scope of this book, but a brief look at the general classification of causal factors is useful. There are two broad etiological (causal) categories, endogenous or primary and exogenous or secondary. In the exogenous group the cause stems mainly from environmental factors or outside causes. Such factors as infections or illnesses, poisons, accident or damage (sometimes called "trauma"), or endocrine (glandular) disorders are the leading causes. Endogenous or primary defects, on the other hand, are determined mainly by genetic factors and run in families, although they occasionally skip a generation. However, in spite of an increasing volume of research, investigators still don't know what causes over 80% of all cases of mental retardation.

The Retarded Child in School

Of the four categories of mental retardation, one most concerns the classroom teacher—the educable mentally retarded. Children in this category are seldom identified until they reach school age. While there will undoubtedly be some early signs such as difficulty or delay in communication, problems of socializing, or poor physical development, these are seldom severe enough to cause great concern and do not greatly affect the child in the preschool years. With the more demanding set of conditions in school, a child who functioned marginally at home is faced with increasingly difficult tasks that ask for more than the child can give. The key words here are "increasingly difficult," for the mentally retarded child is usually unable to follow the academic regimen of mastering one skill or task and moving on to a more complex or demanding one. Because of this and because many teachers have not had even an introductory course in special education, many educable mentally retarded children may not be identified until they have spent a year or more in school. Unless there has been a policy of early screening or group testing, such children will remain in a regular classroom trying to keep up with the others. It is often not until they are failing miserably in second grade or becoming behavior problems that their difficulties become too acute to ignore. Failure and bad behavior are indeed brutal but effective diagnostic signs, arriving after considerable damage to the child's self-image has already been done.

As a result of poor performance and behavior, the teacher usually makes a referral to the school psychologist, who will administer tests designed to explore and assess the child's functioning in the areas of intelligence, personality, and perception. Other members of the school staff such as the nurse, principal, and the teacher may help in this assessment, and together they will attempt to determine the child's potential. Sometimes other professions such as a pediatrician, social worker, or psychiatrist may be consulted. If the problems are mainly due to low intellectual potential, and it becomes clear that the child cannot be expected to keep up with the regular classroom program, the staff will probably make a referral to a special class.

The most prevalent special education program for the educable mentally retarded child involves a special classroom that is generally situated within the regular school. Classes are usually small, numbering between 12 and 15, but this will depend on age range and also the range of mental abilities. At the primary level emphasis is upon language and speech development, social adjustment, good work habits, following directions, basic reading readiness. There is no undue emphasis on academic skills, and there is an acceptance that such skills will develop slowly and to a lesser extent than in the normal child. There will, however, be some emphasis on counting and word recognition. At the elementary level (ages 9 to 14) there is an increasing emphasis on basic skills of reading, writing, and math. Basic social studies and some practical science are also included. However, these subjects are based on practical application so that the secondary program becomes a consolidating unit to prepare the child for work and home living. Many educable mentally retarded children develop functional reading and writing skills; moreover, they have opportunities to mix with normal peers inasmuch as they often attend regular classes in physical education, industrial arts, and home economics. Towards the end of their formal schooling, these young people will become increasingly involved in vocational training or work study programs often run by agencies or organizations outside the school. Thus the educational focus for educable mentally retarded children is the development of basic academic skills but not to the exclusion of social and personal adjustment, so that, to the best of their ability, they will become self-sufficient and able to pursue occupational roles in society.

The trainable mentally retarded child, unlike the educable mentally retarded, is usually identified before reaching school age. For example, Down's Syndrome (mongolism) and many other conditions involving physical abnormalities can be identified shortly after birth. However, even in the absence of such abnormalities, there are critical signs. Children who don't respond to objects and events around them, don't smile or babble, and are unable to walk or talk within the normal times are suspect. Such children may be referred by a pediatrician to a clinic for evaluation by a pediatric neurologist, psychologist, or other specialists for a thorough diagnosis. Although some public education facilities are available for the trainable mentally retarded, they more typically attend special day schools. Here they work on basic school activities such as communication skills, developing a reading sight vocabulary to recognize signs and labels, counting, time telling, and so on. Self-help activities, such as dressing, grooming, eating, and caring for personal belongings are also emphasized. Many of these children live at home and may later work happily or productively in sheltered workshop situations.

From this description, it is clear that the majority of mentally retarded children can not only learn but also become self-supporting. Many attend public schools, often with only minor modifications to the regular program. It is important that teachers become aware of their role in working with the mentally retarded so that they do not burden such children with unrealistic expectations or, equally importantly, that they do not underestimate their potential.

EMOTIONAL DISTURBANCE

A second category of special education, emotional disturbance (E.D.) entails a maze of controversial findings. Even the definition is so elusive that each concerned profession seems to have its own set of diagnostic determinants. Traditionally, exceptional children have been classified under three broad definitions: mentally retarded, emotionally disturbed, or learning disabled. Administratively, this seems very tidy, but unfortunately these problems do not come in such neat, mutually exclusive packages. The difficulty of defining such a broad concept as emotionally disturbed is typical of the overlapping among categories, for by almost any definition, the emotionally disturbed will often include aspects and degrees of mental retardation as well as learning disabilities.

Most children exhibit some symptoms of emotional disturbance at some time in the course of growing up. Though they are normal most of the time, they occasionally become fearful, hyperactive, destructive, or withdrawn. It is doubtful, however, that they will ever be labeled "emotionally disturbed." At what point the incidence of these behaviors will qualify the child as emotionally disturbed depends a great deal upon the setting in which they occur and the tolerance of the observer. In the classroom, children who exhibit such characteristics to the extent that their work consistently fails to meet expectations or their behavior consistently disrupts the class are most likely to be considered emotionally disturbed.

Although we cannot discuss all of the definitions or professional perspectives on this general disorder, it will help to look at some of its broader psychiatric features. The psychiatric model consists of three broad categories: first, primary behavior disorders, that is, habit disturbances, conduct disturbances, and neurotic traits; second, psychosomatic disorders including allergic conditions, fevers, headaches, colitis, and so on; and third, psychotic reactions, which are more severe and include bizarre preoccupations, excessive fantasy or inability to separate fantasy from reality, and schizophrenia. The most severely disturbed child is called autistic. Autistic children demonstrate extreme ritualistic behavior, head banging, rocking, and a total withdrawing from the world around them. They often fail to develop speech and show an intense concern with routine.

The Emotionally Disturbed Child in School

The educational approach to emotionally disturbed children is behavioral in nature. Although surveys conducted among large numbers of teachers reveal many different terms descriptive of emotional disturbance, they reveal more general agreement upon three broad dimension behaviors. First, conduct disorders include children described as defiant, uncooperative, irritable, and impertinent. Second, laziness, lack of interest, preoccupation, and inattentiveness typify the group of immature or inadequate behaviors. The third dimension includes personality problems such as inferiority or feelings of worthlessness, fearfulness, and depression. Another characteristic frequently cited is delinquency, but there is considerable disagreement about whether this maladjustment is truly part of the emotionally disturbed syndrome or if it represents a separate category.

In view of the great divergence of opinion as to what does and does not constitute emotional disturbance, it is very difficult to make a meaningful assessment of the incidence of emotionally disturbed children. In 1970, the U.S. Office of Education estimated that about 2% of all school age children in the country were emotionally disturbed. However, the variance is large, ranging from about 1% to 20% depending on the criterion used to define emotionally disturbed. Another factor that tends to confuse the estimates is that many children improve quite dramatically as they grow older so that children considered emotionally disturbed in the fourth grade are no longer classified as such when they reach seventh or eighth grade. With so many conflicting viewpoints and criteria, attempting to estimate the incidence of the problem is difficult.

The causes of emotional disturbance are also subject to controversy. It is generally conceded that they arise from two main sources, brain damage or dysfunction and experiential factors such as familial, cultural, and social influences. The supporters of the brain damage position cite the high correlation between complications during pregnancy and birth and later behavior and learning problems. They also point to the effectiveness of drug therapy in cases of children with suspected brain damage and also to the behavioral differences between siblings reared in similar environments. To confuse the issue further, problem behaviors such as impulsiveness, hyperactivity, and distractibility frequently found among brain-damaged children are also seen in emotionally disturbed children. This raises the question whether the difficulties are primarily organic in nature. In fact, the term "minimal brain damage" was developed to describe children whose behavior resembled that of children with demonstrable brain damage but in whom no brain damage could be discerned.

In educational practice one of the most common criteria for identifying emotionally disturbed children is the judgment of the classroom teacher. Judgments of observant teachers correlate very highly with identifications made by psychologists and psychiatrists of children with emotional disturbance. This is also true in other cases of special needs such as learning disabilities and communication disorders.

Most emotionally disturbed children remain in the regular classroom, and there will be 2 or 3 in almost any class of 30 children. However, whether or not these children are referred for diagnosis and possible placement in a special class depends on many things, not the least of which is the teacher's tolerance for behavioral and academic differences. Such tolerance will vary considerably from teacher to teacher; some cannot stand any "acting out" or destructive behavior, yet shy, fearful, and withdrawn children are completely ignored because they are so unobtrusive. Other teachers can handle the destructive student, yet they may be quite rightly concerned about the shy, withdrawn child as well.

Teachers are generally more tolerant of academic differences than they are of behavioral differences. However, the child who is emotionally disturbed and underachieving will often remain in the regular classroom as long as the teacher can cope with the disruptive or underachieving behavior. We will discuss the pros and cons of placing emotionally disturbed children in the regular classroom as opposed to a special class when we look at the principle of mainstreaming. There is conflicting evidence as to emotional, social, and academic advantages of one placement over another.

Many school districts maintain separate schools for the more severely emotionally disturbed or will assist parents financially in placing children in private day schools. However, there is an increasing tendency to develop classes for the emotionally disturbed within the regular school setting. Such classes are conducted under many different labels such as social adjustment classes or classes for behaviorally disordered children. The class size is small, usually from 5 to 15 under the supervision of a teacher holding a special certificate or with training in special education. Classes of this type may be self-contained so that the children will spend the entire school day there. "Resource rooms" or "crisis rooms" are an alternative in which part-time help is offered by a specially trained teacher.

Children who are severely disturbed may be placed in a residential school, especially when the home situation is poor. If facilities or finances are not available for this, the child will, as a last resort, be placed in a state institute for the mentally ill. Although emotionally disturbed children may be in a situation other than the regular classroom, the important objective is that of providing therapy to help them return to a normal setting rather than simply containing them.

CHILDREN WITH SENSORY HANDICAPS

Another group of handicaps comes under the general heading of sensory handicaps—handicaps involving sensory acuity in the modalities of vision, hearing, and speech. Although speech difficulties may seem unrelated to vision and hearing, there may often be a definite link between speech and hearing problems.

Visually Handicapped

Visually handicapped children are divided into two groups: the partially sighted and the blind. Children categorized as partially sighted have a degree of vision that, from an educational point of view, allows them to tackle reading and other school-related tasks. Blind children, on the other hand, have so little, if any, useful vision that they must use braille for the reading process. The American Foundation for the Blind defines blindness in a way generally used for educational purposes. In essence, it says that individuals are considered legally blind if they have 20/200 vision or less in the better eye with the best possible correction. The partially seeing are defined as having between 20/200 and 20/70 vision in the better eye with the best possible correction, or who, in the judgment of eye specialists, can benefit from the use of some form of special educational program. The fractions or ratios mentioned above are measures of visual acuity or clearness of vision. One way to measure visual acuity is by means of the familiar Snellen wall chart. The test distance for the Snellen chart is 20 feet and the top, large letters appear to be the same size from 200 feet as the standard size letters appear from 20 feet.

If this sounds complicated, an example might help. If an individual is able to read from 20 feet the line of letters that a normal person can read from 20 feet, the individual is said to have 20/20 vision. If from 20 feet the person is able to read only the letters that normally sighted persons can read at 40 feet, the person is said to have 20/40 vision. Legal blindness means a person can read from 20 feet only a letter size that a normal person can read at 200 feet. In addition to this test, many other measures of visual behavior must be checked.

Almost half of the visual problems in partially sighted children are due to refractive errors. Refraction is the way light is bent by the lens to make it focus on the retina. If the light is focused beyond the retina, this is called hyperopia or farsightedness. If the focus is in front of the retina, it produces myopia or nearsightedness. Astigmatism is caused by an uneven focusing—partially behind and partially in front of the retina. Other causes of defective vision may be structural defects such as cataracts or defective muscle functioning. About 10% of defects are due to infection and injury. Approximately 50% of blindness is due to prenatal causes, most of which are unknown. The remaining cases are due to poisoning, disease, or injury.

Children with serious visual problems are usually identified before they start school. However, the partially seeing child may not be identified until the early school years when visual skills become of great importance in performing school work. Again, the observant, informed teacher usually makes the all-important early referral.

In 1965, the National Society for the Prevention of Blindness[1] listed ten behavioral signs that may be symptomatic of some form of visual defect: (1) excessive frowning and rubbing of eyes; (2) closing or covering one eye, tilting the head or thrusting it forward when looking at objects; (3) difficulty in reading or other close work; (4) excessive blinking, irritability, or crying when doing close work; (5) stumbling or tripping over small objects; (6) holding books or work material very close to eyes; (7) inability to participate in games requiring distance vision; (8) excessive sensitivity to light; (9) red-rimmed, encrusted, or swollen eyelids, recurring sties, inflamed or watery eyes; (10) complaints of dizziness, headaches, or nausea following close eye work, blurred or double vision.

Children who show any or several of these symptoms should be referred to the nurse or an eye specialist for a thorough examination. There are two kinds of eye specialists. One is the ophthalmologist, a medical doctor specializing in diagnosis and treatment of diseases and defects of the eye. This doctor is a surgeon and may also prescribe medication or corrective lenses. The other is an optometrist, a nonmedical practitioner who prescribes glasses for refractive errors and eye muscle defects.

The content of instruction for both the blind and the partially sighted is the same as that for seeing children, but the media may be different, including braille, audio aids, visual aids, or large type. However, there is an additional component for the visually handicapped that relates to their mobility and the orientation training they need to cope with the physical and social environment. The objective of such training is to help them function independently, and a program usually covers both self-care and social skills.

The most efficient and useful means of reading for the blind is braille. It comprises a "cell" of 6 raised dots. There are 63 combinations of these dots, which can be used to represent almost any numerical, literary, or scientific material. Although it seems rather like a code, it is a complete reading and writing system. Braille is taught in the same sequence as reading instruction is to small children. Readiness skills are emphasized in kindergarten and grade one, and a mental age of about 6 is considered necessary for a successful start with braille.

The residential school plan is still the generally accepted one for blind children. However, by using itinerant (traveling) teachers and resource rooms, together with tutorial assistance, training, and special materials, partially sighted children are being increasingly provided for in the public schools. Although regular schooling is most feasible for the partially sighted, there is also a growing trend to follow this pattern with the blind child, particularly for a child with good earlier training.

Hearing Handicapped

A form of handicap that is often greatly underestimated is hearing impairment. Traditionally, children with hearing handicaps are divided into two categories that are distinguished by the degree of hearing loss. The reason for this is that a hearing loss, if severe, will affect the acquisition and development of language. Thus, the hard of hearing are defined as children whose hearing loss does not prevent language development during and after the "prelingual period," which is about two to two and a half years. Children are categorized as deaf if they have such a severe hearing loss at birth or during the prelingual period that language development does not occur.

Many people feel that such classifications are limited since they do not place enough emphasis on the age at which the hearing loss occurs. A child of 9 or 10 who suffers a total hearing loss could be defined as hard of hearing rather than deaf if language had developed normally. Consequently, some authorities have proposed a definition based on a functional educational premise rather than a sensory deprivation one. Such a definition would consider deaf children in two categories according to when the hearing loss occurred. The prelanguage deaf would be children in whom deafness occurred before speech and language were firmly established. Postlanguage deaf would be those who would otherwise be considered "hard of hearing," that is, functionally incapable of recognizing auditory stimuli, but for whom speech and language have already been acquired. Thus the age at which the hearing loss occurs in terms of the stage of speech and language development is of great importance in deciding on definitions of degrees of deafness. The degree of hearing loss is determined using two factors, frequency and intensity. Frequency is the pitch of sound, while intensity, or amplitude, is the loudness. Frequencies are measured in cycles per second (more recently called Herz). Speech frequencies are usually considered to be between 500 and 2000 Herz, but an audiogram for a hearing evaluation will measure frequencies between 125 and 8000 Herz. Intensity is measured in decibels (dB). These are actually logarithmic units of sound intensity that are measured from an arbitrary point of reference. The point of reference is the average level at which normally hearing people using both ears can detect the faintest sound they are capable of hearing. Slight hearing loss occurs at a level of more than 26 decibels and less than 40 decibels. Here difficulty is encountered only with very soft speech. Loss of about 41 to 55 decibels represents a mild hearing impairment and may interfere with the reception of speech at normal loudness. A loss of between 56 and 70 decibels is a marked hearing loss, while between 71 and 90 decibels is considered severe. Individuals who are severely handicapped will understand only amplified speech. Extreme hearing loss requires more than 90 decibels of intensity, and this precludes reception of even amplified speech.

The causes of deafness are categorized under two general headings in much the same way as retardation. Endogenous deafness is some inherited defect, while exogenous deafness is caused by disease or injury. The so-called children's diseases, mumps, measles, scarlet fever, whooping cough, and pneumonia can all cause damage to the delicate ear mechanisms. Chronic infection of the inner ear, called otitis media, is another cause of deafness, but in recent years the incidence of deafness from otitis media has declined due to antibiotics and improved surgical techniques. However, the origins of the largest proportion of cases of deafness are undetermined.

A large proportion of mild hearing loss goes undetected in children because they learn to talk at an average age and can understand normal conversation. The kind of behavior evidenced by these children such as inattention, poor achievement, or poor listening skills is often attributed to low intelligence or emotional problems. Teachers should be especially alert for children who consistently turn their heads and crane forward, who continually ask their classmates, "What did she say?" or who seem to misunderstand instructions and directions. Certainly, all children should be given a periodic screening, and those who appear to have hearing loss should be given a thorough individual hearing evaluation by a specialist.

Educational provision for hard-of-hearing children can usually be made in the regular classroom. With the use of a hearing aid, most are able to keep up academically, although there may be some problems in the areas of speech and language. Special teachers may work part time with the children to help them with the appropriate use of a hearing aid, to provide training in discrimination skills such as lip reading to help "fill in" missing words, and to provide speech training.

For deaf children, education is provided in residential schools, day schools, and special classes in public schools. There is some controversy over the best method of communication for the deaf. The oral method requires communication through speech and lip reading. The manual method provides communication through use of gestures and movements of the hands and arms together to represent words and letters of the alphabet. Both methods are in use, and most authorities agree that there is a place for both, although some schools are strictly oral in their approach and discourage the manual system.

Deaf children have great difficulty acquiring abstract language skills. Subtle shades of meaning of the same word and complex grammatical skills must be systematically taught to the deaf child. A further difficulty encountered by deaf children is one of which all classroom teachers should be aware. Obviously, the acquisition of speech is laborious and difficult for such children and their speech, even after many years of training, may be somewhat labored and distorted. This sometimes conveys an impression of retardation and may result in diminished expectations of the child. Such interpretations, based upon speech patterns, can be very damaging, both emotionally and academically.

Speech Handicapped

Speech handicaps are closely related to hearing problems. Speech, the basic tool of language, evolves from the infant's cooing and babbling to the imitation of sounds. Before children are a year old they can generally put syllables together. Early in the second year normal children are beginning to use meaningful speech. At two, they are combining words, and by three they are able to use sentences. The rate of development of speech patterns is greatly dependent on how parents respond to and reinforce the child's efforts.

While it is not easy to define a speech handicap, there are certain criteria that are useful guidelines. If the speech pattern is so different from normal that it interferes with communication, and becomes a source of attention and emotional distress for the child, then it is categorized as a speech problem. Speech problems in particular tend to overlap into many other categories of exceptionality such as mental retardation, hearing handicaps, physical handicaps, and so on. For example, about 50% of all cerebral palsy children have some form of speech disability. Defects in speech may be classified under seven general headings: (1) delayed speech development, (2) articulation disorders, (3) voice disorders, (4) clef palate, (5) stuttering, (6) disorders associated with hearing impairment, (7) disorders associated with cerebral palsy.

Delayed speech occurs when children's speech does not develop according to their age or when they develop only partial verbal expression. The causes of such delay may include hearing loss, mental retardation or cerebral dysfunction, or damage. The term "aphasia" is used to describe loss or lack of development of speech or language and usually refers to damage or dysfunction of the central nervous system.

Voice disorders include such problems as vocal quality, pitch, and intensity. Such defects appear in the production of sound and include huskiness or hoarseness. Sound resonance may occur in the nasal cavity, which results in a nasal quality of speech. Problems of vocal pitch are often related to defective development of the larynx.

Another voice disorder, cleft palate, occurs when the bony tissue of the palates in the mouth fail to join during the third month of pregnancy, resulting in a cleft or division in the roof of the mouth and often with a division of the upper lip. Typically, such children will have speech that is very nasal and misarticulated.

Of all speech defects, stuttering has probably received more study and attention than any other. The dysfluency that is typical of the stutterer is often noticed in young children who are still acquiring language. This is alarming to parents but seldom persist into later years. It is not until dysfluency persists or occurs with such severity and frequency that it becomes frustrating to the speaker and the listener that the condition is called stuttering.

Children with hearing difficulties often have articulation problems with speech, although much depends on the severity and kind of hearing loss. There may be omissions and distortions of sound as well as indistinctness of word endings. They also tend to have poor discrimination between voiced and voiceless sounds. In children with mild hearing loss, sounds like *s, sh, z, th, t, ch,* and *f,* all of which have high frequency but low intensity or acoustic power, are most likely to be misarticulated.

It is difficult to determine with much accuracy what the incidence of speech disorders really is; since so much depends on what criteria are used to define speech or language problems. Furthermore, speech problems tend to diminish sharply during the first two years of school and continue to decrease through the twelfth grade. In 1970 the U.S. Office of Education placed the total percentage of school age children with speech problems at about 3.5.

As with so many learning problems, early referral as a result of teacher observation is most important. Many schools use a survey method, screening each child in the school. The teacher referral method involves having the teacher listen to and observe the students for any noticeable deviation in their speech patterns. Children who show such deviations may then be referred to a speech clinician for further testing to determine the specific problem. Most articulation tests evaluate the production of consonant sounds at the beginning, in the middle, and at the end of words. Such tests as the Goldman Fristoe Test of Articulation, the Hejna Developmental Articulation Test, and the Templin-Darley Test of Articulation are typical examples of the types of tests used by speech clinicians.

Speech is, of course, fundamental to the process of communication. Because of this, speech problems are high on the priority list in special education. Help for children with articulation problems may be provided by a speech clinician in individual or group sessions held at least twice a week. However, both parents and teachers should play an important part in helping the child practice and transfer the program into daily living. The teacher will usually carry on a program of remediation in the classroom to reinforce the work done by the clinician or specialist. These classroom programs include such activities as auditory discrimination, reading, spelling, and specific speech skills.

CHILDREN WITH PHYSICAL HANDICAPS

The category of physical handicaps includes a broad range of conditions that obviously cannot be covered adequately in this chapter. Physical handicaps are primarily medical problems that may be the result of neurological, orthopedic, or chronic health disorders. The term might, of course, include children with visual and hearing problems, but it is more usually applied to children whose problems are not sensory. There are two major physical handicaps that teachers are most likely to encounter. The first is the crippling condition, cerebral palsy, and the second a chronic health disorder, epilepsy.

Cerebral Palsy

Cerebral palsy is a complex disorder of the neuromuscular system caused by injury to the brain either before, during, or after birth. The condition is characterized by several types of disturbance to the voluntary motor or movement system. Spasticity describes the involuntary contraction of the affected muscles, which causes tenseness and inaccurate, uncoordinated movement. Ataxia describes poor body balance and a disorder of spatial orientation. Athetosis refers to an almost constant, involuntary motion of the extremities. Two other conditions are "rigidity," a state of constant abnormal muscle tension, and "tremor," characterized by small rhythmic movements or an uncontrolled shaking. Cerebral palsy also accounts for a large number of visual, hearing, and speech defects.

Prenatal factors that may give rise to cerebral palsy include incompatibility of blood type, diabetes, prematurity, toxemia (the presence of toxic substances in the mother's blood stream), and certain kinds of maternal infections such as rubella. During birth, prolonged labor or anoxia (lack of oxygen) may cause central nervous system damage. Subsequently, factors that may damage the central nervous system include infections to the brain such as encephalitis, accidents, poisoning, and progressive neurological disorders.

Many specialists may be involved in the treatment and educational programming of cerebral palsy children. Orthopedic surgery and the use of braces may help them gain better control over their limbs. Occupational and physiotherapy may offer activities to help improve muscle coordination and self-help skills. Educational facilities also vary. One type of facility for the cerebral palsy child is the special day school or class. However, the majority of cerebral palsy children who have mild handicaps and normal intelligence function well in regular classrooms in public schools, where minor modification to classrooms and informed, understanding teachers can greatly compensate for their physical impairments. What is most important is that educators evaluate the disability in terms of the problems it presents to learning, such as the ability to move about the classroom and manipulate learning materials.

Epilepsy

The second major physical handicap that we shall consider is one of the chronic health problems. These include congenital heart defects, tuberculosis, cystic fibrosis, diabetes, and epilepsy, which is historically the most misunderstood of the chronic health problems. Causes of epilepsy may be rooted in a variety of neurological disorders, but the seizures themselves are due to electrochemical disturbances in the activity of the brain cells.

A grand mal seizure can be most distressing to people who have never seen one before. The child will grimace and roll the eyes; there may be a change in facial color, along with laborious breathing and gnashing of teeth. Shrill cries may accompany spasmodic convulsions that cause the child to fall to the ground. Drowsiness and unconsciousness usually follow and may be prolonged but seldom last for more than 30 minutes. During the seizure, little can be done to help. It is best to try to ease the child to the floor, allowing the body to move as it will. Try to remove dangerous objects or move the child gently away from precarious positions, and place a coat or blanket under the head, turning it to one side to help discharge saliva from the mouth and make the child more comfortable. Many people who suffer from such seizures have learned to detect warning signs, called auras, visual or auditory sensations that occur before the onset of the seizure. The auras may give sufficient notice for precautions to be taken before the seizure begins, but in other cases they are experienced only a few seconds before the seizure.

A less serious form of epileptic seizure is known as petit mal, which involves a short period of mental confusion often accompanied by a vacant stare, a nodding of the head, and heavy sighing or gasping. These seizures may last only a few seconds during a conversation or even during physical activity and may be mistaken for daydreaming or lack of attention. Following such a seizure a child may have no recollection of what happened and may take several minutes to "pick up the thread" of whatever was going on before.

Epilepsy is predominantly a disorder of young people, with over 75% of all cases occurring before the age of 20. In the majority of these cases, epilepsy is only temporary. With appropriate medical or surgical treatment half of those with elipsy will become seizure free and another 20% may have such a reduction in the frequency of seizures that they are able to maintain a good social adjustment. The advances made in the control of epilepsy by drugs means that most afflicted children can participate in regular classroom programs. In fact, many cases of petit mal go undetected or are first noticed by an observant teacher who is familiar with the symptoms of epilepsy. The most significant educational problem this and other chronic health disorders presents is the loss of the child's strength, vitality, and alertness. However, the teacher's primary concern may lie in the distress to the other children when they witness a seizure. By moving slowly and deliberately to help the child and not treating the incident as a major crisis, the teacher can do much to allay the alarm of the other class members. In addition, discussion of the disorder during health and hygiene classes can promote a realistic understanding and acceptance of the situation.

CHILDREN WITH LEARNING DISABILITIES

Many categories of special education or exceptionality are surrounded by controversy over definitions and incidence. The category of learning disability is no exception. Many children with average intellectual potential and no physical or sensory problems seem to have great difficulty in acquiring certain academic skills. The key component of a learning disability is thus a discrepancy between intellectual potential and academic achievement. The U.S. Office of Education proposed a definition that was the basis for the Learning Disabilities Act of 1969.[2] This definition appears in almost every text on special education published since and is worth repeating:

> Children with specific learning disabilities exhibit a disorder in one or
> more of the basic psychological processes involved in understanding

or in using spoken or written language. These may be manifested in disorders of listening, thinking, talking, reading, writing, spelling or arithmetic. They include conditions which have been referred to as perceptual handicap, brain injury, minimal brain dysfunction, dyslexia, developmental aphasia, etc. They do not include learning problems which are due primarily to visual, hearing, or motor handicaps, to mental retardation, emotional disturbance or to environmental disadvantage.

Although this definition excludes children with emotional or behavioral disturbances, many authorities tend to emphasize that causal conditions are of secondary importance unless they point to specific remedial techniques. The most important and enigmatic aspect of learning disabilities is that they concern a group of children who appear to have the capacity to succeed academically but break down in specific skills. Kirk and Bateman[3] developed a definition of learning disability in 1962 that is still widely accepted because it points to some fairly specific factors that may provide clues to remediation. That definition is as follows:

A learning disability refers to a retardation, disorder or delayed development in one or more of the processes of speech, language, reading, writing, arithmetic or other school subjects resulting from a psychological handicap caused by possible cerebral dysfunction and/or emotional or behavioral disturbances. It is not the result of mental retardation, sensory deprivation, or cultural or instructional factors.

The diversity of definitions tends to produce bewilderment and suspicion. The fact is that different definitions of learning disabilities serve different purposes. Definitions generated by state or federal departments are generally concerned with economic, administrative, or sociological considerations. Such definitions cannot possibly be responsive to the different theoretical approaches that are part of both research and practice in the field. From a practical point of view, most authorities consider the discrepancy between intellectual potential and academic achievement as the most useful approach. This definition usually goes on to exclude mental retardation, severe emotional disturbances, educational or cultural deprivation, or sensory loss or impairment. This means, of course, that diagnostic instruments should be able to distinguish the learning disabled child from the excluded categories. Once again, an observant teacher is usually the first person to see the early symptoms of a learning disability. These may show up in kindergarten and almost certainly by the first or second grades. Such behaviors as restlessness, inattention, constant daydreaming, poor perceptual skills (inability to copy and match shapes), as well as lack of coordination or poor motor skills are often associated with learning difficulties. As the pressure of school work increases children often show a marked deficiency in visual auditory memory, sequencing or discrimination or sometimes a combination of these difficulties. Many of these children tend to have specific problems in learning to read or in manipulating or understanding numbers and concepts of quantity. If teachers are able to make a referral before the child lags too far behind, they may help to avoid the frustration and behavior problems that so often accompany the learning disability.

Once the child has been referred for a possible learning disability, individual testing will be conducted. Diagnosis is often done by means of elimination—finding what is not causing the problem. However, the causes of learning disabilities are varied and may extend from neurological impairment to a mild temporary emotional upset. If the causes are, in fact, neurological, it often becomes a matter of treating the symptoms or trying to help children to compensate for their difficulties.

Test instruments include an individual intelligence test in order to judge the child's academic potential. There will also be an assessment of vision and hearing, a speech and language evaluation, and achievement testing in reading, spelling, and arithmetic. In some cases the child may be referred for neurological testing and possibly an EEG (electroencephalogram) to trace electrical activity in the brain. Many authorities disagree with the emphasis on cerebral dysfunction in learning disabilities, arguing that it is most important to concentrate on the behaviors that make learning difficult or impossible. While this is true up to a point, it is also important to realize that truly learning disabled children are not just "lazy" or "badly behaved" but may be the victims of a subtle cerebral dysfunction that impairs some very specific skills such as linking or sequencing visual and auditory stimuli. In severe cases, it is sometimes impossible to overcome this deficit (or only at the cost of great emotional stress), and it is better to look for compensatory techniques.

The Learning-disabled Child in the School

Because of the broad range of conditions existing within the framework of learning disabilities, it is not surprising to find that educational programs are based on a variety of theoretical approaches. Many approaches stress fundamental, preacademic aspects of learning considered to be the underpinnings for acquiring such complex skills as reading and writing. Perceptual motor training and a variety of similar activities including balance exercises, laterality, and directionality training have enjoyed much attention during the past decade. However, there is very little research to support these highly theoretical positions, and indeed the overwhelming majority of the research indicates they are of little value beyond chance probability. In general, it seems that the most successful approach to remediation of learning disabilities is a direct one, that is, tackling the child's specific problems as they arise. This approach is not always palatable since it often involves a great deal of patience, drill, and "overlearning."

Remedial programs for learning disabled children tend to be individualized and specific to the areas involved, such as reading, arithmetic, language, and so on. Most children remain in the regular classroom, and the teacher implements the remedial plan with the help of an itinerant learning disability teacher. Some children may go to a resource room for a period each day to receive special help in subject areas. Since most of these children are of average or above average intelligence, it is important that they be afforded the opportunity to learn at their grade level in spite of their specific difficulties in reading or writing, perhaps through the use of alternative media. In the past, too many children who were capable of learning at, for example, a grade six level were locked into a grade three curriculum because that was their reading level. As a result, emotional and behavioral problems further complicated the learning disability.

A most controversial topic in learning disabilities is hyperactivity. Symptomatically, the hyperactive child is continually on the go, restless, destructive, uninhibited, and seemingly incapable of settling down to any task for more than a few miinutes. Whether this should be categorized as a learning disability in itself is debatable. More probably, the inability to attend, together with the negative feedback from classmates and the teacher, conspires to leave the child further and further behind academically. Another problem is that no single cause of hyperactivity has been isolated although two general etiological factors seem responsible—one neurological, the other, emotional. There are many correlates (signs that go along with hyperactivity but may not be causal). Most mothers of hyperactive children report, for example, that the child was always restless and slept poorly even as an infant. Some form of brain damage or dysfunction is often considered to be the cause, yet, very often, no such damage can be found.

Another interesting speculation as to the cause of hyperactivity is that some food additives cause an allergic reaction that produces the symptoms of hyperactivity. Some empirical evidence has been gathered to support this possibility. However, to date there is no sound research evidence to indicate that food additives are responsible for hyperactivity.

Medication is often prescribed for hyperactive children and amphetamine-like drugs such as Ritalin, Dexedrin, and Cylert are often quite successful in helping the child, although in no way can they be considered cures. Although there have been accusations of children being drugged en masse into a state of happy acquiescence, there is no evidence to support such dramatic and generalized accusations. However, it does seem that such drugs are ineffective in some cases. Minor tranquilizers may be more effective with children who demonstrate hyperactive behavior that results from emotional disorders.

The field of learning disabilities has developed from a nebulous beginning in which children were labeled anything from "lazy" to "perceptually handicapped." Despite the imprecise definitions and a preoccupation with neurological dysfunction, a concentration on basic and specific disorders in the learning process has emerged rather than on medically or neurologically based categories.

GIFTED AND CREATIVE CHILDREN

There is a tendency to use the words "handicapped," "exceptional," and "special needs" synonymously, usually implying social, intellectual, or academic limitation. However, the other extreme of exceptionality categorizes children as superior or "gifted." The definition of gifted, once again, depends on the criteria used. Two definitions are most prominent in the literature, one includes outstanding ability in any field and the other is focused on creativity and intellectual superiority. The difficulty of measuring the various factors quantitatively has led to the general use of an I.Q. score for identifying the gifted child.

How many gifted children are there? The percentage based on I.Q. scores tend to vary depending on geographical and socioeconomic factors. Assuming that an I.Q. of 140 is the lower limit for the definition of gifted, we will find in an average community that only one half of one percent have reached this level. However, in a superior socioeconomic community, approximately two percent may be expected to be within the gifted range.

The causes of giftedness are obscure and are not, as is commonly believed, related to brain size. Although there are many correlates, none are necessarily causal. Early childhood experiences such as encouragement from parents, opportunities to practice skills, and stimulating social contacts seem to be conducive to the development of reasoning ability and the understanding of abstract concepts. These factors are emphasized on most intelligence tests and are generally considered indicative of intellectual capacity.

While an observant teacher can often identify many incipient cases of special needs, research indicates that teachers do not fare well in identifying gifted children. In fact, they tend to select many children who are not gifted while overlooking many who are. Teachers tend to concentrate on such things as academic success, social success, and talent in areas such as drama or art. Children who are shy, underachieving, or nonconforming are generally excluded from consideration as gifted. Group intelligence and achievement tests are similarly ineffective in identifying gifted children, since they tend to penalize children who have reading, emotional, or motivational problems. The individual intelligence test is probably the most effective method of identification, but it is expensive and time-consuming.

Some characteristics are typical of gifted children. They learn rapidly and easily and seem to retain what they learn. They have good vocabularies and demonstrate originality of thought and expression. Most enjoy reading at a mature level and seem to enjoy the company of older children or adults. They show a great ability to generalize, to see relationships, and to make logical associations. So far, we have listed the positive characteristics, but there is another side to the story. Gifted children often show such negative characteristics as restlessness, carelessness, and impatience with rote learning, drill, and handwriting. They are often critical towards themselves and others. The surprising fact is that gifted children may often be underachievers and behavior problems in school.

There are many strategies and approaches to help the gifted child. Accelerated advancement and special enrichment classes are designed to decrease the time the child spends in school and, in general, they seem to profit from this. The idea that acceleration causes social and emotional stress is not supported by the facts. The great majority of gifted children adjust very well to advanced grades. One of the great problems with the gifted is the teacher's limitations in time, knowledge, and skill. This is not to belittle the teacher but to emphasize the gifted child's voracious appetite for knowledge, skill, and learning. Such children require input from many teachers and counselors as well as increased guidance and extracurricular services. Many programs for the gifted include part-time attendance in nearby colleges before graduation from high school.

SUMMARY

In attempting to identify children with special needs, educators and medical personnel use a wide variety of tests. Many of these are highly specific, especially in the fields of neurology and medicine. In education and psychology there is less specificity and indeed many of these tests have questionable validity. Although teachers may not become involved in administering most of these tests, they must have a working knowledge of their existence and their usage. Two broad categories of tests are used in schools, namely, group and individual tests. There is considerable controversy as to which is more desirable for screening children. Clearly, group tests are more practical and economical in dealing with large numbers of children. The proponents of group testing also argue that such tests put a child in a criterion setting, that is, in the classroom and not in a clinical or laboratory setting. This means that learning characteristics are assessed in a setting like that in which the child is expected to learn. On the negative side, most group tests measure only academic areas and seldom consider behavioral problems that may affect learning performance. There are also many functions that cannot be measured by group tests; for example, sequencing of information and oral expressive skills require individual assessment. Another disadvantage to group testing is the lessening of control over the administration of the test, such as keeping time limits, maintaining suitable supervision, and giving instructions. The greater the variability of administrative procedures, the more likely the results are to be biased.

Individual testing is, of course, much more expensive and time-consuming and often requires highly trained specialists. It is, therefore, not always practical as a screening technique but becomes much more important as a follow-up instrument to assess problems revealed by the initial screening.

Educational and psychological tests cover a range of functions such as language development, perceptual motor skills, emotional status, intelligence, and achievement. The number of such tests is monumental and ever increasing. Such works as Buros Mental Measurements Yearbook,[4] published by the Gryphon Press, provides a ready source of information about the purposes and administration of a great range of tests. It also furnishes details about validity, reliability, cost, and so forth.

Some cautionary observations must be made about testing in special education. Children who have learning disorders may vary considerably in day-to-day performance. What may be considered to be a severe weakness as evidenced by a test result could disappear or be almost undetectable a few weeks later. In addition, while many tests have been carefully standardized with validity and reliability coefficients and item analyses, they are generally based on performance of a normal or representative sample—and these are the very children with whom the tests are not used. Even when the sample reflects the population there is not much evidence that any standardized test will be appropriate for children who are mentally retarded, hyperactive, perceptually handicapped, or emotionally disturbed—in other words, for children who cannot be standardized.

A final warning should be made with regard to tests that purport to evaluate or measure certain theoretical underpinnings of learning problems. Such areas as dominance, laterality, motor coordination, and so on are often tested because difficulties or abnormalities in these areas often seem to accompany learning problems as coexisting behaviors or correlates. Unfortunately, they are often assumed to be causes by people who should know better. Correlation is *not* necessarily causation. All too often this approach leads to a remedial onslaught against symptoms, and children are condemned to spend hours practicing such things as gross motor skills, perceptual skills, or coordination exercises in order to remedy so-called hypothetical deficits. As a result they are often removed from the very kind of programs they need, programs providing specific remediation in reading, arithmetic, and so on. Teachers must use a definitive approach to such testing in order to satisfy themselves that the test will lead to the development of remedial activities for actual problems and not for theoretical constructs that are only peripherally involved.

We have tried to present in this chapter an overview of the various types of special needs and the kinds of services that are provided for each. The most important thing to realize is that the field of special education is the concern of all teachers and not just specialists. The more all teachers know about this challenging area, the better they are equipped to help identify, understand, and provide for the many children with special needs who look to them for help in the regular classroom.

IMPORTANT POINTS TO THINK ABOUT

1. As a regular classroom teacher, you will be responsible for evaluating and understanding the learning potential of children with a variety of special needs. Think about some of the ways you will have to change your own behavior as you set about to observe the behavior of a child who is confined to a wheelchair.

2. What kind of information will you expect to receive from specialists concerning a fourth grade child with epilepsy?

3. A child with a "learning disability" has been enrolled in your seventh grade history class. What questions will you ask of those who determine the child's ability?

4. You have noticed that one of your first grade children constantly reads "was" for "saw." What steps will you take to determine the seriousness of this behavior?

5. How might you recognize "gifted" or "creative" behavior in your children?

6. If you were a principal, how would you caution your teachers not to teach inadvertently to the "symptoms" of a learning problem rather than to the problem itself?

NOTES

1. *Helping the Partially Seeing Child in the Classroom*, Pub. T-300, National Society for the Prevention of Blindness, New York, 1965.
2. National Advisory Committee on Handicapped Children, for the United States Office of Education, 1968.
3. S. Kirk and B. Bateman, "Diagnosis and Remediation of Learning Disabilities," *Exceptional Children* 29 (1962): 72.
4. O. K. Buros, ed., *Mental Measurements Yearbook*, 2 vols. (Highland Park, NJ: Gryphon Press, 1972).

ADDITIONAL READINGS

H. D. Babbidge, *Education of the Deaf* (Washington, DC: Department of Health, Education, and Welfare, 1965).

I. Beery, *Models for Mainstreaming* (San Rafael, CA: Dimensions, 1972).

E. Bleck and D. Nagel, *Physically Handicapped Children: A Medical Atlas for Teachers* (New York: Grune & Stratton, 1975).

E. M. Bower, *Early Identification of Emotionally Disturbed Children in Schools* (Springfield, IL: Charles C. Thomas, 1969).

T. Bryan and J. H. Bryan, *Understanding Learning Disabilities* (New York: Alfred Publishing Co., 1975).

M. Byrne and C. Shervanian, *Introduction to Communicative Disorders* (New York: Harper & Row, 1977).

W. M. Easson, *The Severely Disturbed Adolescent* (New York: International Universities Press, 1969).

Federal Register (Part IV), Department of Health, Education, and Welfare, Public Law 94-142, Education for All Children Act (Washington, DC, 1977).

G. O. Johnson, "Special Education for the Handicapped—A Paradox," *Exceptional Children* 29 (1962).

M. Kindred *et al.*, eds., *The Mentally Retarded Citizen and the Law* (New York: Free Press, 1976).

B. Lovenfeld, ed., *The Visually Handicapped Child in School* (New York: John Day, 1973).

J. W. Melcher, "Law, Litigation and Handicapped Children," *Exceptional Children* 43 (1976).

J. B. Mercer, *Labeling the Mentally Retarded* (Berkeley and Los Angeles: University of California Press, 1973).

H. R. Myklebust, *Progress in Learning Disabilities* (New York: Grune & Stratton, 1975).

J. P. Rice, *The Gifted: Developing Total Talent* (Springfield, IL: Charles C. Thomas, 1970).

N. E. Silberberg and M. C. Silberberg, *Who Speaks for the Child?* (Springfield, IL: Charles C. Thomas, 1974).

CHAPTER TWELVE

EVALUATING CHILDREN IN A SCHOOL SYSTEM— A MODEL

IMPORTANT POINTS TO WATCH FOR

Each school system is as unique and individual as its students. Each must develop its evaluation plan in terms of philosophy and goals.

Physical, personal, and cognitive development must be evaluated continuously through the grades, not in isolation from each other but as all three interact dynamically in the individual's total growth.

An effective evaluation plan provides information to help teachers compare youngsters' progress with others around the country.

An effective evaluation plan provides information to help teachers plan for and meet individual needs *at any time* during the school year.

A good systemwide evaluation plan measures physical, personal, and cognitive progress against well-established theories of human development.

An effective evaluation plan includes reporting pupil progress to parents through forms and parent conferences that clearly indicate each youngster's *individual* growth.

School systems must make decisions about the testing, measuring, and evaluating programs they think are appropriate to their needs. In this chapter, we will describe briefly one process by which a school system attempts to evaluate the progress of its children and some of the ways in which it reports this progress to parents and others who need to know.

We will not attempt to build a perfect evaluation model or a model that is guaranteed to meet the needs of all involved. The diversity of the population from area to area and among cultural groups necessitates careful assessment of the individual needs of each school population.

Therefore it is essential that school systems consider themselves as individual as the children they educate. Two small towns sharing a common boundary may well have significantly different populations of children due to socioeconomic, racial, and other differences. The evaluation programs will need to be different for each. Even with a larger community or a big city, widely differing cultural groups necessitate that two schools very close to each other employ testing programs that are quite different. A neighborhood populated by middle or upper class citizens, for example, may border on a neighborhood of lower socioeconomic status. If a group whose native language is Spanish, French, or Chinese populates the lower class neighborhood, or perhaps a group that has not been fully integrated into American culture, the school system cannot expect the children to succeed on standardized tests consisting of information unfamiliar to them. In the past, the use of the same tests for all children created serious problems. In some cases, poor administrative judgment in the use and interpretation of tests allowed unfortunate comparisons between groups, violating the dignity and human rights of many children. It was not unusual for cities to consider entire groups of youngsters as inferior, either in actual potential or in real achievement. As a result, curricula and the physical facilities of individual schools reflected this attitude to some degree. In short, whenever test scores alone are allowed to determine actual ability, the danger arises of decreased attention to the needs of the children involved. Decreased attention leads to diminished resources and the attitude that one group of children is less important to the total human effort than the children of cultural groups that tests more heavily favor.

Testing programs must be considered in terms of children's needs. Even though great pressures are often brought to bear to treat children from various backgrounds differently, testing programs should be used only to diagnose children's individual needs. Whether a school or school system stresses standardized group intelligence and achievement tests, criterion-referenced material, or teacher-made assessment tools, they are important and useful components of a testing program only if they serve this vital purpose. Even when tests are given to gather data for national comparisons, the results should be used to provide important clues about the needs of the particular group and, ultimately, through further testing and evaluating, about particular students.

TESTING, MEASURING, AND EVALUATING CHILDREN IN A SMALL COMMUNITY

Smaller towns have the advantage of more homogenous populations and simplified communication. Most of the teachers know each other, and the administrative group is well known to the community. Parents in a small town tend to be closer to their schools and more involved in school affairs.

Individual school committee members are generally known personally to teachers, administrators, and parents. These close relationships among professionals, policymakers, and parents not only make communication more effective, they also help to ensure active participation in school affairs. Thus, when decisions are made concerning testing procedures, nearly everyone in town knows about them. This provides two advantages. First, it allows input from those involved and concerned with children's needs, and second, it helps to prevent professionals or policymakers from producing unilateral decisions that are not acceptable to parents. Although such decisions have been made as a matter of course for generations, recent demands by parents and other nonprofessional parties to know more about educational decisions and the reasons for them have led to legislation we will review in Chapter 13. This legislation guarantees parents access to all information gathered about their children and to all practices that affect their children in any way.

What, then, are the general needs of children in a small community? How can they be stated so everyone in town can understand and accept them? And most important, after general needs have been determined, how does the school system assess the degree to which they are being met? Finally, how are the individual and unique needs of each child assessed and diagnosed to provide teachers with the information they require to develop teaching strategies to meet their needs appropriately?

PHYSICAL DEVELOPMENT

Children need to be physically capable of success in the demanding environment of the classroom. Therefore, teachers will assess three aspects of youngsters' physical needs and development as they enter kindergarten.

Vision First, teachers need to know whether children's vision and hearing are adequate for the learning environment. the initial testing for vision consists of standard procedures for determining visual acuity and focus. All children are required to take this test as a screening device to help the school identify specific vision problems. For instance, the nurse who gives the test might notice that Ted seems to have difficulty in focusing on objects. His eyes are not working together to focus on the chart. This initial screening activity gives the school an important clue that Ted has a serious physical need.

Hearing The initial hearing test is given for the same reason. It is a test to identify children whose auditory ability seems to be impaired. Without good hearing, children cannot recognize sounds and therefore may not develop adequate speech and language and may have difficulty learning to read. Without good auditory discrimination and acuity, children bring inappropriate sounds to the printed word and are unable to read it accurately.

Children with apparently normal vision and hearing will receive no further testing for a while and can begin the school learning process. Those like Ted, who are identified as having an apparent deficit of some kind, either in vision or hearing, will be referred to specialists who will administer more sophisticated tests, including mechanical tests by audiologists and optometrists and thorough assessments by doctors specializing in vision and hearing to determine whether identifiable deformities or physical damage might exist. In a few cases, no such obvious cause for the problem will be discovered, so the children will be referred to doctors specializing in diagnosis and treatment of disease or damage to the central nervous system.

Speech Another common problem occurring in young children entering school is inadequate speech. Although many early speech problems are the result of immature speech behavior, this must be recognized and corrected for optimal use of speech in the learning process. For children whose speech defects seem more severe, special tests are available and are given by speech therapists.

In short, before children are asked to begin the demanding process of learning to read and write, for which vision, hearing, and speech are essential, the school will make every effort to discover the degree to which they are ready and able to do so. Those who seem to have difficulty will undergo further evaluation to determine the precise nature of their impairments. Only then can teachers prepare materials and strategies to help them learn in spite of their impairments. Without such thorough testing of vision, hearing, and speech, some children will be doomed to failure and frustration, an unnecessary situation given the current knowledge of how to test, diagnose, and correct vision and hearing difficulties.

General physical condition A second aspect of physical assessment has to do with general physical condition. Good physical condition provides abundant energy for both motor and intellectual tasks. Consequently, the school must identify children who seem to be run down or otherwise lacking in physical strength. For this assessment, the school requires a complete physical examination of all children entering school. Thus a child who seems extremely lethargic will be referred to the family doctor for more specific testing of blood conditions, metabolism, and the like. If more specific or serious physical problems seem to exist, specialists will be asked to provide precise information about the child's condition along with directions for overcoming or living successfully with the handicap. Knowing that Bill is diabetic will help teachers tailor the teaching environment to accommodate his special needs. Such knowledge will also remind teachers to observe him for evidence of fatigue or other specific behaviors that signal a decline in learning energy. Similarly, knowing that Joe's lack of enthusiasm and spirit is caused by a long history of poor motivation and diet will help teachers have patience with him until his health improves.

The list of physical deficits is long and includes everything from such obvious impairments as physical deformities and crippling diseases to subtle problems associated with the central nervous system. Since teachers can now know about a great many more disabilities than ever before, they can find ways to provide special learning strategies to help compensate for each. Most important for teachers is understanding the dynamic ways in which physical health interacts with and affects the learning process.

Thus the testing program in a small community begins by determining the degree to which each child is physically able to thrive in the demanding environment of the classroom.

Physical Growth through the Grades

As children move into and beyond kindergarten, assessment of physical growth will continue in both formal and informal ways. Vision and hearing will be checked again in grade one, and special testing will be called for whenever the screening tests indicate the need for more precise diagnosis. General physical examinations will be encouraged each year, although this will be the responsibility of the parents rather than the school

Informal physical assessment will be an ongoing process throughout each child's school career. As we suggested in Chapter 2, observation by teachers, nurses, physical education instructors, and guidance counselors will provide the major clues to physical problems that might affect overall development. Since classroom teachers have more direct contact with children than anyone else, they are more likely to spot possible physical problems. When this happens, the decision to send a child to the nurse may well be the beginning of important treatment. Identifying possible physical deficits early is a vital aspect of testing, measuring, and evaluating often overlooked in the schools. It can be just as important to the success of some children as the assessment of achievement or intelligence.

Physical Development as a Continuum

A schoolwide program for assessing children's physical well-being, then, should be thought of as a continuum. As youngsters enter the school system, all will receive formal tests for vision and hearing, and those with apparent speech difficulties will be given specific tests to determine whether the inadequacy is related to the maturing process or whether it has some physical basis. Physical examinations to assess overall health will also be required for all children to identify those who might have some specific condition that requires further attention and diagnosis. These initial testing experiences are largely screening activities, important in providing as much information about new children as possible.

The continuum will subsequently include additional physical examinations before the beginning of each year of school as well as vision and hearing tests during grades two and three. From then on, the observation and assessment of physical growth will be largely the responsibility of knowledgeable teachers who understand the importance of good health to learning. In some cases, the observation will be formal, with physical education teachers or coaches watching carefully for evidence of physical problems. In other cases, the school nurse will be important in identifying problems. However, for the most part the initial clues that a physical condition may be inhibiting learning will be the teachers' responsibility. At all grade levels, in all subjects, teachers are expected to observe constantly for indications of physical deficits. In observing carefully and making appropriate referrals, teachers are testing, measuring, and evaluating children's physical development to meet individual needs and improve instruction.

PERSONAL DEVELOPMENT

Children need to be personally and emotionally ready to plunge into the formal learning environment of the school. Good physical health provides the stamina and strength required to learn. Sound personal development provides the emotional strength necessary for successful handling of the anxieties and tensions that are often part of the challenge of learning.

A school system takes into account the growing body of information concerning the dynamics of personal growth. Consequently, teachers know how to identify behaviors that indicate inadequate personal development and can begin to help children compensate for their emotional limitations while finding ways to help them gain greater personal strength.

Assessment of Personal Growth Begins in Kindergarten

As children enter kindergarten, the ongoing assessment of personal development begins. In fact, even before the children arrive on the first day of school, teachers meet with them and their parents for an informal but vitally important visit. It is the first opportunity for school personnel, including the teacher, to get some feeling for each child's personal and emotional readiness for school.

We have emphasized in Chapter 2 and again in Chapter 10 the difficulty of evaluating personal growth. We also emphasized—and we repeat it here—that as difficult as it might be, personal evaluation is absolutely essential if a school testing program is to be considered complete. Personality evaluation is difficult mainly because few formal instruments for its assessment are considered adequate. Many textbooks in tests and measurements, although they describe such instruments as personality inventories, self-report inventories, attitude scales, and sociometric instruments, stop short of recommending them for general use in the overall testing program. We agree that such instruments are probably too limited in their usefulness for such purposes. However, to exclude personality assessment from an evaluation program on the basis of inadequate formal instruments is to ask teachers to understand their children by examining only one facet of growth and development.

In the school system for which we are describing a program of tests, measurement, and evaluation, teachers are not expected to be clinical psychologists or highly trained guidance counselors. Yet all classroom teachers should be knowledgeable enough about personal growth to recognize when it is inappropriate or inadequate for effective learning.

In meeting their prospective kindergarten children, then, teachers carefully observe and record the children's behavior and what they learn about each child's background. For example, Dara's parents will provide important clues to Dara's personality and will help the teacher understand the reasons for some of her behavior. If their description includes strong evidence of overindulgence, the teacher can expect that Dara will demand extra time and energy because she will expect the indulgence to continue. If the parents indicate feelings of resentment or expressions of neglect, the teacher can expect other kinds of emotional responses from Dara—possibly withdrawn behavior or general unhappiness with life.

Dara's parents supplement the information that the teacher's observations provide. In addition, Dara's responses to the new situations and her behavior will provide tentative but important signals about her personal development—signals that may be confirmed later when more evidence accumulates about her strengths and weaknesses. These initial observations represent the first of an ongoing process of evaluation that will help the teacher build a more definitive picture of her personality and how it relates to the stresses and strains of school. If she refuses to answer questions or withdraws from the teacher, she reveals insecurities that will surely inhibit her chances for success in kindergarten. Teachers do not need to know the psychological dynamics that cause insecurity, but they do need to recognize when a child is troubled and unable to relate to others without fear and anxiety.

As we pointed out in Chapter 10, the variety and divergence of personal development among the children sometimes seems overpowering. However, the stability and security of a good kindergarten will often bring about remarkable changes in how children relate to their world. Dara may quickly discover an environment filled with affection and genuine interest unlike she has ever known before. Her insecurity may well fade quickly as she learns that her kindergarten is safe and that no one there wishes to neglect or hurt her.

The initial prekindergarten interview, like the tests of vision and hearing, is a screening process. It is a way to identify youngsters who probably will move into their formal learning environments with sufficient personal strength to thrive there. It is also a way to spot those whose emotional strength is not adequate for the challenge. Once again, the major objective for this first evaluation is to identify probable causes of learning difficulty—in this case, difficulties of an emotional and personal nature that might inhibit success in the learning process. As teachers identify these difficulties and make tentative judgments that one child seems extremely insecure or another seems resentful and hostile, they are implementing a philosophy of meeting individual needs. Teachers test, measure, and evaluate personal growth to find ways of improving instructional strategies and making them fit children's specific needs when their personal development seems inadequate for success in school.

Referring Children to Specialists

Sometimes the initial screening interview will be followed by referrals, in some cases, to school psychologists or adjustment counselors for additional evaluation. Specialists from the department of pupil services are trained to diagnose thoroughly the specific personal problems teachers identify. Their diagnosis will lead to a number of alternatives. For children whose personal behavior is thought to be only mildly troublesome, they will work closely with the kindergarten teacher to help develop teaching strategies to meet each child's needs. Like the child with physical deficits, those with emotional weaknesses will be helped to compensate, and ways will be sought both to teach around the deficits and to help children acquire the personal strength they lack.

In other cases, the specialists may point out that the initial assessment was not accurate and that personal development was probably quite sufficient. In still others, a child or two may be very seriously handicapped by emotional immaturity or by some deeper personal problems, and the parents may be asked to seek psychiatric help or to keep the child out of school until emotional strength improves. Although specialists may use certain testing materials to determine the nature of personal growth, their decisions will also be based on their own observations, and they will either verify or modify the teacher's initial and tentative assessment of each prekindergartner's emotional ability to learn.

As children move into the kindergarten, teachers are responsible for continuing their observation of personal growth. Some remarkable changes in the youngsters' emotional behavior is likely as they settle in to the learning process. Some, who seem frightened by the scene at first, may well recognize that there is safety here and their behavior will change accordingly as they become more comfortable and begin to relate better to the other children. More than likely, the initial assessment has sensitized the teacher to these problems and the ensuing teaching strategies will help such children feel more comfortable. As they feel more secure, they will tackle the learning process with increased assurance and will perhaps make good progress toward adequate personal development.

Initial assessments are not always correct. Sam, for example, who was so friendly and outgoing in the interview and who seemed so emotionally ready for school, is really a very hostile child. Many children surprise teachers with the depth and seriousness of their personal inadequacies— inadequacies that went unrecognized in the first meeting. Assessing personal growth is a difficult process requiring not only knowledge of developmental theory, but, even more important, sensitivity to and patience with a wide variety of behavior patterns. Therefore first decisions must be tentative. Teachers simply cannot know enough about the unique personal characteristics of each child to make a definitive evaluation; they may *never* know enough. Thus keeping decisions tentative assures the best chances for success for each child. Tentative findings encourage teachers to seek help from specialists when they feel the problems need that kind of attention.

Reserving judgment also helps teachers maintain a degree of flexibility in the programs they plan. Flexibility of programming based on tentative assessments of personal development does more to help any child adjust to school than rigidity and inflexibility based on judgmental and unyielding decisions about the child's personal and emotional status.

Personal Growth through the Grades

The process of evaluating personal and emotional growth will continue throughout the school system much as it began in kindergarten. With few pencil and paper tests to yield valid information about personal development, teachers need to depend largely on their knowledge of developmental growth and their ability to make detailed and discerning observations. Behavior that is antisocial or hostile or frightened demands even closer observation to discover whether it is temporary or deeply rooted. Teachers cannot respond impulsively. They must take enough time to make tentative decisions and test their validity.

This process continues throughout the elementary grades, into junior high, and on through high school. Each classroom teacher is part of the first line of defense and protection of children's emotional needs. They receive the first clues that events in children's lives are bearing down on them and creating emotional barriers to successful learning. If teachers are secure in their understanding of human behavior and how personal growth proceeds through a developmental continuum, much the way physical growth does, they are more likely to spot the important clues as soon as they appear. This knowledge also makes their relationships with such specialists as psychologists, guidance counselors, and psychological examiners more productive. Such teachers are not only more accurate in describing children, they are also better able to interpret the specialists' findings and translate them into appropriate remedial action in the classroom.

Difficulties of Assessing Personal Growth

A number of criticisms are likely to arise from this approach to the evaluation of personal growth. First, even in a small school system, teachers are often seriously lacking an adequate understanding of personality development. This will lead to misdiagnosis and inappropriate strategies for helping children. Second, even if most or all of the teachers are knowledgeable about personal development, their individual perceptions of the behavior they see will vary so much as to make agreement impossible. Even trained psychologists in the same school system sometimes arrive at different conclusions and disagree on the remedial action to be taken. Third, some teachers will protest that their job is to teach and not to be responsible for children's emotional well-being. Personal problems and emotional deficits, they may say, are the responsibility of specialists hired for this work.

In the first instance, we agree that lack of knowledge about personal development has been a problem in the past and perhaps will continue to be so in some school systems. However, we believe that teachers are fully capable of acquiring such knowledge and, in fact, are doing so to a much greater degree than ever before. Even though there is still much to be learned about personal development, psychological research has provided important information that is available to everyone. It is demeaning and condescending when specialists claim that teachers are not capable of understanding personal growth. We are convinced that all teachers should assume full responsibility for this knowledge and that they are fully capable of doing so.

In the second instance, we also agree that teachers will differ in their interpretation of the personal needs of a given child. This will be a problem only if different teachers are not willing to take another look or to listen with an open mind to the interpretations of others. With more knowledge of personal development, more and more teachers will enter the classroom with this ability to reserve judgment and to seek the opinions of others. Sharing information and working together with other teachers and specialists to understand Dara's emotional responses will increase her chances of overcoming her difficulties than will a single diagnosis or a quick, unthinking referral to the psychologist. With the availability of more courses and information about human behavior and with a growing understanding of the importance of good personal development to successful learning, more effective identification and remediation of personal problems is now possible.

In the third instance, some teachers persist in disclaiming responsibility for the personal well-being of their children. As teachers enter the classroom with more awareness of the needs of the total child this condition is improving. The problem seems to have been most severe among junior and senior high school teachers whose training included a great deal of study in their chosen subjects and minimal study of human behavior. Secondary school teachers, having learned that successful handling of preadolescent and adolescent behavior often holds the key to successful teaching, are making the effort to understand the dynamics of adolescent behavior. As they do, more teachers willingly accept responsibility for observing personal growth in order to improve each child's opportunities for success.

All three criticisms have some validity in the model school system. It would be unrealistic to expect otherwise. However, as the schoolwide program of testing, measuring, and evaluating develops, it can be assumed that all teachers are professionally committed to their jobs. Before they are asked to systematically observe personal behavior, the administration will develop training programs to help them know what to look for and how to use their information both for referral to specialists and for meeting personal needs in their classrooms. Eventually, all teachers will operate from the same base of information, and all will be knowledgeable about current behavior theories. All will know that specialists are available who will not simply send children back to the classroom with a few suggestions for the teacher, but who will work closely with the teacher and share available information. This team effort, with teachers making the first tentative decisions, sharing them with colleagues, specialists, and parents, and then developing strategies for helping children compensate or change their behavior, is possible in the model school system. Committed and knowledgeable professionals will make the team effort a vital component of a sound program of testing, measuring, and evaluating personal development.

COGNITIVE DEVELOPMENT

Most authors of test and measurement textbooks stress academic achievement when they discuss schoolwide testing programs and tend to treat physical and personal development somewhat lightly. We believe that since all three components of development interact dynamically, to concentrate evaluation efforts on one to the exclusion of the others will not serve children's best interests, nor will it afford teachers a clear view of the total child. Without wishing to diminish the importance of evaluating academic performance, we ask you to review Chapter 2 and the discussion of the importance of understanding the physical, personal, and cognitive aspects of behavior for effective evaluation.

Traditionally, school systems have spent more time and money in measuring academic progress than in the other two components combined. This may seem only natural since parents see the schools primarily as transmitters of the world's knowledge and as builders of the basic skills necessary to understand, communicate, and build upon that knowledge. Another reason for the emphasis on cognitive achievement is that group tests for measuring both cognitive potential and achievement have been available for many years, while such tests are not available for the other two areas of development. Yet standardized tests that have been used in enormous numbers and widely accepted by educators and parents alike are now being severely criticized for their alleged shortcomings. Educators are reevaluating the practical value of standardized tests of intelligence and achievement to measure children's real progress. While the model will include such tests because the best of them are useful, other, equally important techniques will be included as well.

Assessment of Cognitive Growth Begins in Kindergarten

As in the evaluation of physical and personal factors, teachers in the model system will want to know the degree to which each child entering kindergarten is "ready" for the learning process. In effect, teachers will try to establish a rough estimate of each child's cognitive potential to tackle the intellectual demands of school. It may seem strange to worry about a child's academic promise for such a low level academic endeavor as kindergarten. However, since cognitive development, like physical and emotional development, is a continuum, each successive cognitive level requires that sufficient and appropriate experiences have been gained in the preceding levels. Without such experiences to build upon, children will be frustrated by the demands of cognitive functioning that are beyond their ability.

Kindergarten represents an important level of cognitive development—one that marks the beginning of Piaget's concrete operations. At this level the children will be called upon to apply the language and sensori-motor experiences they have acquired during their first four or five years. Teachers will attempt to evaluate the quality of those early experiences during the initial interview with the children and their parents. By listening carefully to speech and vocabulary patterns and by learning of the kinds and varieties of experiences each child has had, the teacher begins to form a tentative judgment.

Readiness Testing

Along with these observational techniques, the teacher will administer the first standardized test, a reading readiness test, to provide a rough idea of how successful each child will be in beginning the formal reading process. Basically, the test asks each child to recognize rhyming or matching sounds and to use oral vocabulary to identify or describe pictures on the test. Since oral language and pictures are the primary activities on such tests, a child with limited experiences will probably be limited in vocabulary and will do poorly. Rich and varied experiences in the early years help to build good vocabulary including knowledge of the meanings of many words. These cognitive experiences constitute the memories that help children recognize and bring meaning to words as they begin to read them. Without adequate experiences, kindergarten and first grade children are unable to cope with the difficult abstract process of reading.

By identifying the various readiness levels of the children, the teacher has begun to use the evaluation process to meet individual needs. A child whose vocabulary and use of language seems limited and who recognizes few of the pictures on the reading readiness test will be given an intensive program of readiness materials to compensate for the lack of experience. Another child who has traveled widely and who seems to recognize all of the pictures on the test will be placed in an advanced group of children who will be reading very quickly.

Thus the schoolwide testing program begins with a determination of the children's reading readiness levels. Through the combination of formal and informal techniques, each of limited usefulness when employed individually, the teacher has obtained a tentative evaluation (an evaluation that will be modified many times in the future) by which to begin planning instructional strategies to meet children's individual needs.

The Basic Skills in the Primary Grades

Throughout the primary grades (K-3), emphasis on cognitive testing will be in the basic skills. Since most reading textbooks are accompanied by reading tests prepared by the publisher, teachers carry on a rather continuous program of measurement of this basic skill. As each unit is completed, tests are available to determine how well the children have learned the skills taught in the unit. At any time, a child may have difficulty with word recognition or syllabication or word meaning, and teachers will respond by modifying the reading program.

In addition to the reading tests provided by publishers, teachers will probably give a standardized reading test at the beginning of each year. This test will be used to screen each child's progress in reading. It will also help determine the reading status of the school system as it compares with others in the nation.

The standardized reading test gives a rough estimate of each child's progress in comparison to national norms. It also provides a rough ranking of individual children. Beyond that, it tells very little about individual progress in reading. For that assessment teachers must rely on both teacher-made tests and the publishers' ongoing tests. Used in combination, this variety of assessment tools provides a more accurate picture of reading ability and progress than will any one of them when used alone. The basic skills of arithmetic are measured in much the same way as reading but without the standardized test at the beginning of each year. Teacher-prepared tests and tests included in the arithmetic text series suffice until grade two.

Achievement Batteries in the Primary Grades

At the beginning of grades two and three, the school will administer a standardized test of achievement. In addition to arithmetic, this test will include sections on reading, language, and listening. The comparisons with national norms that result may encourage teachers to reexamine their teaching methods or the materials and curriculum they are using. They may also encourage a look at the population of children in the school system to determine whether it is comparable to the national norms.

The results of this standardized achievement test do not describe the specific and individual progress of each child. For this teachers must depend largely on their own observation techniques and on tests designed to measure individual achievement within the school system. These will most certainly include criterion-referenced tests, which we discussed in Chapter 9. With these tests, teachers can be satisfied that the children have met established criteria.

Achievement in the Upper Elementary Grades

In grades four through six, achievement becomes more advanced as children begin to apply their basic skills to the various subjects taught in those grades. If standardized achievement tests are administered during these years, the first will probably be given at the beginning of grade four. This will provide a rough idea of the children's status in the various content and skill areas as they enter the intermediate grades. It will help somewhat in the overall planning for curriculum, but mostly it will indicate how the children have achieved compared with the average beginning fourth grader around the country. Once again, in order to evaluate effectively individual youngster's achievement in basic skills, and in science, social studies, and English, teachers must depend upon their own well-planned and executed assessment techniques and perhaps on criterion-referenced tests in each subject or skill.

Intelligence or Scholastic Aptitude Tests

Given the controversy about the nature, origins, and measurement of intelligence, intelligence tests can be variously used in the school system. Due to recent criticisms of the use of intelligence tests, along with the belief of some testing experts that intelligence tests measure the skills called for in achievement tests, such standardized instruments are sometimes referred to as either intelligence tests or scholastic aptitude tests. Whatever they are called, they are used as instruments to measure intellectual potential. Whether inherited, experienced, or both, such potential is essential to the cognitive learning process. If it does not exist in adequate amounts, children will have difficulty using their experiences to learn more facts or solve new problems. In fact, limited cognitive potential will seriously inhibit the acquisition and memory of the experiences themselves.

Standardized group intelligence tests are not given in grades one or two because of the great variability of cognitive behavior in individual children during these years. The results would not be reliable or stable due to the wide differences in experience levels among very young children. It is not unusual, in fact, for I.Q. scores of young children to vary by 10 or 15 points from one year to the next. Several stabilizing years of school in which children share approximately the same kinds of experience are necessary before an intelligence test is of much use. Until then, teachers must depend on readiness tests to assess potential for specific cognitive tasks.

When group intelligence or scholastic aptitude tests are administered for the first time in grade three or four, teachers already have a fair estimate of each child's academic potential. The standardized test helps verify the estimate and provides a prediction of cognitive potential for future academic success.

In the upper elementary and secondary grades, the results of standardized intelligence tests are somewhat more reliable, since the children have had many more learning experiences to bring to the tests. Unless there are pressing needs to assess intelligence with group I.Q. tests, schools administer them only every several years, perhaps in grades six, eight, and ten. Once again, we emphasize that such tests indicate how a group of children compares in cognitive potential to the normative or standardizing group. Also, by comparing their intelligence scores with their academic achievement, teachers can assess the degree to which youngsters are living up to their potential. Teachers can make this comparison in two ways. First, they might give the intelligence test and, from the results, estimate children's probable ability to do well in school studies. Second, they may compare the intelligence test scores with their accumulated observations of children's academic progress. Either way, teachers use the intelligence test to verify predictions of academic potential or to make the prediction in the first place. In Chapter 9, we showed how closely intelligence test results correlate with results on achievement tests.

SPECIAL TESTS OF INTELLIGENCE AND APTITUDE

Since general group tests do not adequately evaluate individual progress, they are helpful primarily in initially screening youngsters to determine who needs special attention. To be sure that the school system honors its commitment to meeting individual needs, teachers must be prepared to give specialized tests of intelligence and aptitude. In the case of suspected low intelligence, individual intelligence tests should be administered by trained psychological examiners to determine more accurately the nature of the child's potential and to provide diagnostic information for improving the learning environment. When the child comes back to the classroom, the teacher should have a more thorough and detailed picture of intellectual ability.

As psychological researchers and testing experts agree more and more on the similarity between intelligence tests and achievement tests, they will recommend that special or multifactor aptitude tests play a more important role, particularly in the upper elementary and secondary school years. For verifying or predicting the mathematics potential of a seventh grade child, a general intelligence test will not be of much help, but a test of mathematical aptitude will. As we mentioned in our chapter on intelligence testing, there are special aptitude tests for everything from music to woodworking to physics. With the ever-increasing number of separate subjects available for study in the upper grades, teachers need to be ready to order and administer one of these special aptitude tests when it seems appropriate. A teacher may wish to screen an entire group of ninth grade music students to get a rough idea of instrumental aptitude or administer such a test to an individual child who seems to have special promise in music. Each test is useful in assessing potential and in planning curricula so long as teachers remember the limitations of such tests and take them into account.

The school may wish to make an initial assessment of all of the children's aptitudes. In the seventh grade and perhaps again in the ninth or tenth, a multifactor intelligence test such as the Differential Aptitude Test (DAT) described in Chapter 8 might be administered. This standardized test, covering verbal reasoning, numerical ability, abstract reasoning, space relations, mechanical reasoning, clerical speed and accuracy, and language usage, is one of several available for a general screening of the major special aptitudes thought to comprise the totality of intelligence. Any one of the seven aptitudes might well have several more specific factors, and when a teacher sees that a child does either very well or very poorly on a particular section, the administration of more specialized aptitude tests may be desirable.

We have not built an elaborate model for a school testing program. To do so would imply that all school systems have the same needs and the same kinds of children. Neither have we identified and described all of the standardized tests that might be used in various grades, nor have we specified the months and days the tests are to be given. Our purpose in building the model is to emphasize the major purpose of any school testing program—to meet the needs of individual children. The total child— physical, personal, and cognitive—must be considered when teachers give any test or make any assessment. The emotionally disturbed child will not test well; neither will the child who is preoccupied with a painful physical defect. All three components affect each other and the only way teachers can know the extent of the interaction is to understand the developmental nature of each. Only then can they choose or construct the testing, measuring, and evaluating tools for effective assessment of each component. By knowing the developmental nature of children, by knowing how to measure developmental growth, and by knowing how to diagnose individual needs from the results of measurement, teachers will be able to modify their curricula and their teaching strategies to meet individual needs and to improve instruction.

REPORTING DEVELOPMENTAL GROWTH TO OTHERS

We have placed the emphasis in this book on teachers' responsibility for assessing growth and using the information to improve instruction. In the final analysis, teachers are the child's best hope for continued success in school and ultimate success in life. However, teachers' responsibility must also include reporting and interpreting growth to those even closer to the children—their parents. Reporting growth must be included as a vital part of our model.

If all the report cards issued by school systems throughout the country were collected, one would be amazed at the variety of forms they take. If the minutes of all the professional meetings held by educators to discuss better ways of reporting growth were assembled, a person would be unable to read them in a lifetime. They have resulted, over the years, in a bewildering array of grading systems, nearly all of which have been unsatisfactory for one reason or another. This is not difficult to understand given the complex and difficult task of measuring human growth and development. Except for physical growth, which can generally be measured in quantitative and objective terms, educators deal primarily with hypothetical constructs they do not even understand fully. Intelligence, aptitude, ego strength, emotional maturity—these are abstract terms for elements of the human condition that cannot be measured directly. It is no wonder that reporting growth and development has consistently fallen far short of perfection.

When the testing movement was making its first heavy impact on the schools, educators placed a great deal of faith in the scores themselves, and translated them into letter or number grades on report cards. The test results and their quantitative expressions were thought to be objective measures of the characteristics the tests were assessing. This assumption changed gradually as parents and educators began to understand more about the tenuous nature of such issues as intelligence and individual differences. More descriptive information was sought and grades were explained by brief narratives about one child's reading progress or about another's improved attitude.

Currently, report cards can be found with every conceivable marking format. Some have number grades based on a school system's philosophy that children's progress should be reported in concrete, no-nonsense terms and according to a set of rigidly specified behaviors that constitute a particular grade. Some have departed completely from quantifying marks such as letter or number grades and do all of their reporting in narrative form. A few have even done away with formal report cards and have adopted the personal conference to describe growth and development. A recent innovation is the computerized report that saves much administrative time but allows for only brief cryptic statements from the teacher.

There is no perfect reporting system, and perhaps there never will be. For one to exist, educators would need perfect knowledge and understanding of all of the components of growth and development. Hypothetical characteristics such as intelligence would no longer be hypothetical, and teachers would be able to describe their nature exactly. Testing and measuring procedures would be based on this perfect knowledge and the instruments would be completely objective and accurate. All would agree on the precise meaning of each score and on what exact behavioral or cognitive requirements must be met for an A or B or a 93.

Since such knowledge is far from perfect, teachers must still report growth in terms that cannot be completely objective. These subjective and sometimes judgmental assessments may well get teachers into trouble with parents whose different perceptions of their children are probably just as subjective and judgmental. In spite of the shortcomings in reporting systems, teachers must find ways to interpret, to parents and children alike, the progress the children are making as well as their potential for the future. Although there are very practical reasons for report cards, such as the certification of success or achievement for promotion, there is, finally, one major and overriding reason for them—to communicate to parents and children as accurately as possible the status of the child's individual growth and development at a particular point in time. Reports to parents should be consistent with the educational goals and objectives of the profession. If these objectives have been stated clearly enough for both teachers and parents to understand, there will be less chance for misunderstanding. Knowing what growth should include makes it easier to describe. Then when teachers speak with parents, they can readily see that a child has met most of the objectives in reading but still falls somewhat short of a few of them, or that another child's arithmetic achievement shows excellent grasp of computation skills but definite weakness in problem solving.

Setting objectives and reporting progress in terms of the degree to which children have achieved them is much like the building of a criterion-referenced test. Criterion-referenced tests serve as report cards to teachers of how well the children met the teacher's specific instructional objectives, in other words, how well they learned the material and skills the teacher set out to teach. Similarly, a reporting system can be essentially a criterion-referenced one. Although teachers may report to parents the degree to which their children stack up against national achievement norms, they will stress children's progress in achieving local objectives, which are more realistic, more understandable, and more valuable in individualizing instruction. In short, teachers can describe to parents and children the real growth that took place during a given marking period. Each child's report card grades and comments will thus reflect the amount and quality of achievement actually gained. From concrete information such as this, teachers can provide a realistic picture of growth and, together with parents, set individual objectives for the next period. In a very real sense, this form of reporting serves as one more important step in the continuing efforts toward good diagnostic evaluation to meet individual needs and to build curriculum strategies that recognize individual differences.

SUMMARY

This chapter ends with an outline of the testing program we have described for a model school system. It is based on carefully stated educational goals we believe to be relevant for youngsters. It also includes the three components of growth we have stressed in this book—physical, personal, and cognitive—components that interact and that must be considered together in evaluating children. Our plan, although it includes standardized tests of readiness, intelligence, and achievement, places more importance on daily observation and evaluation by classroom teachers. The teacher is the only one who can know each child well enough to evaluate the real progress each makes every day throughout the year.

Along with an outline of the testing program, we have included a sample of report forms for elementary and for secondary grades. The report cards are direct outgrowths of our philosophy of evaluation. They reflect the individual objectives set for each grade level as well as the long range educational goals of the school system. In short, they represent an important component of our overall testing, measuring, and evaluating plan—one that communicates honestly and clearly to parents the actual progress each child has made in a given reporting period, and one that can help parents and teachers work together to understand and meet the needs of each child.

TESTING, MEASURING, AND EVALUATING THE CHILDREN IN THE SPRINGMEADOW PUBLIC SCHOOLS

Educational Goals

The parents and citizens of Springmeadow believe that each child who enters and is influenced by its schools should receive the best available professional attention to their developmental needs. The school system maintains the philosophy that each child is to be considered unique and individual and that the physical, personal, and cognitive needs of each is to be nurtured to the greatest degree possible. Through careful attention to these three aspects of growth—physical, personal, and cognitive—children will reach their fullest potential as participating and contributing members of the human family. School committee members, administrators, and teachers share the responsibility for developing educational strategies most appropriate to this goal. In close and constant cooperation with parents, curricula will be chosen and teaching methods evaluated to assure that the best traditions are retained while the most promising innovations are considered.

Springmeadow's evaluation program reflects this goal as it measures and reports the developmental growth of its children. The following outline of Springmeadow's ongoing evaluation effort is presented to help parents and citizens understand the ways in which the school system conducts its program of educational assessment.

Year	Evaluation Activity	Purpose
Preschool	Parent-teacher conference Teacher-child conference Physical exam by doctor	To help teacher and parents determine degree of readiness—physical, personal, and cognitive—of each child *before* entering kindergarten. To identify specific problems *before* school begins in order to plan with parents and specialists for individual treatment.
Kindergarten	Vision, hearing, and speech evaluation	To determine children's ability to discriminate visually and auditorily and to assess ability to articulate sounds and words. To identify children who will need immediate help or referral.
	Reading readiness test	To assess each child's readiness to begin reading and to help in grouping children for their first reading experiences.
Grades 1-3	*Physical assessment:* Vision and hearing at beginning of each year. General physical assessment by family physician each year.	To assess and identify specific vision and hearing deficits that might inhibit learning and to help in planning special activities for those with vision, hearing, or other physical barriers to learning.
	Continuous observation of physical growth.	To identify specific physical deficits that might inhibit learning or healthy personal development.
	Personal assessment: Continuous observation of personal behavior.	To identify serious personal problems or personality deficits that might inhibit learning or cause personal distress.

Year	Evaluation Activity	Purpose
Grades 1-3 (continued)	Specific personality or psychological testing by specialists as deemed necessary.	To plan classroom strategies that will help children with personality deficits to gain ego strength sufficient for the learning task.
	Cognitive assessment: Standardized tests of basic skills (reading, arithmetic, spelling).	To assess the primary grade skills of of our children compared with those in other school systems around the country.
	Continuous observation and teacher-made assessment of basic skills. Use of basic skills testing materials supplied by authors of textbooks in reading and arithmetic.	To continually assess *individual* growth and ability in the basic skills and to plan for individual needs.
Upper Elementary	*Physical assessment:* Ongoing observation by teacher.	To identify physical deficits that might inhibit learning and good personal growth and to refer to the nurse and doctor whenever appropriate.
	Standardized physical education tests.	To assess motor coordination and general athletic ability and to identify physical traits or deficits that should be referred to a physician.
	Personal assessment: Ongoing observation by teachers.	To identify emotional barriers to good cognitive growth and to plan strategies for helping troubled youngsters feel secure. To identify and refer to specialists (such as the school psychologist) cases of severe personal disturbance.
	Special tests of personal and emotional growth.	To determine exact nature of personal deficit in order to plan effective classroom strategy and remedial action.
	Cognitive assessment: Standardized group intelligence test.	To determine children's general capacity to perform cognitive tasks and to compare their cognitive potential with national norms. To verify teachers' assessments of the cognitive potential of each child.
	Grade 4—Standardized achievement test.	To determine achievement and skill status compared with national norms. To compare achievement with cognitive potential as measured on intelligence test.
	Individual intelligence test.	As needed to pinpoint specific cognitive strengths.

Year	Evaluation Activity	Purpose
Upper Elementary (continued)	Special tests of aptitude (music, mathematics, art, etc.).	To further identify specific strengths and interests as indicated on group intelligence or aptitude test.
Junior High (7-9)	*Physical assessment:* Standardized physical education tests of motor coordination and athletic skills (swimming, basketball, etc.).	To assess general physical development and identify special athletic skills and abilities. To identify specific physical deficits.
	Ongoing observation by teachers.	To watch for physical changes that might signal cognitive or emotional problems (such as the onset of puberty).
	Personal assessment: Personality assessment inventory.	As a screening test to identify possible emotional or personal deficits usually related to adolescence.
	Ongoing observation by teachers.	To identify emotional responses to adolescence and plan ways to help youngsters negotiate these complex times.
	Special sessions with guidance specialists as needed.	To assist teachers, parents, and children in understanding special problems and to help in planning for individual development.
	Cognitive assessment: Grade 7—Multifactor intelligence test (standardized).	To make initial assessment of children's aptitudes.
	Special aptitude tests as required (mathematics, language, etc.).	To further identify and foster special areas of cognitive strength and to plan for remediation of weaknesses.
	Standardized achievement tests.	To verify assessments and predictions of ability on the basis of intelligence tests and teacher observation and to compare achievement with national norms.
	Ongoing observation by teachers.	To continually assess individual progress and to plan for remediation or enrichment. To observe the dynamic interaction among physical, personal, and cognitive growth factors so important during the adolescent years. To plan strategies to help youngsters overcome deficits in any of these areas.

Year	Evaluation Activity	Purpose
Senior High (10-12)	*Physical assessment:* Standardized physical education tests of motor skill and athletic ability.	To identify growing abilities in specific athletic skills as well as specific deficits in physical functioning.
	Ongoing observation by teachers.	To watch for deficits that might occur (hearing loss, vision impairment, etc.).
	Personal assessment: Ongoing observation by teachers.	To observe and identify changes in behavior that might signal significant personality change or disturbance.
	Guidance counselor and psychologist.	To follow up teacher's initial assessment of personal problems and to administer special tests of personality if necessary.
	Cognitive assessment: Grade 10—Multifactor intelligence test.	To verify ongoing teacher asessment of ability. To screen for special problems or strengths. To compare with national norms.
	Special tests of aptitude.	To further identify or verify special areas of cognitive strength or weaknesses.
	Standardized achievement tests.	To verify the ongoing assessment of youngsters' cognitive potential and to compare their achievement with national norms.
	Ongoing observation by teachers.	To continually assess each youngster's *individual* progress for clues to better teaching strategies for meeting individual needs.
	PSAT (Practice Scholastic Aptitude Test)	To give juniors an opportunity to become familiar with the SAT and to help them identify and strengthen areas of weakness.
	SAT (Scholastic Aptitude Test)	To assist in college and career placement decisions.

The report forms on pages 278-285 are used to communicate to parents the progress of their children through the grades. The teachers and administrators recognize the difficulty of recording fully all of the details of each child's developmental progress and ask that these forms be considered in that light. They represent a straightforward effort by each teacher to report the *individual* progress of each child four times each year. To supplement these periodic written reports, parents are asked to visit with teachers at least once a year, more often if necessary. Periodic written reports combined with face-to-face discussions between parents and teachers afford the best means of communicating information about children's growth and development—physical, personal, and cognitive—and provide the bases for mutually acceptable decisions about each child's learning activities through the grades.

Since each school system is as unique and individual as each of its students, no two report cards are exactly alike, and no two school systems evaluate their youngsters in exactly the same ways. The foregoing evaluation outline and the report card samples are included to help prospective teachers visualize the totality of the evaluation process and to get some feel for its components. Through a combination of published and teacher-made tests along with continuous and systematic observations, each youngster is tracked through the grades. At any time, individual needs can be diagnosed and new learning strategies devised to meet them. Whenever serious physical, personal, or cognitive deficits are noted, they can be referred immediately to specialists for further evaluation. Continuous and systematic evaluation, then, keeps teachers aware of the unique developmental characteristics of each youngster and always ready and able to meet the needs of each.

IMPORTANT POINTS TO THINK ABOUT

1. Think about a child you know who is about to start kindergarten. What physical characteristics does he or she have that might inhibit or assure success in school?

2. If you were the kindergarten teacher whose class this child were about to enter, how would you conduct a prekindergarten conference to help you spot physical deficits?

3. Imagine that this child is now in grade three and doing poorly in all academic (cognitive) work. How would the evaluation plan for your school system help you to pinpoint and diagnose the child's specific weaknesses?

4. What components of your evaluation plan would provide more precise information to help you meet the child's needs?

5. Using the report forms in this chapter, assign grades that reflect this child's poor achievement and include a written statement explaining the grades to the parents.

6. This child's mother is coming in for a parent-teacher conference, and she is very disturbed by your report. What information will you gather from your ongoing evaluation and how will you conduct the interview?

SPRINGMEADOW PUBLIC SCHOOLS
Kindergarten Progress Report

Name: Timothy   Teacher: Mrs. Margolis

Personal Adjustment	1st Quarter				2nd Quarter				3rd Quarter				4th Quarter			
	H	S	I	U	H	S	I	U	H	S	I	U	H	S	I	U
Relates with consideration to:																
other children	✓															
classroom duties	✓															
learning tasks		✓														
recreational activities		✓														
Shows courtesy and willingness to share.		✓														
Recovers quickly from personal setbacks.	✓															
Shows evidence of independence.	✓															

Learning Activities	H	S	I	U	H	S	I	U	H	S	I	U	H	S	I	U
Uses classroom materials with confidence (scissors, crayons, pencils, etc.).		✓														
Completes assigned tasks.			✓													
Works neatly.			✓													
Follows directions.		✓														
Speaks clearly.		✓														
Recognizes likenesses and differences in pictures and objects (visual and auditory discrimination).	✓															
Relates groups of objects to numbers.	✓															

	H	S	I	U	H	S	I	U	H	S	I	U	H	S	I	U
Knows and uses initial reading skills.		✓														

Physical Development	H	S	I	U	H	S	I	U	H	S	I	U	H	S	I	U
Hearing.	✓															
Vision.	✓															
Coordination in games and recreation.	✓															
Coordination in use of learning materials (scissors, etc.).		✓														

H = Highly Satisfactory
S = Satisfactory
I = Improving
U = Unsatisfactory—requires special attention

SPRINGMEADOW PUBLIC SCHOOLS
Kindergarten Progress Report
(continued)

Parent's Signature and Comments

1st Quarter

2nd Quarter

3rd Quarter

4th Quarter

Parent-Teacher Conference Notes and Decisions: Date:

SPRINGMEADOW PUBLIC SCHOOLS
Primary Grade Progress Report

Name: Tomilee   Grade: 3   Teacher: Mrs. Moynihan

	1st Quarter				2nd Quarter				3rd Quarter				4th Quarter			
Personal Adjustment	H	S	I	U	H	S	I	U	H	S	I	U	H	S	I	U
Relates confidently with others.			✓													
Shows courtesy and sensitivity toward others.			✓													
Works and plays with self-confidence and independence.		✓														
Learning Activities																
Reading:																
Reads orally.		✓														
Reads with understanding.		✓														
Reads independently.			✓													
Knows and uses word attack skills effectively.			✓													
Arithmetic:																
Understands basic number facts.	✓															
Solves problems.	✓															
Language:																
Speaks clearly.	✓															
Expresses thoughts orally.		✓														
Expresses thoughts in writing.		✓														
Uses rules of writing.			✓													
Handwriting		✓														
Spelling:																
Spells well in spelling lessons.		✓														
Spells well in general written work.			✓													
Science:																
Follows rules in experiments.		✓														
Understands science concepts.		✓														
Social Studies	✓															
Art:																
Uses art materials correctly.		✓														
Music:																
Knows language of music.		✓														
Participates in music activities.	✓															
Physical Development:																
Coordination in games and physical education.	✓															
Coordination in learning tasks (artwork, construction projects, writing, etc.).		✓														

SPRINGMEADOW PUBLIC SCHOOLS
Primary Grade Progress Report
(continued)

H = Highly Satisfactory
S = Satisfactory
I = Improving
U = Unsatisfactory—requires special attention

Parent's Signature and Comments

1st Quarter

2nd Quarter

3rd Quarter

4th Quarter

Parent-Teacher Conference Notes and Decisions: Date:

SPRINGMEADOW PUBLIC SCHOOLS
Intermediate Grade Progress Report

Name: Sam   Grade: 5   Teacher: Mr. Hoffman

Personal Adjustment	1st Quarter				2nd Quarter				3rd Quarter				4th Quarter			
	H	S	I	U	H	S	I	U	H	S	I	U	H	S	I	U
Accepts responsibility.				✓												
Works independently.		✓														
Cooperates and shares.			✓													
Is respectful and sensitive to others.			✓													
Knows and obeys rules and regulations.			✓													

Learning Activities	A	B	C	U	A	B	C	U	A	B	C	U	A	B	C	U
Reading:																
Reads orally.			✓													
Reads with understanding.			✓													
Uses reading skills effectively.			✓													
Language:																
Speaks clearly and with expression.			✓													
Expresses ideas in speech.			✓													
Expresses ideas in writing.			✓													
Knows and uses rules of language.				✓												
Spelling:																
Knows rules of spelling.			✓													
Spells correctly in general written work.			✓													
Handwriting (neatness and legibility)		✓														
Arithmetic:																
Understands number facts.		✓														
Uses number facts to solve problems.		✓														
Science:																
Knows and uses scientific method.			✓													
Understands science facts and concepts.		✓														
Social Studies:																
Understands relationships of man to his world.			✓													
Understands social studies facts and concepts.		✓														
Art:																
Uses art materials correctly.			✓													
Uses art materials creatively.			✓													
Music:																
Reads music.			✓													
Participates in music activities.			✓													

SPRINGMEADOW PUBLIC SCHOOLS
Intermediate Grade Progess Report
(continued)

Physical Development	H	S	I	U	H	S	I	U	H	S	I	U	H	S	I	U
General coordination. Athletic skills.	✓	✓														

H = Highly Satisfactory
S = Satisfactory
I = Improving
U = Unsatisfactory—requires special attention

A = Outstanding progress
B = Better than average progress
C = Average progress for grade level
U = Below grade level progress. Needs attention.

Parent's Signature and Comments

1st Quarter

2nd Quarter

3rd Quarter

4th Quarter

Parent-Teacher Conference Notes and Decisions: Date:

SPRINGMEADOW PUBLIC SCHOOLS
Junior-Senior High Progress Report

Name: Andrew   Grade: 10   Homeroom Teacher: Mr. White

Subject	1st Qrt.	2nd Qrt.	3rd Qrt.	4th Qrt.	Teacher and Comments
English Composition	B				Written work and spelling needs improvement but expression and creative ideas are very good. J. Adams
Math: Algebra	C				Andrew has difficulty remembering basic facts and this makes problem solving difficult. A. Brown
Science: Biology	B+				Understands the method of scientific discovery and uses it effectively in experiments. Good grasp of science facts. T. Williams
Social Studies: Anthropology	C				Seems to have minimal interest in people and their problems. Does not see relationships of man to environment. B. Larson
Foreign Language: Spanish	A				Andrew recognizes words quickly and uses them correctly in sentences. Speaks with excellent pronunciation. B. Chouinard
Art: Drawing	C				Uses pencils and charcoal without much enthusiasm or creative expression. B. Cleary
Music: Instrumental	B				Quickly caught on to the trumpet. Plays well from sheet music. P. Quinlan
Physical Education: Swimming	A				A natural athlete. Very well coordinated. Backstroke and crawl especially strong. C. Blake

A = Outstanding progress
B = Better than average progress
C = Grade level progress
D = Somewhat below grade level progress
W = Well below grade level progress—indicates need for serious attention

SPRINGMEADOW PUBLIC SCHOOLS
Junior-Senior High Progress Report
(continued)

This junior-senior high progress report reflects the increased emphasis on academic achievement in the upper grades. Physical development is evaluated largely through physical education classes. Personal and emotional development are observed by all teachers and any evidence suggesting a personal problem or inappropriate behavior is reported immediately to the guidance teachers. The guidance teachers, in turn, are instructed to contact parents immediately for consultation and assistance in helping the student.

ADDITIONAL READINGS

N. E. Gronlund, *Improving Marking and Reporting in Classroom Instruction* (New York: Macmillan, 1974).

O. Milton and J. W. Edgerly, *The Testing and Grading of Students* (New York: Change Magazine, 1976).

G. R. Musgrave, *The Grading Game, A Public Fiasco* (New York: Vintage Books, 1970).

R. L. Thorndike, "Marks and Marking Systems," *Encyclopedia of Educational Research*, 4th ed. (New York: Macmillan, 1969).

CHAPTER THIRTEEN

MAJOR ISSUES IN TESTING, MEASURING, AND EVALUATING

IMPORTANT POINTS TO WATCH FOR

Teachers will need to know how to describe to parents both the results of testing and the current principles and issues in the testing movement.

One major issue is the heritability of intelligence, whether different national and ethnic groups *inherit* different amounts of intelligence and whether such information can be determined from the results of intelligence tests.

A second issue is accountability for teaching and evaluating the basic skills, an aspect of education many critics feel has been seriously neglected.

A third issue is parents' growing demand for more cautious use of tests to determine such things as intelligence and placement in special educational settings.

A fourth issue is the trend toward "mainstreaming" children with special needs into the regular classroom and the need for regular classroom teachers to understand testing procedures for identifying and diagnosing these children's special needs.

A fifth issue is constructing tests that are "culture free" and "culture fair." As difficult as it is to adhere to the principle of tests that are fair to *all* segments of the population, educators must make every effort to avoid evaluation procedures that discriminate on the basis of cultural experience.

A sixth issue is finding an appropriate balance between the use of norm-referenced tests by which progress is measured against national norms and criterion-referenced tests that are more useful in assessing *individual* growth.

The testing movement has come under severe criticism in recent years, and all evidence points to increasing pressures in the immediate future. New laws protecting children's rights and demanding the schools' full disclosure of information about students will require an increased understanding of testing and measuring procedures. No longer will school authorities be allowed to deny test results to parents on the presumption that "they will only misinterpret and misunderstand the results." No longer will it be sufficient for teachers to choose and administer a standardized test and then simply record the results on the children's permanent records.

Teachers of elementary and secondary school youngsters must know not only the mechanics of testing, measuring, and evaluating but the critical issues as well. They will answer to more and more parents who have also become knowledgeable about testing and who are demanding more information about their children. The issues are emotional ones since they revolve around the children. The only way teachers can reduce the emotionality is to know and think deeply about the issues and be ready to discuss them rationally and objectively with children's parents. Teachers should not reject all criticism, nor should they accept it blindly. Thoughtful criticism by informed people can be a source of important and constructive input.

This concluding chapter will touch briefly on several of the most persistent trends currently at issue in the testing movement. Since each could easily be the subject of an entire book, teachers are expected to read widely and become professionally knowledgeable about each. In fact, we believe that the most important of these issues is the need for better understanding of the testing movement by teachers and increased competency in using and interpreting these instructional tools.

TEACHERS NEED TO UNDERSTAND MORE ABOUT TESTING, MEASURING, AND EVALUATING

Commercial publishers prepare most of the tests used in classrooms, and school administrators usually choose them. But teachers are the ones who give the tests—over 40 million each year at a cost of well over a quarter of a billion dollars. Teachers are also the ones who must interpret the scores to parents and explain to them the meaning of an achievement score or a percentile rank or a deviation I.Q. However, for many years teachers were instructed not to divulge I.Q. scores and to give out as little information as possible about children's performance. Consequently, since parents never speak to publishers and rarely to administrators, they have had good reason for their growing anger and frustration when they have been unable to get straight answers to their questions.

Unfortunately, teachers themselves have not had to know the issues, a great many have been sadly lacking in an understanding of sound testing practices. Parents will no longer tolerate this lack of understanding. Teachers, along with administrators, must become accountable for what they do in the name of education. If a standardized achievement test is given, each teacher must know how the test was conducted and standardized and must be ready to justify the use of the test for a particular population of children.

Knowing the hows and whys of testing is only the beginning. These are the mechanics of evaluation that are necessary for accurate administration, scoring, and interpretation. A more subtle aspect of standardized testing is whether it should be conducted at all. The many complaints that have surfaced recently amount to a moral dilemma. To some, standardized tests are immoral since they claim to test and measure aspects of learning and human potential about which little is known. The subsequent labeling and identifying of children on the basis of their test scores has become a moral issue of the first magnitude.

Educators need to make evaluation one of the most important aspects of any teacher education program. Before teachers can be considered ready to discuss intelligently with parents the reasons for testing as well as the results of tests, both the mechanics and the moral issues of the testing movement must be known and understood. We hope this book has adequately explained the mechanics. The moral and philosophical issues will constantly shift and change through the years. An excellent case in point is the old controversy over the nature of intelligence, particularly as it has led to the labeling of an entire cultural group as intellectually inferior to others.

THE HERITABILITY OF INTELLIGENCE

Perhaps on of the saddest commentaries on the misuses of testing has been that of labeling the Black population as intellectually inferior to the white. Using the specious logic of statistics, highly respected researchers have claimed that the I.Q. test scores of thousands of Blacks prove, by approximately 15 points, that they are less intelligent than whites. It would be one thing if this were an incident that occurred when the testing movement was in its infancy. During the early part of this century, immigration quotas were set by Congress on the basis of I.Q. score data. In 1923, C. C. Brigham used the World War I Army Alpha and Beta test results to rank the peoples of Europe according to a hierarchy of inherited intelligence.[1] On the basis of his findings, immigration quotas were deliberately set to reduce the number of "biologically inferior" immigrants from Southeastern Europe. A quotation from Brigham's book will serve to indicate the social force exerted by such early testing data:

We must face a possibility of racial admixture here that is infinitely worse than that faced by any European country today, for we are incorporating the Negro into our racial stock, while all of Europe is comparatively free from this taint. . . . The decline of American Intelligence will be more rapid than the decline of the intelligence of European national groups owing to the presence here of the Negro.

That is an indication of the moral overtones of the testing movement. Brigham's was not the only case in history in which genetic inferiority was "proven" by test results. A man of no lesser stature than Henry Goddard[2] administered the Binet Intelligence Test to thousands of immigrants as they entered the United States through Ellis Island. His amazing results established that 83% of the Jews, 80% of the Hungarians, 79% of the Italians, and 87% of the Russians were "feebleminded."

Similar practices continue today. Arthur Jensen[3] has raised a storm of criticism with his statement that Black intelligence scores are evidence that they have "inherited" less intelligence than have whites. Jensen has argued that inheritance plays a more important role in the establishment of intelligence than does the environment. If Jensen's research findings were accepted, the social impact of his study would be monumental. To paraphrase Jensen, since Blacks are genetically and intellectually inferior, programs such as Head Start cannot work. Because such programs assume environmental conditions are more important in the formation of intelligence, they are doomed to failure.

When teachers are faced with pronouncements such as these, the dilemma is clear. If teachers accept the findings of a Jensen, they must treat Blacks as inferior beings. If not, they must assemble information that refutes Jensen's data in order to justify their moral outrage that a racial substructure can be declared inferior.

The moral issue here transcends the use of test results. When such events occur, some will always accept them eagerly as evidence of "truths" for which they lacked proof. However, this particular issue has recently taken an amazing turn, one that should serve as a warning to the most astute researchers. Jensen has discovered that most of the data upon which he based his findings were erroneous, having been virtually manufactured out of thin air. Rather than rely on information he gathered himself, he used test data gathered by Burt,[4] who has been proven fraudulent in his research methodology.

Jensen is considered a respected researcher, and his willingness to admit a significant change in position provides a hopeful commentary on researchers' capacity to approach findings cautiously and to reevaluate them when necessary. It is also fortunate that the pronouncements of a Goddard or a Brigham are no longer slavishly followed and accepted without question. Despite the individuals who wait anxiously for such socially explosive announcements, there is a growing number who instantly challenge such findings. The role of the teacher is to challenge thoughtfully and to continue to think deeply about such issues as the nature and origin of intelligence, recognizing that there is much to learn and that the most brilliant of scholars have not yet begun to scratch the surface. For teachers, the issue is to maintain the child's individual integrity and worth, which demand the best estimates and efforts at all times. Jensen will probably not be the last to declare one race inferior to another. Informed teachers will be the child's best defense against such devastating abuses of the testing movement.

ACCOUNTABILITY FOR TEACHING THE BASICS WILL BE EXPECTED OF EVERYONE

School systems' performance in educating children has been the target of a growing demand for accountability. For generations, parents and society in general have accepted the educational system and its products with little question. Despite thoughtful critics who have sought to demand more of the schools, the system has gone on much as before. More recently the dissatisfaction with schools has become increasingly significant, and hard questions are being asked by more and more people, including parents and educational leaders.

The major question has focused on children's competency in the basic skills of language and mathematics. The critics point to a steady decline in ability to read, write, and compute—a decline that seriously undermines intellectual success in college and in life. Interestingly enough, the evidence for this decline comes not from failure on the job or in college, but from the results of standardized tests. And here arises a paradox.

On one hand, schools have been called to account for their indiscriminate use of standardized tests. They have been accused of allowing the material on the tests to dictate the curriculum. On the other hand, when the test results are in, critics have been shocked to discover that the children are not able to perform adequately on tests they supposedly have been prepared for. It is no wonder that, in the search for someone or something to blame for the decline in achievement, the tests have been singled out as major contributors. And yet, when cities have reacted by demanding accountability from their teachers and administrators, they, too, have turned to the results of standardized tests to determine whether their teachers are in fact teaching the basics.

"Back to basics" programs are catching on fast and, at this writing, at least 11 states have adopted laws requiring "minimal competency" testing. Many others are watching carefully and are studying the feasibility of such programs for their school systems. "Accountability," "minimal competency," "competency based teaching"—are all phrases describing "back to basics" programs. At heart, the issue here is whether standardized testing programs should be allowed heavy influence on curricula and teaching strategies.

Accountability must be demanded of everyone involved in evaluating children. The question is whether tests, particularly standardized tests, are the most appropriate means of ensuring accountability. Whether tests are used to determine how well youngsters are learning the basics, to place them in special classes, or to accept them in college, the use of tests in making decisions about children has become so widespread and so enormously influential that they control significant aspects of the educational system.

An encouraging trend away from slavish dependence on test results has occurred among educational administrators—a group that has long defended testing and has been largely responsible for adoptions of one standardized test or another for their school systems. In 1975, the National Association of Elementary School Principals devoted two issues of its journal, *Principal*,[5] to the abuses and misuses of standardized testing. In doing so, these professionals demonstrated a willingness to publicly criticize their behavior of many years. This is a form of accountability of the highest order. When those holding responsibility for the testing programs of their schools can rise above the usual defensive posture of the education establishment, perhaps there will be continued and intensified attempts to put testing in its proper perspective—as one of many constructive and valid tools to help educate children.

Test publishers must also concern themselves with accountability. These companies produce millions of tests each year for which school systems annually pay many millions of dollars. They are receiving more and more attention from critics for allegedly placing the profit motive above the needs of children. Yet educators must be careful in listening to violent tirades against test publishers. Since publishers are in business to make money, the challenge to them should be that they must work harder to construct better tests and to make them more understandable to teachers and parents alike. Theirs is a highly competitive business, and accountability is not as easily achieved as for educators who have everything to gain by improving testing.

For teachers, accountability is very real and very immediate. To be held accountable for teaching basic skills means that teachers are being tested as surely as the children. When teachers know that the results of a standardized test will tell whether or not children have learned as much and as well as administrators have declared they should, the temptation to teach for the tests can be very strong. Further, when teachers know that teaching will be evaluated in terms of children's performance, they can begin to understand the influence standardized tests can have on the professional.

Accountability for the judicious use of tests is a vital component of the more general and complex issue of overall accountability for the knowledge and skills taught to students. Test publishers, administrators, teachers, and the public must come to understand the appropriate use of tests for measuring progress in the basic skills. Each must agree to stop pointing the finger of blame at the others, and all must assume greater responsibility for the educational process. School committees have the right and the responsibility to demand effective teaching, but their demands must be reasonable and based on an understanding of children's needs in their particular settings. As the makers of educational policy for their communities, they, too, should be held accountable for the decisions they make.

Administrators and teachers who carry out the policies of school committees must in turn use good professional judgment in doing so. They must know their children's needs better than the school committees and, in fact, must use their professional knowledge of children to guide the school committees in their decisions. If accountability programs are instituted and standardized tests are used to measure "minimal competencies" or "basic skills," both policymakers and professionals must be held accountable for choosing the most appropriate tests.

Finally, to demand accountability of the test publishers means to demand tests that are constructed for the purposes intended. Such demands impose financial pressures on publishers, and they must respond by building appropriate testing instruments. Accountability is everyone's responsibility, but classroom teachers feel the responsibility more keenly than anyone else. However educators choose to measure children's progress—whether by standardized or locally prepared tests or both—the classroom teacher is held most immediately accountable when the results are in.

LITIGATION OVER TESTING

Closely allied with the growing demands for more accountability has been the increased court activity related to the use and misuse of tests. Most of the suits have been based on new federal legislation protecting the rights of children and guaranteeing to those who are handicapped equal treatment under the law. This legislation will bring about more and more cases in which parents and other interested parties challenge not only the misuse of tests but the use of certain others.

One such case, in California, involving the use of I.Q. tests[6] is being watched closely by many educators concerned with evaluation. A lawsuit filed on behalf of the children alleges that they were mislabeled as mentally retarded after being screened by standardized intelligence tests. The attorneys for the children have charged that the tests were racially and culturally discriminatory. They have cited the new antihandicapped discrimination regulations, which state in part that tests must be used "that have been validated for the specific purpose for which they are now being used." They also claim that the school system has violated the new Education for All Handicapped Children Act, which calls for testing and evaluation procedures for all children to be free of racial or cultural discrimination. This is a tall order, and school systems everywhere are hard pressed to find evaluation materials that do not discriminate in some way against some children.

The issue here is whether the California case will succeed in eliminating I.Q. tests as a means of screening children and placing them in special educational settings. The case is even more dramatic considering that, until very recently, children were placed in special settings with far less attention to careful assessment than was the case in California. Alice, for instance, was only one of many children diagnosed as retarded on the basis of a single group intelligence test. The California children were each diagnosed with three separate *individual* intelligence tests, each considered to be among the best available.

At issue, also, is the growing awareness that very real differences appear in the results of tests taken by Black children and white children. The litigation, despite its emotional overtones, will call needed attention to the fact that many tests are not culturally or racially fair and that educators have sometimes been deluded into accepting the differences in scores between Blacks and whites as indicating true differences in ability. Whatever the outcome in California, those who must test, measure, and evaluate children will do so with a renewed and strengthened awareness of the need for extreme caution and professionalism.

The teaching profession is both fortunate and unfortunate in the timing of such court cases. The profession is unlucky because, once again, educators are under fire for practices that critics claim to be unprofessional at best and downright destructive and immoral at worst. Educators are fortunate because they are part of a dramatic episode in the history of testing and education that may well be the beginning of a major shift in the ways children's ability and achievement are assessed. Public pressure and the threat of lawsuits will force educators to test more cautiously and to seek more effective ways to screen and place children in special settings. For the same reasons, test publishers will most certainly work harder to develop testing materials that are less discriminatory and more appropriate. Once again, classroom teachers will be closest to these developments, and their awareness of good evaluation procedures will help protect youngsters against inadvertent discrimination by test results.

MAINSTREAMING

In Chapter 11, we touched upon the variety of special-needs children. Largely on the basis of test results, educators have done a more effective job of identifying children's specific handicaps. More important, educators have learned that special settings for most children with special needs is a form of discrimination that is destructive of sound learning opportunities. The most beneficial setting for emotionally disturbed, learning disabled, or physically handicapped children is not a place of isolation. Since they must live their lives among the rest of society, the place to learn how to cope with life is in the regular classroom, among the people who will constitute the rest of society.

Psychologists and educators have learned that special-needs children perform better academically and emotionally if they spend the maximum time possible in the regular classroom. Public Law 94-142—The Education for All Handicapped Children Act—spells out the regulations that school systems must obey to guarantee handicapped children equal protection and equal opportunity. "Mainstreaming" is the heart of the law, demanding free public education in the "least restrictive environment" for all handicapped children.

Children with special needs must be tested, measured, and evaluated just as all children are. However, to ensure the effectiveness of mainstreaming, these youngsters need more careful assessment, both for initial diagnosis and placement and for determining how best to meet their special needs in regular classrooms. As philosophically and psychologically sound as mainstreaming may be, it presents significant problems for the classroom teacher. When it was introduced, most teachers accepted the concept of mainstreaming gladly, believing that they could find relatively easy ways to integrate handicapped children into their classrooms. However, they quickly learned that many handicapped youngsters require attention and services the teachers were not prepared to give. A single emotionally disturbed child, for instance, can make crushing demands on the teacher's time and energy—demands that take time and energy away from others in the room. Some school systems were forward looking enough to anticipate these problems, and they provided extensive orientation and training programs for their regular classroom teachers. Others did not, and the results have been painful for all concerned. Teachers have been frustrated in their attempts to understand and provide for special-needs youngsters. The youngsters have experienced frustration and unhappiness at finding themselves in what seemed to be hostile, unsympathetic environments. Some parents, too, have been less than enchanted with the progress their children have made in mainstreaming situations. However, for the most part, mainstreaming seems to be working in the states and cities in which it has been tried so far. Ongoing studies and research are needed to provide more information on the effects of mainstreaming than is currently available.

Almost every class has a few handicapped children. The range of handicaps as well as their degree of severity varies tremendously as we pointed out in Chapter 11. This adds some very definite responsibilities to a teacher's already awesome task of teaching. Each handicapped child must have a thorough evaluation. Teachers are expected to take part in the evaluation and bring their expertise to bear. In many cases, teachers initiate the evaluation process since they are trained to recognize the various handicaps. Teachers also work with school principals, special education teachers, psychologists, and guidance counselors to evaluate each child as cautiously and as thoroughly as possible. When the assessment has been completed, an educational prescription will be prepared spelling out all remedial activities for each special-needs child. Teachers are more immediately responsible than anyone else for seeing that each child's program is implemented.

However, before they can begin, they must, as part of the new law, seek the parents' approval of the plan. This provision has created some very special problems. Although most parents are sensitive to their children's needs and are cooperative in approving and implementing the educational plans for their children, a few are not. Under the new regulations, they may ask for an outside team of evaluators to conduct a second evaluation and write a new educational plan. If the school system and the parents cannot agree on the assessment or the plan, the parents may take the case to court. In at least one state, enormous amounts of time, energy, and money are now being expended in this activity—time, energy, and money already in short supply for carrying on the normal functions of the school day.

For teachers, the issue here is assessment. In order to avoid the pitfalls of inadequate evaluation and the subsequent waste of valuable resources in lengthy, emotional arguments, teachers must be versed in the techniques and principles of testing, measuring, and evaluating to a far greater degree than they would have been before the introduction of mainstreaming. They must know the categories of handicaps, how to identify them, and how specialized evaluation materials are used for the assessment of special-needs children. Teachers' professional awareness of the needs of handicapped children and their commitment to meet those needs will make mainstreaming more productive for children and more fulfilling for themselves.

CULTURE-FAIR AND CULTURE-FREE TESTS

One of the major complaints against standardized tests is that they discriminate against certain groups within the culture. In fact, one of the most common charges in many court cases now pending against testing procedures is that the material on standardized tests is often unfamiliar to minority groups whose experiences have not included this material. Test makers have been charged with standardizing their tests on middle-class white populations of children, thus giving those children an unfair advantage. The language and the content are said to be taken from the middle-class social structure, and Blacks, Indians, Hispanics, and other minority groups are unable to understand many of the questions.

Educators and test makers have only recently begun to understand the validity of this complaint. Arthur Jensen, for instance, declared the Black population to be genetically inferior to whites on the basis of standardized test results. His subsequent admission[7] that tests are discriminatory on the basis of information called for in the questions signals a farther-reaching realization about test discrimination than its apparent effect on specific minority groups. In testing the hypothesis that Black children in the rural South are thought to exhibit cumulative deficits in I.Q. scores over a period of years in school, he discovered that environmental conditions and cultural background were major factors in the steady decline of I.Q. scores among rural Blacks. Consequently, Jensen revised his earlier assertion that intelligence is formed largely by inheritance and now maintains that environmental factors play at least an equally important role in the formation of I.Q. In testing Blacks in California, whose environmental circumstances are much better than those in the South, Jensen found no such cumulative decrement in I.Q. scores.

The issue is not really whether standardized tests discriminate against Blacks or any other specific minority group, but that they discriminate seriously against *any* child in *any* cultural group whose background lacks the language and experiences used in the tests. Cultural disadvantage, although it occurs most frequently among the Black population, also occurs in segments of the white population. Some of the most telling evidence of this fact can be seen in the test results of economically and culturally deprived whites in Appalachia. In other words, the evidence is growing that cultural deprivation adversely affects any child's performance on standardized tests.

Perhaps it is impossible to produce a group test of intelligence or achievement that is truly culture fair. To do so would mean that all the test items sample the experiences of every child in every cultural group in the country. To be fair to all children taking the test, the test would have to provide each child with the same number of familiar items as every other child. In a nation of diverse subcultures and economic groupings, there probably is no test that can be thought of as being fair to all.

To overcome the problems of cultural unfairness, some test publishers have attempted to produce tests that are not culture fair but culture *free*. Since any use of language at all will most certainly be unfair to some children, culture-free tests are designed without the use of written language. However, the effectiveness of so-called culture-free tests has been questionable to date. Even though written language and vocabulary are absent, the need to give directions requires oral language, and all children will not understand the directions with equal success.

Culture-free and culture-fair tests are ideals toward which educators should strive in their testing, measuring, and evaluating procedures. But perhaps more important for those who assess children's intelligence, achievement, and personal growth is the recognition that no standardized test can be totally free of discriminatory materials. Neither can any test be totally free of language, pictures, or information that are as familiar to one cultural group as to another. The controversy over the discriminatory nature of standardized tests will thus continue, and teachers will feel its effects directly. Such practices as busing and mainstreaming will increase the numbers of culturally, economically, and educationally disadvantaged children in classrooms, and of necessity the evaluation of each will be less in terms of national norms and more in terms of individual differences. If the controversy has made one positive contribution to more effective evaluation, it is that teachers are able to dispel long-entrenched beliefs that racial and cultural differences are responsible for lower intelligence or inadequate achievement. Instead, poor performance on standardized tests and persistently lowered achievement may well be evidence that there is a single, large minority group in the nation. It is made up of all children in all cultural and geographic groups whose environment has deprived them of the experiences and information necessary to succeed.

Whether tests are culture fair or culture free is really an unimportant issue for those who understand how to interpret test scores in light of each child's unique experiences. The test will be culture fair because teachers make it so, and an assessment of any child will be fair if teachers remember the degree to which experience affects performance on tests.

CRITERION- VS. NORM-REFERENCED TESTS

Most standardized tests used in the schools are norm-referenced tests standardized on certain populations of children to determine normative scores for each age group and, in some cases, for each grade level. Although these tests provide comparisons with the scores of the children in the standardizing group, such comparisons tell little about individual progress or about a youngster's talent or potential. For this reason, the critics of standardized tests claim that norm-referenced tests, no matter how carefully they are standardized and constructed, do not describe individual progress.

Parents and educators are recognizing these criticisms of standardized tests and are looking for ways to measure actual progress. Criterion-referenced tests provide an important new alternative to norm-referenced tests. As we pointed out in Chapter 9, setting learning objectives for children and then testing to see whether they have achieved the objectives seems, to many, to be a more realistic and meaningful way to assess learning. It places the responsibility and authority for determining learning objectives squarely on local school authorities. However, to be successful, criterion-referenced testing must be developed and implemented with as much attention to detail and good testing practice as goes into the standardizing of a norm-referenced test.

Theoretically, at least, criterion-referenced tests will help teachers avoid the pitfall of "teaching to do well on the standardized tests." And yet, the same pitfall exists in criterion-referenced testing programs. Someone has to establish the objectives. Once they are established, teachers *must* teach to achieve them. If they succeed, the established criteria have been met and individual progress has been measured. The pitfall appears when teachers become dependent upon people outside the school system to establish learning objectives. In fact, test publishers recognize that educators will be looking for help in writing objectives or criteria, and they have begun to develop "banks" of objectives. These libraries of objectives are collected by sampling learning behaviors around the nation and by writing those that seem to be adequate or appropriate to most children. If teachers go to these banks for their objectives, they are once again allowing others to determine their courses of instruction, which may not be relevant to a particular group of children.

The major advantage to criterion-referenced tests should be obvious. By establishing the learning objectives children are expected to reach, and by stating them in measurable behavioral terms, teachers can chart progress or lack of it for each child. Knowing the specific learning activities each youngster should achieve allows teachers to diagnose accurately the unique problems and strengths of each. This attention to individual differences is not possible with norm-referenced tests. With criterion-referenced materials, teachers engage in *diagnostic testing* and are better able to develop teaching strategies to meet individual needs.

For teachers, the issue is discovering alternative forms of testing that meet children's individual needs most effectively. Whether criterion-referenced testing finally replaces norm-referenced testing or only supplements it as an evaluation technique, teachers must understand how both forms are developed and how each can contribute to a better understanding of youngsters. In spite of the intense efforts of some critics to eliminate standardized testing completely, this probably will not happen. Both are useful forms of assessment for specific purposes. As we have said previously, tests are not dangerous, but people who use them can be. Teachers have the responsibility to use tests of any kind with caution and good judgment. In doing so they reduce the emotion-laden and often unproductive controversy over standardized testing.

SUMMARY

The issues we have discussed are among the most important contemporary concerns to teachers. As the individuals who administer and interpret tests, teachers will often bear the brunt of direct criticism from parents and others.

They must be prepared to meet this criticism, not with emotional response, but with thoughtful and well-reasoned explanations of what good testing, measuring, and evaluating is all about. Teachers can do this only by understanding the strengths and weaknesses of testing. Emotional and unreasonable attacks on the testing movement will not stand up to solid knowledge of the facts and the courage to express them—not defensively, as educators too often do, but firmly and with the self-assurance that comes from knowledge.

Many thoughtful and reasonable critics have forced educators to look more closely at traditional ways of testing. They have shown weak and even destructive aspects of traditional evaluation techniques. They have pointed out specific tests that are poorly constructed or that discriminate against certain segments of the population. They have also shown the need for updating many popular standardized tests, tests used in some cases for many years without major revision.

As professionals charged with the responsibility of accurately evaluating and diagnosing children's individual needs, teachers should not have to be told by others that their house needs to be put in order. They should strive constantly to find better ways of evaluating children and to use more accurately the instruments that are available. Whether these instruments are standardized or teacher-made tests, they should have as their one major purpose the goal of improving instruction. Used diagnostically, tests provide the information teachers need to achieve a goal they often hear but rarely reach—that of individualized instruction. And that should be the major purpose of all testing, measuring, and evaluating—to identify, diagnose, and meet the individual learning needs of all children.

IMPORTANT POINTS TO THINK ABOUT

1. If you were a superintendent of schools, what decisions would you make about testing that would help assure that *no* child's future is placed in jeopardy because of tests?

2. If you were a classroom teacher, what steps would you take to be sure you understood the special needs of a visually handicapped child who was mainstreamed into your room? A child with a learning deficit? An emotionally disturbed youngster? A child with cerebral palsy?

3. How would you explain to the parents of a Hispanic child who speaks limited English the reasons for his poor performance on a standardized achievement test?

4. What components would you build into a testing program for your senior high school that would hold the teachers accountable for teaching the basics?

NOTES

1. As quoted in P. L. Houts, ed., *The Myth of Measurability* (New York: Hart, 1977), p. 59.

2. *Ibid.*, p. 55.

3. A. R. Jensen, "How Much Can We Boost I.Q. and Scholastic Achievement?" *Harvard Educational Review* 39 (1969).

4. C. Burt, "The Evidence for the Concept of Intelligence," *British Journal of Educational Psychology* 25 (1955).

5. "The Scoring of Children: Standardized Testing in America," *The National Elementary Principal* 54, 6 (1976).

6. *Ibid.*

7. A. R. Jensen, "Cumulative Deficits in IQ of Blacks in the Rural South," *Developmental Psychology* 13, 3 (1977): 184-191.

ADDITIONAL READINGS

R. W. Tyler and R. W. Wolf, eds., *Crucial Issues in Testing* (Berkeley, CA: McCutchan, 1974).

G. Weber, "Uses and Abuses of Standardized Testing in the Schools," Council for Basic Education, Occasional Paper No. 22 (1974).

Readings in Mainstreaming (Guilford, CT: Special Learning Corp., 1978).

W. J. Popham, ed., *Criterion-referenced Measurement* (Englewood Cliffs, NJ: Educational Technology Publishers, 1971).

B. Hoffman, *The Tyranny of Testing* (New York: Collier Books, 1962).

J. W. Holt, *On Testing* (Cambridge, MA: Leodas, 1968).

R. J. Herrnstein, *I.Q. in the Meritocracy* (Boston: Little, Brown, 1973).

L. J. Kamin, *The Science and Politics of I.Q.* (New York: Wiley, 1974).

GLOSSARY

The following list of terms and their definitions is a quick reference only. It is by no means a complete listing of measurement and evaluation terms. We hope it will be helpful as a supplement to the more detailed discussions of each term found in the text.

Achievement test: Achievement tests—either commercially prepared or teacher made—measure the degree to which students have acquired information or skills taught in a formal or school setting.

Age equivalent: The age level at which students perform. For instance, if the average score for 10 year olds on an achievement test is 88, any child, regardless of age, who achieves that score will be assigned an age equivalent of 10.

Age norms: The normative values assigned to the achievement levels of students of specific chronological ages (see **Age equivalent**).

Alternative: One of the choices in a multiple-choice test item.

Aptitude: Those abilities, both inherited and acquired through the environment over a period of time, that allow an individual to achieve or learn.

Aptitude test: A test that helps predict the degree to which an individual will succeed in any area of cognitive learning.

Arithmetic mean: The most widely used expression of average in statistics. Obtained by dividing the sum of a set of scores by the number of scores in the set (see **Median; Mode**).

Average: The general expression of the measure of central tendency (see **Arithmetic mean; Median; Mode**).

Battery: The term given to a group of two or more tests that have been standardized for the same population and that measure different aspects of behavior (California Test of Mental Maturity, for example).

Behavioral objective: An objective that describes the behavior expected of a student to demonstrate successful learning.

Central tendency: The tendency for scores to cluster or group around a measure of central tendency such as the mean, median, or mode.

Chronological age: The actual age of an individual, usually expressed in years and months.

Completion test: One of the objective tests. Incomplete statements are completed by the student.

Coefficient of correlation: A mathematical expression of the relationship or "closeness of fit" of two variables. In measurement, it is most commonly used to express the degree to which one score will vary as another does. For instance, we would expect a close relationship between a measure of intelligence and a measure of reading ability.

Criterion: A standard by which behavior will be judged. If the behavior on a test or other learning experience occurs as predicted, the student has met the criterion.

Criterion-referenced test: A test having a predetermined level of success that will show whether a student has met the established criteria.

Culture-fair test: A test that does not discriminate by including items unfamiliar to members of a specific cultural group.

Decile: Any one of the nine points that separate a distribution of scores into ten equal parts. A decile of 50 means a point below which 50 percent of the scores fall.

Deviation: The degree or amount by which any score deviates or differs from some specified point such as the mean.

Deviation I.Q.:   A method of standardizing I.Q. scores to describe intelligence. All scores are converted to z scores by multiplying each by 16 and adding 100.

Diagnostic test: An evaluation instrument designed to assess an individual's specific strengths and weaknesses.

Distracter: The incorrect alternative choices on a multiple-choice item.

Distribution: A distribution of scores showing the number of scores that fall at each point along the distribution (see **Frequency distribution**).

Equivalent form: A form of a standardized test that closely approximates another in difficulty and content.

Face validity: A quality of a test that indicates that it apparently measures the variable the examiner wishes to test.

Frequency distribution: A tabulation of large numbers of scores showing the frequencies with which persons obtain scores within each of several divisions making up the tabulation.

Grade equivalent: The grade level for which any given score represents the average. A child who achieves 4.6 on a reading test is said to be reading at the level of an average reader in the sixth month of grade four.

Intelligence quotient (I.Q.): A mathematical expression for intelligent behavior. Derived by comparing an individual's score on an intelligence test with the scores of "average" pupils of the same age (see **Deviation I.Q.**).

Item analysis: The procedure used to determine appropriateness of a single test item. Items are analyzed for difficulty, ambiguity, and discrimination.

Matching test: A test requiring the matching of a series of items in one list to a corresponding series in another.

Mean: See **Arithmetic mean**.

Median: The middle point or midpoint in a distribution of scores above and below which lie 50% of the scores.

Mental age (M.A.): The age level at which a child achieves an average I.Q. score. If a student scores 86 on an intelligence test, a table will tell us that this score is average for children who are 12 years and 4 months of age. Regardless of the child's chronological age, mental age will be 12-4.

Mode: The score that occurs most frequently in a distribution of scores.

Multiple-choice item: A test item containing a "stem" and several alternatives from which the correct one is chosen. Incorrect alternatives are called distracters.

Normal distribution (Normal curve): A distribution in which a series of scores are distributed symmetrically about the arithmetic mean. The heaviest concentration of scores will be around the mean, with decreasing numbers clustered at points above and below the mean. The symmetrical distribution takes the form of a bell-shaped curve and is known as the normal curve.

Norm group (Standardization group): A group of individuals randomly sampled from a total population and selected as representative of the population at large.

Norm-referenced test: A test designed to measure individual traits or variables such as achievement as compared with the scores of individuals from the norm group.

Norms: The test performances of norm or standardization groups against which pupil's individual scores are compared.

Objective test: A test having clearly agreed upon criteria for scoring so that different scorers will not disagree on the correctness or incorrectness of the answers.

Percentile: A point along a distribution of scores that indicates, for example, that the percentage of scores falling below the 80th percentile is 80%. The median is the 50th percentile.

Performance test: A test requiring the performance of a task rather than the answering of questions. Such tests may be pencil and paper types such as shorthand or bookkeeping. They may also be "hands on" tests of mechanical ability to run lathes or repair engines.

Personality test: A test for the measurement of noncognitive characteristics such as introversion, sociability, attitudes, and other affective traits.

Population: In statistics, the total number of individuals from which a random sample is taken. The population could include all the people in the United States or all the children in a school.

Practice effect: The increase in a test score when the test is taken a second time. Experience with the test allows memory to play a role in improved performance the second time.

Profile: A method of showing the results of a number of tests taken by an individual. The profile helps paint a picture of several traits or characteristics and is usually presented graphically.

Projective technique: A method of assessing personality traits by asking the individual to look at unstructured pictures or incomplete sentences and to express feelings concerning them. Individuals "project" their personality into the stimuli by completing or describing them in terms of their perceptions and experience.

Quartile: The term used to express the division of a distribution into four equal groups or quartiles (the first quartile is the 25th percentile).

r: Symbol for coefficient of correlation.

Random sample: A sample chosen from the population strictly according to chance. Random sampling gives every individual in the population an equal opportunity to be selected (see **Population**).

Range: The difference between the highest and lowest scores in a distribution of scores.

Raw score: The original score obtained when scoring a test. Most raw scores in measurement and evaluation are later converted to more statistically usable scores—such as percentile ranks, deviation I.Q.'s, and grade equivalents.

Rating scale: A device for systematically and and accurately recording observations of individuals.

Readiness test: An evaluation instrument used to assess a child's current experiences to determine whether they are adequate to begin some new learning activity. Reading and arithmetic readiness tests are most commonly given.

Reliability: A term applied to a test's dependability or consistency in measuring the trait it is supposed to measure. Reliability is enhanced by test items that are very carefully written and that are said to "discriminate" (see **Item analysis**).

Sample: The group of individuals randomly selected from the population.

SD: The symbol for standard deviation.

Split-half coefficient: A coefficient of reliability derived by scoring two halves of the same test and applying the Spearman rank-difference formula (Rho).

Standard deviation: A measure of the way scores vary or disperse themselves around the mean. The more closely the scores cluster around the mean, the smaller will be the standard deviation. Approximately 68% of all scores will be included in 1 standard deviation.

Standardized test: A test constructed according to rigid specifications with careful attention to validity, reliability, and original sampling procedures. Norms are obtained and become the "standards" to which teachers compare their youngsters' scores.

Stanine: One of the nine divisions of the normal curve used to express scores in single digit "standard" scores from 1 to 9. The "stanine" is derived from the words "standard nines."

Stem: The open-ended statement in a multiple-choice test item.

T-score: A standard score having a mean of 50 and a standard deviation of 10.

Test-retest coefficient: A coefficient of reliability obtained by correlating the scores from the same test given twice over a short period.

Validity: The degree to which a test actually measures the characteristic or trait it was designed to measure.

z score: A standard score with a mean of 0 and a standard deviation of 1.

AREAS OF THE CURVE

Z	Between the X and Z	Z	Between the X and Z	Z	Between the X and Z
0.00	.0000	0.25	.0987	0.50	.1915
0.01	.0040	0.26	.1026	0.51	.1950
0.02	.0080	0.27	.1064	0.52	.1985
0.03	.0120	0.28	.1103	0.53	.2019
0.04	.0160	0.29	.1141	0.54	.2054
0.05	.0199	0.30	.1179	0.55	.2088
0.06	.0239	0.31	.1217	0.56	.2123
0.07	.0279	0.32	.1255	0.57	.2157
0.08	.0319	0.33	.1293	0.58	.2190
0.09	.0359	0.34	.1331	0.59	.2224
0.10	.0398	0.35	.1368	0.60	.2257
0.11	.0438	0.36	.1406	0.61	.2291
0.12	.0478	0.37	.1443	0.62	.2324
0.13	.0517	0.38	.1480	0.63	.2357
0.14	.0557	0.39	.1517	0.64	.2389
0.15	.0596	0.40	.1554	0.65	.2422
0.16	.0636	0.41	.1591	0.66	.2454
0.17	.0675	0.42	.1628	0.67	.2486
0.18	.0714	0.43	.1664	0.68	.2517
0.19	.0753	0.44	.1700	0.69	.2549
0.20	.0793	0.45	.1736	0.70	.2580
0.21	.0832	0.46	.1772	0.71	.2611
0.22	.0871	0.47	.1808	0.72	.2642
0.23	.0910	0.48	.1844	0.73	.2673
0.24	.0948	0.49	.1879	0.74	.2704

Z	Between the X and Z	Z	Between the X and Z	Z	Between the X and Z
0.75	.2734	1.15	.3749	1.55	.4394
0.76	.2764	1.16	.3770	1.56	.4406
0.77	.2794	1.17	.3790	1.57	.4418
0.78	.2823	1.18	.3810	1.58	.4429
0.79	.2852	1.19	.3830	1.59	.4441
0.80	.2881	1.20	.3849	1.60	.4452
0.81	.2910	1.21	.3869	1.61	.4463
0.82	.2939	1.22	.3888	1.62	.4474
0.83	.2967	1.23	.3907	1.63	.4484
0.84	.2995	1.24	.3925	1.64	.4495
0.85	.3023	1.25	.3944	1.65	.4505
0.86	.3051	1.26	.3962	1.66	.4515
0.87	.3078	1.27	.3980	1.67	.4525
0.88	.3106	1.28	.3997	1.68	.4535
0.89	.3133	1.29	.4015	1.69	.4545
0.90	.3159	1.30	.4032	1.70	.4554
0.91	.3186	1.31	.4049	1.71	.4564
0.92	.3212	1.32	.4066	1.72	.4573
0.93	.3238	1.33	.4082	1.73	.4582
0.94	.3264	1.34	.4099	1.74	.4591
0.95	.3289	1.35	.4115	1.75	.4599
0.96	.3315	1.36	.4131	1.76	.4608
0.97	.3340	1.37	.4147	1.77	.4616
0.98	.3365	1.38	.4162	1.78	.4625
0.99	.3389	1.39	.4177	1.79	.4633
1.00	.3413	1.40	.4192	1.80	.4641
1.01	.3438	1.41	.4207	1.81	.4649
1.02	.3461	1.42	.4222	1.82	.4656
1.03	.3485	1.43	.4236	1.83	.4664
1.04	.3508	1.44	.4251	1.84	.4671
1.05	.3531	1.45	.4265	1.85	.4678
1.06	.3554	1.46	.4279	1.86	.4686
1.07	.3577	1.47	.4292	1.87	.4693
1.08	.3599	1.48	.4306	1.88	.4699
1.09	.3621	1.49	.4319	1.89	.4706
1.10	.3643	1.50	.4332	1.90	.4713
1.11	.3665	1.51	.4345	1.91	.4719
1.12	.3686	1.52	.4357	1.92	.4726
1.13	.3708	1.53	.4370	1.93	.4732
1.14	.3729	1.54	.4382	1.94	.4738

Z	Between the X and Z	Z	Between the X and Z	Z	Between the X and Z
1.95	.4744	2.30	.4893	2.65	.4960
1.96	.4750	2.31	.4896	2.66	.4961
1.97	.4756	2.32	.4898	2.67	.4962
1.98	.4761	2.33	.4901	2.68	.4963
1.99	.4767	2.34	.4904	2.69	.4964
2.00	.4772	2.35	.4906	2.70	.4965
2.01	.4778	2.36	.4909	2.71	.4966
2.02	.4783	2.37	.4911	2.72	.4967
2.03	.4783	2.38	.4913	2.73	.4968
2.04	.4793	2.39	.4916	2.74	.4969
2.05	.4798	2.40	.4918	2.75	.4970
2.06	.4803	2.41	.4920	2.76	.4971
2.07	.4808	2.42	.4922	2.77	.4972
2.08	.4812	2.43	.4925	2.78	.4973
2.09	.4817	2.44	.4927	2.79	.4974
2.10	.4821	2.45	.4929	2.80	.4974
2.11	.4826	2.46	.4931	2.81	.4975
2.12	.4830	2.47	.4932	2.82	.4976
2.13	.4834	2.48	.4934	2.83	.4977
2.14	.4838	2.49	.4936	2.84	.4977
2.15	.4842	2.50	.4938	2.85	.4978
2.16	.4846	2.51	.4940	2.86	.4979
2.17	.4850	2.52	.4941	2.87	.4979
2.18	.4854	2.53	.4943	2.88	.4980
2.19	.4857	2.54	.4945	2.89	.4981
2.20	.4861	2.55	.4946	2.90	.4981
2.21	.4864	2.56	.4948	2.91	.4982
2.22	.4868	2.57	.4949	2.92	.4982
2.23	.4871	2.58	.4951	2.93	.4983
2.24	.4875	2.59	.4952	2.94	.4984
2.25	.4878	2.60	.4953	2.95	.4984
2.26	.4881	2.61	.4955	2.96	.4985
2.27	.4884	2.62	.4956	2.97	.4985
2.28	.4887	2.63	.4957	2.98	.4986
2.29	.4890	2.64	.4959	2.99	.4986
				3.00	.4987

STATISTICS: SOME REVIEW AND SOME NEW

The exercises that follow review the material found in Chapter 7. In this review, we amplify our discussion of statistics and offer some sample computations.

DISTRIBUTIONS

The concept of the bell-shaped curve was discussed in Chapter 7. The curve is shown in Fig. C.1.

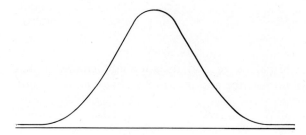

Fig. C.1 Normal curve.

Distributions that do not distribute normally are frequently referred to as "skewed." Positively skewed and negatively skewed curves are shown in Figs. C.2 and C.3, respectively.

The positively skewed curve has the tail of the curve on the positive end, and thus the scores cluster away from that end; the negatively skewed curve tails at the negative end, and thus scores cluster away from that end.

The normal curve is perfectly symmetrical; that is, one side mirrors the other. This characteristic allows the percentages of cases that fall between given points, called standard deviations, and the center (mean) to be known. This curve, repeated from Chapter 7, is shown in Fig. C.4.

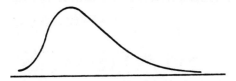

Fig. C.2 Positive skew.

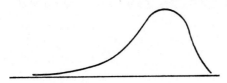

Fig. C.3 Negative skew.

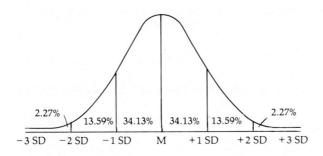

Figure C.4

The concept of the normal curve and its attendant characteristics provide a number of ways to describe and interpret individual and group scores.

CENTRAL TENDENCY

The three measures of central tendency are the mean, median, and mode. The mean is probably the most frequently used and is by far the most meaningful.

Mode: the score that appears most frequently.

Median: the midpoint of the distribution—with the same number of scores above and below it.

Mean: the average, the sum of the scores divided by the number of scores.

Compute and state the mean, median, and mode from the following distributions:

	A			B	
	20	13		30	13
	18	10		31	12
	18	8		25	11
	17	7		22	9
	14	5		22	

Remember the formula for the mean is:

$$\overline{X} = \frac{\Sigma X}{N}$$

The answers:

	A	B
Mean	13	20
Median	13.5	22
Mode	18	22

All three measures of central tendency are useful and provide us with the methods to better interpret scores meaningfully.

VARIANCE

The range is the difference between the highest and lowest score and indicates the spread of a distribution. What is the range for distributions A and B? If you stated 15 and 26, respectively, you were correct.

The standard deviation is a most useful statistic. It is the "average deviation" of a set of scores. The deviation is the difference between a score and the mean. For example, in distribution A, the deviation for the (X) of 20 and the Mean ($\overline{X}$) of 13 is 7.

The standard deviation refers to the group and describes a group characteristic. The standard score statistic refers to the interpretation of a specific score within the group. The z score is a standard score, the expression of a raw score in standard score units. The formula is

$$z = \frac{X - \overline{X}}{s}$$

Refer to distribution A and compute the z scores for the raw scores of 20, 17, 10, and 5. Recall that the $\overline{X}$ = 13 and s = 5.

If you stated +1.4, +.8, −0.6 and −1.6 you were right. In the z score distribution the mean is 0 and standard deviation is 1. The signs in the individual scores give the direction, and the numbers give the units of standard deviation above or below the mean.

For practice, take these four z scores, and using the table in Appendix B, state the percentiles for these z scores:

$$
\begin{array}{rcl}
+1.4 & = & P92 \\
+0.8 & = & P79 \\
-0.6 & = & P27 \\
-1.6 & = & P\ 5
\end{array}
$$

The z score is valuable, but the + and − signs could be troublesome. The T score is a common way to convert z scores and retain the meaning.

The formula is : $T = 10\ (z + 50)$, and the T scores for the above z scores would be 64, 58, 44, and 34, as the T score distribution has $\overline{X}$ of 50 and s of 10.

The formula for the computation of the standard deviation is

$$
s = \sqrt{\frac{\Sigma x^2}{N}} \quad \text{or} \quad s = \sqrt{\frac{\Sigma(X - \overline{X})^2}{N}}
$$

Try to compute the s for distribution A and check your figures below:

X	$\overline{X}$	$X - \overline{X}$	x^2
20	13	7	49
18	13	5	25
18	13	5	25
17	13	4	16
14	13	1	1
13	13	0	0
10	13	−3	9
8	13	−5	25
7	13	−6	36
5	13	−8	64
			250 $= \Sigma x^2$

(The sum of the squared deviations is called the variance.)

$$
s = \sqrt{250/10} = \sqrt{25} = 5
$$

Try computing the s for distribution B. The variance or sum of squared deviations will be 694.

The standard deviation indicates the dispersion of the set of scores; the larger the standard deviation the more heterogeneous the distribution, and the smaller the s the more homogeneous the group.

CORRELATION

The primary measure of relationship is correlation, which is quantitatively expressed as a coefficient of correlation. The coefficient of correlation ranges from −1.0 to +1.0. The sign expresses the type of correlation, and the number expresses the strength of the correlation. The coefficient indicates the kind and strength of the relationship between two variables. To compute a coefficient we need measures of two variables for each individual in a group. Correlation is extremely helpful in determining the validity and reliability of published standardized instruments.

For example, the developer of a new test of reading comprehension could administer the test to a group at the appropriate age and grade level. These individuals could then be tested with another instrument that also measures reading comprehension, and a correlation study could be done that would result in an expression of validity coefficient of correlation. Reliability is a statistical concept and is always expressed as a correlation coefficient.

One frequently used method of estimating the coefficient is the Pearson product moment correlation coefficient, often referred to as the Pearson r. The formula is

$$r = \frac{N\Sigma XY - (\Sigma X)(\Sigma Y)}{\sqrt{[N\Sigma X^2 - (\Sigma X)^2][N\Sigma Y^2 - (\Sigma Y)^2]}}$$

The formula may look formidable, but with a hand calculator and the following it can be worked out:

N = Number of students (not scores)
ΣX = Sum of the scores for test 1
ΣY = Sum of the scores for test 2
ΣX^2 = Sum of the squared scores, test 1
ΣY^2 = Sum of the squared scores, test 2
ΣXY = Sum of the products of tests 1 and 2

Let us assume we have tested five children in reading (X) and in math (Y). The small number of students and small numbers used as test scores are used to illustrate the application of the formula:

Students	X	Y	X²	Y²	XY
A	3	2	9	4	6
B	4	4	16	16	16
C	4	5	16	25	20
D	4	3	16	9	12
E	2	2	4	4	4
	17	16	61	58	58

$$\frac{5(58) - (17)(16)}{\sqrt{[5(16) - (17)^2][5(58) - (16)^2]}}$$

$$\frac{290 - 272}{\sqrt{(305 - 289)(290 - 256)}}$$

$$\frac{18}{\sqrt{(16)(34)}}$$

$$r = 0.77$$

The interpretation of any coefficient of correlation depends on the purposes for computing the coefficient. There can be no cut-off point for good or bad.

Reliability is always stated with a coefficient of correlation, and we have described the various ways of establishing reliability in Chapters 6 and 7, including test-retest, equivalent form, and odd-even.

When the odd-even or split-half method is used, the test is cut in half or divided according to odd and even item numbers. In either method, two variables per student are generated and a correlation coefficient computed. Since the coefficient estimates only half of the test, the Spearman-Brown formula provides an estimate of reliability for the whole test. This formula is

$$r_{xx} = \frac{2r_{\frac{1}{2}\frac{1}{2}}}{1 + r_{\frac{1}{2}\frac{1}{2}}} \quad \text{when}$$

r_{xx} is the reliability of the total test

$r\frac{1}{2}\frac{1}{2}$ is the reliability obtained by computing the correlation of the split halves.

For example: The split-half coefficient is 0.70

$$r_{xx} = \frac{2(0.70)}{1 + 0.70} = \frac{1.40}{1.70} = 0.82$$

Another method for estimating the internal consistency of a test is to administer the test to the appropriate group and apply the Kuder-Richardson Formula 21 to the results. A simplified version of the formula is

$$r_{xx} = 1 - \frac{\overline{X}(K - \overline{X})}{K(s)^2} \quad \text{when}$$

K is the number of items in the test

s is the standard deviation of the distribution

For example: When $\overline{X} = 70$, $s = 10$, and $K = 75$.

$$r_{xx} = 1 - \frac{70(75 - 70)}{75(10)^2}$$

$$= 1 - \frac{350}{7500}$$

$$= 1 - 0.046$$

$$= 0.95$$

The standard error of measurement was described in Chapter 7. It is a function of reliability and states the dimensions that an individual score may vary in a given distribution. If Jimmy received a score of 85 and the standard error was ±6, then we would assume that Jimmy's "true" score would fall between 79 and 91. The valuable aspect of the standard error is that it precludes thinking of any score as one unchangeable fixed point. The formula is

$$s_m = s\sqrt{1 - r}$$

For example: with an s of 10 and an r of 0.85

$$s_m = 10\sqrt{1 - 0.85}$$

$$= 10\sqrt{0.15}$$

$$= 10(0.387)$$

$$= 3.87$$

INDEX